Welfare and Ideology

Welfare and Ideology

Vic George
Professor of Social Policy and Social Work
University of Kent

and

Paul Wilding
Professor of Social Policy
University of Manchester

HARVESTER WHEATSHEAF

NEW YORK   LONDON   TORONTO   SYDNEY   TOKYO   SINGAPORE

First published 1993 by
Prentice Hall/Harvester Wheatsheaf
Campus 400, Marylands Avenue
Hemel Hempstead
Hertfordshire, HP2 7EZ
A division of
Simon & Schuster International Group

Typeset in 10/12pt Times
by Dorwyn Ltd, Rowlands Castle, Hants

Printed and bound in Great Britain by
MPG Books Ltd, Bodmin, Cornwall

British Library Cataloguing in Publication Data

A catalogue record for this book is available from
the British Library

ISBN 0–7450–1344–9

5 6 7 8 9   02 01 00 99 98

To Enid and Janet

CONTENTS

INTRODUCTION

For the past fifteen years or so, welfare states have been under intense scrutiny. The basic line of attack has been that state welfare provision undermines individual freedom, social discipline and national rates of economic growth. Supporters of the welfare state have given considerable ground during this period though now they are beginning to regain some of their old confidence that the welfare state along with parliamentary democracy are the two main advances that civilised industrial states have made during the past hundred years. An attack on one constitutes an assault on the other. These traditional debates between Left, Centre and Right have now been joined by new ideologies that highlight other and equally important social concerns: that is, the position of women in society and the impact welfare states make on them and the threat to the environment posed by the dominant ethic of consumerism that characterises our contemporary world and is supported both directly and indirectly by welfare state policies.

The primary aim of this book is to shed some light on these debates. It examines six main ideologies: the New Right, the Middle Way, Democratic Socialism, Marxism, Feminism and Greenism. Every attempt has been made to present each ideology as impartially as possible though the discerning reader will not find it difficult to ascertain the ideological commitment of the authors. The final chapter makes this clear in any case and raises the issue that defenders of the welfare state will need to do some hard thinking as a fully developed welfare state of the future has to be better than the past one if it is to be in tune with public expectations and help to maintain a just and sustainable society.

CHAPTER 1

IDEOLOGIES OF WELFARE

The role of the state in economic and social affairs has always been an ideologically contested issue particularly since the introduction of democratic forms of government. Social theorists, politicians and governments have always differed on such issues as the relative merits of the private market and of state action, on the distribution of resources in society, and on the role of the family. The force of ideology in these and other issues, however, is dulled as it moves from the treatise of the theoretician to the policy instrument of the cabinet minister. A host of economic, social and political factors intervene to shape particular policy proposals into what governments consider possible at any one time. Relating this to the growth of welfare services, one can say that though ideology has played a part in the development of the welfare state, other factors, too, have played a major and sometimes more important role, as we shall see in subsequent chapters.

Ideology is, of course, important not only for group and government action but for individual behaviour as well. It is difficult to see how individuals can live without some adherence to values and beliefs, that is, to their individual ideology. Individuals may not always live by the beliefs and values which make up their own ideology but, at times, they are also quite prepared to die for them. The role of ideology in the lives of individuals, groups and nations may well be inconsistent but it can also be quite significant and dramatic at times. It is this blend of interacting material, self-interest and ideological factors which makes accurate analysis of the motives behind individual and government behaviour impossible on most occasions.

1

All this, however, begs the question of what ideology is, how it is defined and how it is used. It is important to distinguish from the outset between ideology as a concept and ideology as political or welfare doctrine, which is the main concern of this book. The two can be related but they are different as the following discussion will hopefully show. Beginning with the concept of ideology, McLellan notes that it is 'the most elusive concept in the whole of social science' (McLellan, 1986, p. 1) with the obvious result that there is no agreement on its meaning. Hamilton analysed a large number of writings on the concept of ideology and found that 'there are at least as many definitions of it as there are theorists proposing them' (Hamilton, 1987, p. 18). This, of course, is not unique to ideology. Most social science notions are contested because the way a concept is defined has implications not only for academic study but for government policy as well (Gallie, 1955/56).

Despite all this, it is possible to identify four distinct ways in which the notion of ideology has been defined over the years, each of which has influenced debates in social policy and in politics. The term 'ideology' was first used by de Tracy in 1797 in the immediate aftermath of the French Revolution to counter the dominance of custom, tradition, the supernatural and mystical religion in government policies. For him, ideology was the objective and impartial gathering of ideas gained through experience – it was the science of ideas, a rational new way of gathering information to inform government decisions for the betterment of society. Thus, ideology had a positive connotation both as regards the ways in which ideas are formulated and the uses to which ideas are put. Students of ideology could be impartial enough to deliver the promises of this new science despite the fact that their ideas brought them into conflict with established institutions. It was not long, however, before the students of the new discipline found to their cost that government policies are shaped by many factors with or without 'objective' knowledge. In his anxiety to maintain the support of the Catholic Church, Napoleon turned on the 'ideologues', whom he had previously supported, dismissing their ideas as partisan, biased and impractical. He thus equated ideology with doctrinaire and utopian thinking. This contrast between ideology as objective and biased reality, as rational and doctrinaire, as realistic and utopian has persisted through the centuries and it has influenced the perception of the role of the social sciences in general and in policy-making in particular.

If de Tracy is the author of the notion of ideology, Marx is the creator of the theory of how ideology originates and what its functions in society are. As a historical materialist, Marx claimed that it is not the consciousness of people that determines the course of history but rather it is the conflict over the production process that shapes both the course of history and people's ideology. In Marx's words: 'the mode of production of material life conditions the social, political and intellectual life process in general. It is not the consciousness of men that determines their being, but, on the contrary, their social being that determines their consciousness' (Marx, 1970, p. 181).

In a capitalist society, it is natural that the ideas, values and beliefs of those who dominate the production, distribution and business sectors will become accepted as the ideas of all sections of society, including those who stand to lose out by their application in everyday affairs. Thus, ideology for Marx was tantamount to 'false consciousness' as far as the majority of the population was concerned. It was a means through which the upper class could gain and retain the allegiance of the population. Though ideology comes about through the material processes in society, once in existence it assumes a power of its own and 'becomes an apology for institutionalised inequality' (Manning, 1980, p. 3). Several of Marx's followers, particularly Gramsci, laid even more stress, though with greater subtlety, on the power of ideology and in particular on the way in which it undermined working-class radicalism and thus helped to maintain the 'hegemony' of the upper classes in capitalist societies. Far from being an objective and impartial body of ideas for the benefit of the whole society as de Tracy had argued, ideology is, according to Marx, a partial body of beliefs distorting reality for the benefit of the ruling class. Thus, the derogatory connotation attributed to ideology by Napoleon was further reinforced by Marx with the backing of a materialistic theoretical framework.

The weakness of the Marxist notion of ideology is to be found in its excessive claims. It can be argued quite convincingly that several of the dominant values of a society do serve primarily the interests of the dominant classes or groups, and that these same classes or groups will do their utmost to perpetuate that position.

Where Marxism goes wrong is its claim that all dominant values are partial and its assumption that class power, official propaganda and similar measures can always succeed in indoctrinating the populace. Such values as inequality or private ownership of marketable wealth are to the advantage of mainly the very affluent sections of a society, but it is difficult to see why freedom of choice or honesty necessarily serve the interests of those groups more than those of other groups. Marx was also wrong in his claim that capitalism had little to offer the working class. If that were the case, the working class would not accept and defend the dominant values. Where the content of ideology is incompatible with people's experience, its hold is tentative and superficial. This is shown by the example of Eastern Europe where seventy years of intensive Party dominance and propaganda have failed to capture the fundamental loyalties of the public despite all signs to the contrary. People outwardly behaved as if they accepted the official ideology but this only served to create a climate of public cynicism. As Vaclav Havel, dissident and President of the former Czechoslovakia put it: 'one need not believe all these mystifications, but one must behave as if one did, or at least put up with them tacitly, or get along with those who use them' (Rupnik, 1988, pp. 232–3).

Mannheim was perhaps the next major figure in the debates on ideology after Marx. His treatment of ideology was strangely both an acceptance and a refutation of the Marxist notion of ideology. Mannheim agreed that dominant ideologies are always distortions of reality for the benefit of the ruling groups and to the disadvantage of other groups in society. But all ideologies are historically bound and none can be eternally valid. There are no eternal truths. Thus Marxism was a correct diagnosis of the situation in nineteenth-century Britain, Germany and other European countries but lost its validity in the twentieth century as the socio-economic conditions changed. It ceased to reflect reality and it became a distortion for it relied on evidence from the past (Mannheim, 1936). Thus, contrary to Marxist claims that Marxism was a scientific approach as distinct from Hegelianism, liberalism, and all the rest which were mere ideologies, Mannheim insisted that Marxism was nothing more but an ideology of the nineteenth century. But if all ideas and theories are subjective and historically bound, what future is there for the social sciences? It was to resolve this dilemma that Mannheim put forward the idea that intellectuals with no vested interest in the existing economic and political system and who were thus unconnected to the dominant ideology could be objective and impartial presenters of existing reality, and could thus promote the advancement of social knowledge. Mannheim's treatment of ideology, both in its historical and its methodological sense, however, was so relativistic that it is difficult to take seriously his views on the role of intellectuals. His contribution to our understanding of ideology is his explanation of the influence of the societal environment on ideas and the warning that even definitions of ideology can themselves be ideological.

Finally, several American sociologists in the 1950s and 1960s identified ideology as a system of values and beliefs that increases social cohesion in society for the benefit of all. Parsons, for example, defines ideology as 'a system of beliefs, held in common by members of a collectivity . . . a system of ideas which is oriented to the evaluative integration of the collectivity' (Parsons, 1951, p. 349). This is in contrast to de Tracy's perception of ideology as a body of impartial, empirical knowledge as well as in contrast to Marx's view of the class bias of such belief and value systems. Both Marx and Parsons see ideology as indispensable to the stability of a society though the former sees this as simply benefiting the upper classes while the latter considers it to be to the benefit of all groups in society. This reflects their wider differences on the nature of society with Marx emphasising its class conflict nature and Parsons stressing its consensual features.

Our brief account of debates on the meaning of ideology has demonstrated that, apart from de Tracy, the three other writers see it as a system of values and beliefs which exercises important functions in society though there is clear disagreement as to how ideology is formed, how it is modified and transmitted and which groups in society benefit most from this. The most common usage of the notion of ideology today is a set of values and beliefs held by individuals, groups and societies that influences their conduct. This is a neutral kind of definition which leaves open the question of whose values dominate society and who benefits most from their application.

The notion of ideology is, as mentioned earlier, different from the notion of political or welfare doctrines, such as liberalism, Marxism, socialism, and nationalism. It is, of course, more than possible, as Rejai has pointed out, 'that one's analysis of the concept of ideology may be conditioned "ideologically" (in the second sense) but these questions are analytically distinct' (Sargent, 1990, p. 1). The following chapters will provide numerous examples of how one's values and beliefs influence one's interpretation of social situations. We now move on to examine those political ideologies or doctrines which are relevant to debates on the welfare state.

Political ideologies possess several features, the number of which varies from one writer to another. Macridis lists seven while Jones condenses them to four. The first of these is a view of the world, 'most importantly human nature, the purpose of political activity and the nature of economic activity' (Jones, 1991, p. 101). Thus, socialism sees people as co-operative and altruistic while classical liberalism sees them as selfish and individualistic. Second, all ideologies offer a critique of existing socio-economic systems, largely depending on their view of human nature. It is no surprise that socialism is critical of existing patterns of ownership, distribution, and reward while liberalism sees them as right and proper. Third, stemming from their critique, they offer a vision of the future – the ideal society which its followers should strive to achieve. In order to carry more weight with their followers, all ideologies present a rosy but simplistic picture of the future. They tend to stress all the positives and to ignore all the negatives of their particular utopia. Fourthly, they provide some guidance to their adherents as to what methods should be used to achieve the ideal society. We will see later, for example, that democratic socialism has always rejected the use of violence to achieve its political ends while Marxism has not.

Applying these four features of ideologies to the welfare state, we might suggest that welfare ideologies are value-laden expositions which provide the answers to several questions such as the following. How large should state involvement in economic and social affairs be? What are the positive and negative functions of state welfare provision for the political, economic and social life of the country? What organisational forms should state intervention take? What is the ideal form of the society of the future and how does it differ from existing welfare states? What methods or processes are necessary to attain this ideal type of society?

Even with these guidelines, however, the list of welfare ideologies could be far too long for it may include such isms as anarchism, Maoism, puritanism, fascism, which are very much minority ideologies in today's advanced industrial societies. For this reason a second list of criteria is needed to select the most important ideologies for contemporary industrial welfare states. Macridis suggests four such tests of significance in his work on political ideologies which seem to be very relevant to the taxonomy of welfare ideologies: that is, coherence, pervasiveness, extensiveness and intensiveness.

Coherence refers to the scope, logic and structure of an ideology. Does it have something to say on the various questions raised above and do its answers seem logical irrespective of whether one agrees with them or not? Pervasiveness denotes the length of time during which a welfare ideology has been actively propagated. Thus, some ideologies may be extinct whilst others are so very new that they do not satisfy this test. Extensiveness means simply the number of people who share an ideology. Whilst it is not always possible to give precise figures one can, for example, safely say that feminism in Britain passes this test today but it failed it thirty years ago for it was then a minority viewpoint. An ideology may fail the other tests but still qualify if it satisfies the test of intensiveness for this implies 'emotional commitment, total loyalty, and unequivocal determination to act even at the risk of one's life' (Macridis, 1992, p. 18). The strongest ideologies are those which satisfy all four tests but it would be wrong to exclude an ideology which failed one of these tests, particularly if there is evidence that shows that its appeal is spreading.

On the strength of these two scales, we have included in our study the following six welfare ideologies: the New Right, the Middle Way, Democratic Socialism, Marxism, Feminism and Greenism. We have omitted anti-racism, ageism, nationalism and others, not because we consider them either unimportant or uninteresting but because they do not satisfy our criteria to count as major ideologies of welfare. It should be said that a list of political ideologies in general would differ from our list as the numerous textbooks in politics show (Adams, 1993; Leach, 1991; Eccleshall *et al.*, 1984).

Though each of our six ideologies coheres around a number of themes which make it distinct from others, they may also share several common features at any one time. For example, despite their many differences, all six ideologies today will speak in support of public participation in civic affairs even though they may define it in different ways. What is more, within any one of these ideologies there exist different strands of thought which do not agree on several important issues. Communitarian socialism and Fabian socialism differ quite substantially on the degree of acceptable central government planning; feminist groups disagree on the causes of and solutions to gender discrimination; though the New Right favours minimum government intervention, its various schools of thought disagree on what constitutes minimal. Despite these qualifications, the six ideologies provide very different answers to the questions on welfare raised above as subsequent chapters will show.

As ideologies of welfare, they are related to political parties but they rarely coincide totally with any one political party, let alone government. They inform the thinking, aspirations and policy debates within political parties; they set the broad political agendas, but they do not decide the outcomes. The only exception to this is feminism which has no corresponding political party though its different strands are loosely related to the policies of different parties and have affected government programmes in various ways and degrees. Thus, political ideologies are not bound by national boundaries and their understanding is of relevance to welfare debates in all countries.

All six ideologies are both normative and explanatory approaches to the study of the welfare state. They attempt to explain events and processes as well as make prescriptions for change to various aspects of welfare activity. Marxism provides a conceptual explanation of the forces behind the growth of state welfare in society and it also makes broad recommendations about how a future socialist society should function; feminism provides various explanations of gender discrimination in society as well as detailed agendas for change. Though these two aspects of each ideology can be discussed separately, there is, in fact, a close relationship between them for every explanation contains the seeds for prescription. Thus, the explanatory and the prescriptive function of a welfare ideology are, in fact, two sides of the same coin. It is not logically possible, for example, to combine a New Right explanation of the development of the welfare state with a Marxist analysis of the functions and future of the welfare state!

Typologies of welfare ideologies are commonplace now even though this was not always the case. As Lee and Raban show, the flowering of theoretical debates on welfare typologies in social policy arose out of the collapse of political consensus on the nature of the welfare state in the 1970s and has tended to be along a one-dimensional continuum 'concerning the role the State should play in relation to the private market – whether this be to sustain, supplement or supplant the free play of market forces in achieving an "equitable" allocation of resources or "welfares" ' (Lee and Raban, 1983, p. 22). It is, of course, quite possible, as they suggest, to have two-dimensional or even three-dimensional typologies but it is uncertain whether this will add much to our understanding of the broad issues of welfare states even though they could be quite useful to the understanding of specific issues in particular countries. The first four of our ideologies are indeed positions on the free market/state provision continuum while feminism and Greenism stand on their own even though they have a lot to say about

Table 1.1   Classification of welfare ideologies

1.	Anti-collectivism	Citizenship	Integrationism	Functionalism			
2.	Residualism	Industrialism		Institutionalism			
3.	Anti-collectivism	Reluctant Collectivism	Fabian Socialism	Marxism			
4.	Residualism	Institutionalism		Socialism			
5.	Conservatism	Positive State	Social Security State	Social Welfare State	Radicalism		
6.	Market Liberalism	Political Liberalism	Social Democracy	Neo-Marxism			
7.	Classical Economic Theory	Neo-Mercantile Collectivism	Marxian/Socialist				
8.	Individualism	Reformism	Structuralism	Marxism			
9.	Anti Collectivism	Social Reformism	Fabian Socialism	Radical Social Administration	Political Economy of welfare	Feminism	Anti-Racism
10.	New Right	Middle Way	Democratic Socialism	Marxism	Feminism	Greenism	

Sources: 1. Wedderburn (1965); 2. Titmuss (1974); 3. George and Wilding (1976); 4. Mishra (1977); 5. Furniss and Tilton (1979); 6. Room (1979); 7. Pinker (1979); 8. Taylor-Gooby and Dale (1981); 9. Williams (1989); 10. George and Wilding (1994).

this. Anyhow, the recognition that there are divisions of opinion within each ideology is an acceptance that there are other issues of substance in welfare debates in addition to the issues raised by the continuum used here.

Table 1.1 shows the typologies of welfare ideologies used by several authors over the years. It shows, first, a substantial agreement among the various authors even though the term used to define the same ideological perspective is different. Second, the table shows that since the beginning of the 1990s the range of typologies has increased to include ideologies which previously were not considered as fundamental as the rest. In a way, this reflects the current disquiet with the old ideologies, the feeling that they no longer deliver as much as they once did because we live in a very different world.

Though most social scientists and others agree with the view that ideology is central and inevitable, there have recently been those who have felt that the age of ideologies is now over. During the past thirty years, 'the end of ideology' has made its appearance on two occasions: that is, in the early 1960s and in the late 1980s. On the first occasion, writers like Bell, Lipset and Aron argued that since capitalist industrialisation and welfare provision had secured affluence and raised living standards for all in the advanced industrial countries, the ideological debates between capitalism and socialism had become redundant and any future political conflict 'will be a fight without ideologies' (Lipset, 1963, p. 408). What few problems remained in the industrial world could not be solved through ideological debates but through rational, empirically based arguments. In Bell's words 'the ladder to the city of heaven can no longer be a "faith ladder" but an empirical one' (Bell, 1960, p. 405).

As McLellan points out, behind the 'end of ideology thesis' lurked two premises: that is, the linkage of ideology with totalitarianism and the contrast of ideology with science (McLellan, 1986, p. 52). It was argued that support for socialism was tantamount to support for authoritarianism as socialism was equated with Eastern European regimes. Only ideologues could, therefore, support socialism. Similarly, the belief in technocratic solutions to social problems meant that only 'objective' and 'scientific' social science with a strong quantitative emphasis could provide the answers. In other words, only social science that accepted the status quo could be useful. The 'end of ideology thesis' was a product of its time: unemployment was low, economic growth high, the welfare state was widely accepted and hence party political consensus was at its highest as signified in Britain by the term 'Butskellism'. The deterioration of economic fortunes in the 1970s gave rise first to a revival of Marxism and later to New Right ideology and thus to a resumption of ideological debates between Left and Right, as well as an upsurge of gender and ecological debates that were steeped in ideology.

The 'end of ideology' made its second appearance in the late 1980s under the guise of 'the end of history'. Fukuyama's book in 1992 which elaborated his thesis of an earlier article in 1989 claimed that logic, historical evidence and the recent events in Eastern Europe have shown that democracy and capitalism have triumphed over all other systems and there is no adequate alternative to them. The future belongs to capitalist democracy which he calls liberal democracy. This system represents 'the end point of mankind's ideological evolution' and the 'final form of human government' (Fukuyama, 1992, p. xi). The two parts of the system are inextricably linked for the betterment of all nations for neither authoritarian capitalism nor democratic socialism could compete with liberal democracy. The first would be rejected by the people because of the absence of democracy while the second was not a practical possibility. Some critics consider the Fukuyama thesis to be nothing more than an apologia for American capitalism just as Bell's 'end of ideology thesis' was. Others have claimed that his marriage of democracy to capitalism, particularly American capitalism, is a slur on democracy; and others, such as Miliband, have argued that the concept of 'capitalist democracy is a contradiction in terms' and that the future belongs to 'socialist democracy' (Miliband, 1992, p. 109). As we shall see in the following chapters, socialists, Marxists, feminists and Greens reject out of hand this second version of the 'end of ideology' for they believe that the future belongs to their favourite system. Democracy is acceptable to all; it is capitalism that divides our various ideological perspectives.

Finally, there is the criticism of 'grand ideologies' by postmodernists. There is no agreed definition of postmodernism for it covers not only a variety of perspectives but a multitude of situations from art, literature, architecture, the social sciences, philosophy and science. It is 'one of those words that has a tendency to reduce sensible people to a mad scramble for the nearest and deadliest instrument of destruction that they can find'! (Rengger, 1992, p. 560). In the social sciences it was first used by Lyotard who defined 'postmodern as incredulity towards meta-narratives' (Lyotard, 1984, p. xxiv). The advances of technology, of the organisation of international capital and the ensuing changes in social and economic structures of modern societies have made the old ideologies and theories redundant. Such grand ideologies as liberalism, Marxism, functionalism, and feminism can no longer provide valid explanations for social, economic and political processes nor can they act as guides to the future utopia.

There are elements of the 'end of ideology thesis' in postmodernism in the claim that the old ideologies no longer function adequately but it goes beyond it for the 'end of ideology' is in itself a 'meta-narrative'. The distinctive feature of postmodernism is its twin claim that ideological consensus and political utopia are not possible in modern societies. As Mishra points out 'what is implied is more akin to the end of *utopia* than of *ideology*' (Mishra, 1993, p. 34; emphases in original). But if the old ideologies cannot explain how societies function and cannot inspire individuals, groups or parties, then what is to take their place? The answer is 'local narratives', that is, a diversity of values and beliefs held by a variety of groups and shifting alliances in society with no agreed vision of the future.

Postmodernism has clear implications for social science theory, for everyday politics and for the future development of the welfare state. A party of the Left, for example, should not rely on the working class for it is so splintered that it has lost any political meaning. Rather, it should promote the concerns of women, ethnic groups, the environment, and the various interest groups that function in society. The notion of class should be replaced by gender, age, disability, and ethnicity for they are better reflections of actual situations. Clearly, there is an element of truth and sense but also a mountain of mistaken thinking and irrationality in all this. It is, for example, correct to take into account the significance of race, gender, disability, or unemployment etc. in analysing social situations at any one time but this does not mean the rejection of class. There are as many differences, for example, between the life chances of a middle-class and a working-class woman as there are between men and women in general. Similarly, a black, working-class, disabled woman can suffer from all three handicaps and there is no reason to reject the handicap of class. The challenge facing social scientists is how best to combine overarching and single concepts in explaining social situations. Similarly, the task of political parties is how best to take account of the concerns of new social movements without abandoning the interests of their older constituencies. While its emphasis on the new social groupings in society must be applauded, postmodernism runs the risk of degenerating into political irrelevance because of its commitment to limitless individualised explanations of social phenomena. Its message of more sensitive social analysis is to be welcomed but its demand that all generalised statements are incorrect and irrelevant is to be rejected. As Boyne and Rattansi put it: 'There is little doubt that one must guard against any tendency to collapse support for the new social movements into an indiscriminate pluralism which will lead not to sharpened awareness of difference but to uncritical sponge-headedness' (Boyne and Rattansi, 1990, p. 38).

It is also doubtful whether all grand ideologies have lost their potency. It can be argued that the ideology of the New Right dominates today so much so that even parties and governments of the Left are influenced by New Right principles. It is true that Marxism is not such a strong force today as it used to be, but we should not forget that grand ideologies have their ups and downs as the case of the New Right so well illustrates. The technological and business changes of the past thirty years and the concomitant emphasis on consumerism play into the hands of the New Right and pose problems for ideologies of the Left so that the future of the welfare state is uncertain. It is this that should concentrate the minds of students of social policy rather than postmodern claims that all grand ideologies are a thing of the past.

All this, however, does not mean that the grand ideologies discussed in this book are unproblematic. The discussion in the following chapters will illustrate that many of the old methods and goals of each of these ideologies are now being questioned. Socialists, for example, now accept that their analysis of the impact of welfare provisions in the past neglected the interests of women; the New Right is beginning to realise that their total belief in the benevolent effects of an uncontrolled private market is an economic and political liability; Marxists now accept that their past hostility to parliamentary democracy was both misplaced and harmful to their own cause. There is a general and justifiable feeling that we live in 'new times' and that more subtlety and sensitivity are needed to understand the world and to solve its many problems. To a critical student of welfare ideologies, it is now clear that no one ideology contains all the answers. This 'mini-crisis' in the grand political ideologies of both the Left and the Right has its roots in the growing social, economic and ecological changes and problems which all countries are now experiencing to a greater or lesser extent. The collapse of Eastern European authoritarian planning has been replaced not by 'a triumphant capitalism but by a global capitalist economy in trouble, and recognising that it is in trouble' (Hobsbawm, 1992, p. 59). It is this world crisis which makes claims of the 'end of ideology' or the 'end of history' irrelevant.

Ideological debates have played a part in shaping both the growth and the nature of the welfare state. The range, structure, generosity and distributional effects of social services are the result of several factors of which ideology is only one. In order to obtain as complete an understanding as possible of all this, we need to look at the various welfare ideologies in some historical perspective, for now, as always, 'we live in the shadow, and under the influence, of thinkers long dead' (Ball and Dagger, 1991, p. xi). Ideological debates are inevitable in societies with social conflicts and they will exert as much influence in shaping the future of the welfare state as they did in shaping its past and present. A study of welfare ideologies may help us to have a better understanding of government policies and of 'which side are we on, and why' (Eccleshall *et al.*, 1984, p. 32). What is crucial, now as ever, is whose values and ideology will exert the greatest influence on governments and thus help to shape the course of the welfare state in the future. In the following chapters, we examine the main ideologies which are relevant to debates on the welfare state. It will be clear that all of them are hybrid and though they 'carry immense amounts of inherited, interwoven intellectual baggage, often increasing by the year' (Vincent, 1992, pp. 18–19), they are very influential in shaping people's attitudes towards the nature and future of the welfare state.

CHAPTER 2

THE NEW RIGHT

The New Right came to the fore as an intellectual and political force in the 1970s and achieved a position of power in many countries in the 1970s and 1980s. In a sense, the movement was a product of the economic difficulties which overtook the global economy in the years after 1973, but it was also a reaction to the rapid expansion of public welfare spending in the 1960s and widespread uncertainty about the success and impact of such policies.

What the New Right did, essentially, was to take up, develop and extend classical liberal critiques of state action and apply them to the key contemporary issues of economic and social policy. It was a powerful – if at times strident – critique with a firm ideological base. It posed a clear ideological challenge to the conventional wisdom and forced a range of important and neglected issues back to a central place in the analysis of the role of the state in welfare.

The development of the welfare state

The New Right have various explanations as to how and why the state has come to take a major role in welfare in industrial societies. A number of commentators stress the significance of war – echoing Halevy's famous description of war as 'the grim harbinger of collectivism' (quoted in Greenleaf, 1973, p. 183). Joseph, for example, speaks of the Second World War bringing about the belief that 'government could do almost everything for everybody without infringing freedom or opportunity' and Lawson argues on similar lines (Hoover and Plant, 1989, pp. 135–6). Seldon writes of developments post 1945 being based on false conclusions drawn from wartime experience leading to the view that the wartime production and distribution system should continue into the peace (Seldon, 1990, p. 6).

The essence of the New Right argument is that two false conclusions were drawn from wartime experience. The first was that if a collective purpose is possible in wartime, then it is also possible in peacetime. The second was that because government had successfully planned the war, it could plan the peace. This belief fed and fuelled the conviction that it was possible to build a New Jerusalem in post-war Britain – a belief which Barnett sees as proving ultimately disastrous (Barnett, 1986). The New Right see government's wartime successes, therefore, as an important factor encouraging and legitimising a new and larger role for government in welfare. The doubt and scepticism about the potential and capacity of government which had characterised British politics in the past were swept away. The floodgates of collectivism were opened. Government had shown in wartime what it could do, therefore, it should do it.

For the New Right, there are two people in particular to blame for the new politics which contributed so much to the development of the welfare state – Keynes and Beveridge. Keynes was blamed for three things – his patrician dislike of the profit motive and the pursuit of gain, the way he made deficit budgeting legitimate, which freed governments from a vital financial discipline, and for the way in which his writings 'set the economically literate in Britain on a course where hard work, efficient industrial organisation and the employment of a high fraction of the labour force on productive and profitable work were considered to be of only secondary importance' (Wiener, 1981, p. 92).

Beveridge's influence gave a strong impetus to the belief in the desirability of collective goals and purposes. Marsland's view is that the Beveridge Report 'had the effect, whatever the author's intentions, of discouraging individualism, self-reliance, voluntary organisations, and private initiatives. It tipped the balance in the development of social policy decisively against competition and in favour of planning' (Marsland, 1992, p. 146).

The New Right see the ideas and influence of Keynes and Beveridge as a crucial – and in their judgement malign – influence on the development of the welfare state in Britain.

Also important for the New Right in the development of the welfare state are a number of misunderstandings which welfare state supporters hold about the nature of society. According to the New Right, they fail to grasp the nature of the spontaneous order (that is, the market system) and that its maintenance is 'the prime condition of the general welfare of its members' (Hayek, 1976, vol. 2, p. 6). They fail to understand its importance, its delicacy and its capacity for supplying goods and services through a process of competition and discovery. Welfare state supporters are confident in the possibilities of piecemeal social engineering partly, at least, because they fail to grasp the complexity of the market order.

The supporters of the welfare state believe in the possibility and necessity of common social purposes and their pursuit and expression in, and through, welfare state policies. The New Right see such a belief as a powerful influence on the development of the welfare state. They also regard it as mistaken in two respects. Firstly, they argue that society can be held together more securely by agreement about means than by a search for common ends. Secondly, the New Right believe that those who advocate a welfare state on the grounds of the need for shared social purposes fail to grasp the unifying potential of the market. Self-interest, they argue, following Adam Smith, can be a powerful force for co-operation. Willetts lays great stress on the belief 'that markets bring people together. They help create and sustain communities' (Willetts, 1992, p. 179). Later he speaks of the market as 'the most powerful device for human cooperation that one can envisage' (Willetts, 1992, p. 184). Novak argues that markets are morally superior to socialism and state provision because they draw people into 'reasoned, civil, voluntary interchange with their fellows and promote association and community' (Novak, 1990, p. 14).

Another misunderstanding about the nature of society which, in the opinion of the New Right supporters, has been a factor in the development of the welfare state, is the utopian belief that all – or at least most – of the historic ills which have afflicted humankind, such as poverty, unemployment and ill-health, are avoidable and that, as Glazer puts it, for every problem there is a policy (Glazer, 1988, p. 3). Marsland, for example, speaks of 'the utopian thinking of the reconstructionist movement' (Marsland, 1992, p. 164). Beveridge fired the nation's imagination with his characterisation of the five giants barring the road to reconstruction to be vanquished by collective action. Utopianism is a powerful engine of collective action. The New Right see it as failing to face the fact that problems are inherent in economic and social life.

Welfare state supporters are also, in the opinion of the gurus of the New Right, woefully ignorant of economics. Their preoccupation is with 'the social' and they have an implicit belief that 'the economic' will take care of itself. There is little sense, according to the New Right, that too much social may undermine the productive potential of the economic. This blinkered myopia has led welfare state supporters, according to the New Right, to press ahead with proposals for welfare state developments with scant regard for economic realities.

The New Right charge supporters of welfare state policies with a range of misunderstandings and failures of understanding which, in their view, lead them to press for an ever-expanding role for the state in welfare. They also accuse them of misunderstanding and misinterpreting a number of key concepts, and then arguing for welfare state policies on the basis of these misunderstood concepts – for example, liberty, justice, need and social rights.

For the New Right, liberty is essentially the absence of coercion. Supporters of the welfare state argue that freedom must not just involve being free to do something but must also involve being *able* to do it. Freedom, therefore, comes to involve the presence of real opportunities – which involves the provision of resources and services. Such a view of freedom – mistaken according to the New Right – has been an important influence on the development of the welfare state.

There is a similar dispute about social justice. It has been a powerful impetus for the development and extension of public welfare. The New Right, under the intellectual leadership of Hayek, deny that the concept has any meaning. The New Right view is that where outcomes are not intended, as in market relations, it is impossible to talk of justice or injustice. The term justice can only properly be applied to processes and procedures, not to unintended outcomes. So, for the New Right, it is a conceptual error which has been one of the most significant motors of welfare state development.

Again, the New Right are fiercely critical of the way the concepts of need and social rights have been used as levers for the extension of the role of the state in welfare. Enoch Powell describes the translation of a want or a need into a right as 'one of the most widespread and dangerous of modern heresies' (Powell, 1972, p. 12).

What essentially is at issue for the New Right is the dominance of a social element in all these concepts. All have been *socialised* when they are properly concepts of a different kind. Welfare state supporters have used their emotive power but, for the New Right, the concepts have been misused.

In their accounts of the development of the welfare state, the New Right rely heavily on their beliefs about people – that they are fundamentally self-interested – and their beliefs about the forces which dominate individuals and society – the economic ones. These beliefs lead New Right thinkers to the position which is adopted by John Gray – that 'we best understand the growth of the interventionist state if we apply to it the analysis of the Virginia School of public choice theorists'. That is to say, interventionism grows when politics comes to be dominated by democratic competition for votes. The result is 'a momentum in the trend to statism which transcends the interests, and even the wishes, of the political actors involved' (Gray, 1986, p. 120).

Public choice theorists stress two forces driving interventionism forward – firstly, the competition between parties for votes which stimulates parties to promise more and more, and secondly, the self-interested, budget-maximising behaviour of bureaucrats and professionals. 'Civil servants and welfare administrators', says Lawson, 'are far from the selfless platonic guardians of paternalist mythology: they are a major and powerful interest group in their own right' (Deakin, 1987, p. 159). The argument of the public choice theorists is that politics must be modelled as exchange and that all 'public choosers' – voters, politicians, bureaucrats – must be modelled in strict self-interest terms (Buchanan, 1986, p. 26). Once initiated, welfare programmes are driven on by these powerful pressures.

Beer's analysis of the political contradictions of collectivism depends heavily on this analytical framework. Consensus between political parties, as existed to a significant extent in Britain in the 1950s, leads to the development of group politics and party competition for group support. Groups only have incentives to maximise their claims. Success entrenches new welfare bureaucracies which become a secondary force for expansion as they press the cause of their clients – which is, at the same time, *their* cause (Beer, 1982). The costs of such expansion are always to be paid tomorrow and in any case fall on an abstraction – the community (Deakin, 1987, p. 83).

A final argument which the New Right put forward to account for the development of the welfare state is to stress the significance of definitions of social problems. From the 1890s onwards, there was more stress on the social and structural causes of social problems and less on personal factors. The New Right see this line of thought as encouraging and legitimising social action. If society 'causes' problems, then it is reasonable for society to provide compensation and solutions.

Mead, for example, describes the belief that the source of social problems was unfair social structures and sees it as having fuelled social policy development in the United States (Mead, 1986, p. 18). He also sees what he terms 'the sociological approach' as shaping the kind of policies which were adopted. If the poor are, indeed, made poor by their environment then they are not responsible for their situation, so they cannot be expected or required by government to solve their problems; government must solve them (Mead, 1986, pp. 54–5).

The New Right see 'the sociological approach' as having pushed forward the boundaries of state action in the field of welfare and as shaping the kind of policies which were adopted. They also see it as mistaken and so doomed to failure. But failure then merely strengthens the demand for more action – so the approach itself leads to an expansion in state welfare and its basic errors add to the pressure.

Attitudes towards the welfare state

The New Right do not totally reject any role for the state in welfare, but their general attitude to the idea of the welfare state is one of suspicion and anxiety. The critique has many strands; it is leavened with fact but basically it is profoundly ideological, resting on instinctive beliefs about human nature, human capacity and the nature of economic and social order.

We will examine the New Right attitude to the welfare state under eight headings. Inevitably there is some overlap between them but the eight headings represent distinctive elements in the critique.

1 The impossibility of creating a comprehensive welfare state

The New Right believe, quite simply, that creating this kind of purposeful collective enterprise is impossible. The argument has three related parts – firstly, to seek to create a comprehensive welfare state ignores the nature of spontaneous order; secondly, it assumes that such rational planning is possible and finally it assumes the possibility of a common purpose in society.

Belief in the spontaneous order is at the heart of the New Right critique of the welfare state. The idea of the spontaneous order is essentially simple: that social institutions – and social order in general – arise as a result of human action rather than from human design. Liberalism, said Hayek, 'derives from the discovery of a self-generating or spontaneous order in social affairs' (Hayek, 1967, p. 162). Such a belief asserts the primacy of tacit knowledge, of habit and custom over reason. Man, Hayek, insisted, is 'often better served by custom than by understanding' (Kukathas, 1989, p. 81). He sees social institutions as bearers of knowledge and as expressing accumulated wisdom.

For the New Right, the spontaneous order is a miracle of a self-generating, self-renewing system. It is seen as infinitely superior to any deliberate human construct. 'Order generated without design', Hayek wrote in his last book, 'can far outstrip plans men consciously contrive' (Hayek, 1988, p. 8). And yet, the self-generating, spontaneous order is a plant of great delicacy. Its functioning can all too easily be disrupted. Attempts to 'construct' a welfare state are likely to do this and the result will be disaster.

Secondly, supporters of the comprehensive welfare state assume that rational planning of the kind required is actually possible. The New Right believe that it is not – 'the fatal conceit' is how Hayek styled this belief. Oakeshott speaks of 'the myth of rationalist politics' (quoted in Willetts, 1992, p. 89).

Supporters and advocates of rationalist social planning believe that the relevant facts can be known, that from this knowledge plans to secure desired ends can be developed, that the plans can be successfully implemented and the desired aims achieve. The New Right are highly dubious of all this. They speak with contempt of the fallacies of constructivist rationalism and the failure to accept the limitations of human reason. Gray writes of 'the epistemological impossibilities of successful central planning' (Gray, 1992, p. 7). Raymond Plant, an elegant scourge of the New Right on many issues, accepts that 'the case against central economic planning is at its most decisive on epistemological grounds' (Plant, 1992, p. 120).

Three issues are crucial for the New Right. First, there is the failure of protagonists of welfare state policies to accept that they will never have all the facts they need to plan. Secondly, there is their conviction that human reason is incapable of constructing and implementing the plans to which economic and social planners aspire. Thirdly, there is the failure of the would-be social planners to appreciate the complexity of economic and social life. Such complexity seems to make planning necessary and desirable but in fact, according to Willetts 'It is precisely the increasing complexity of modern life which makes centralised organisation impossible' (Willetts, 1992, p. 25).

The third factor which makes it impossible to create a comprehensive welfare state is the simple – but decisive – impossibility of achieving common purposes in society. Hayek has long argued for the impossibility of achieving agreed social purposes. Agreement about means, yes; agreement about ends, no. A free society cannot, the New Right insist, achieve agreement about ends; that is a fact of its nature. The welfare state, however, depends on such agreement if there is to be support for the required redistribution. Failing such support, there will be disorder, diswelfare and tyranny rather than welfare.

2 Mistaken views of human nature and social order

Fundamental to the New Right critique of the welfare state is the belief that its supporters have a mistaken view of human nature and the nature of society. This conviction pervades the New Right critique and is manifested in a wide range of New Right arguments.

New Right thinkers believe that there are certain unchangeable aspects of individuals and societies, that is, certain laws for successful individual and social functioning. Individuals are seen as needing clear incentives for good behaviour and punishment for failure. Risk and uncertainty and the real danger of failure are necessary to human and social functioning. The attempt of the welfare state, says Gilder, 'to deny, suppress, and plan away the dangers and uncertainties of our lives – to domesticate the inevitable unknown – violates not only the spirit of capitalism but also the nature of man' (Gilder, 1981, p. 253). People need the discipline of insecurity and failure.

The New Right believe that welfare state supporters have a far too optimistic view of human nature. They assume people will continue to be just as innovatory and productive when the rewards of success are reduced by taxation and the costs of failure are reduced by the cushion of welfare benefits. The reality is that people are self-centred and they will only exert themselves for individual gain or to avoid painful punishment. They will not, in normal circumstances, exert themselves for a wider social good, nor will they continue to exert themselves when the rewards of so doing are only marginal. Welfare state policies, in the New Right view, ignore these elementary social laws. They see people, quite wrongly, as primarily social beings who can be motivated by social concerns and social goals. New Right thinkers reject such views as naive and dangerous.

There are two ideas here; firstly, that people are essentially individualistic in their motivation, and secondly that they respond only to the prospect and possibility of individual reward and individual punishment. What Norman Barry calls 'the aggregative approach' (Barry, 1990, p. 122), that is, the pursuit of a general social state of welfare ignores the inherently individual nature of welfare and reduces the chances of achieving it by weakening the basic laws of social functioning. 'It is the attribution of the welfare property to "social states", or aggregates that has been partially, if not mainly, responsible for the theoretical and practical problems that have become endemic to welfare states since their inception' (Barry, 1990, p. 126).

3 Mistaken Ideas about Welfare

The New Right see the welfare state as being based on a number of mistaken ideas or misinterpretations of ideas about welfare. In our discussion of New Right views on the development of the welfare state we looked at how, in the New Right view, misunderstanding of key ideas had fuelled that development. The New Right see the welfare state's development as the product of a mistaken view of the nature of liberty, of misconceptions about social justice, the idea of rights and of the concept of need. They also stress the importance of the construction, by welfare state supporters, of certain conditions as 'social problems' in terms of their causes and the remedies required.

Here we look at five other ideas which represent important elements in the philosophy of the welfare state and which the New Right see as mistaken. First, the New Right criticise the welfare state for putting the emphasis on the pursuit of equality and re-distribution rather than on growth and wealth creation. They believe that growth is more likely to enhance national welfare and to make society more equal than any egalitarian policies. They also see growth as dependent on the motor of inequality. 'The real growth in the 1980s', Brian Griffiths has argued, 'would not have occurred if the thrust of government policy had been egalitarian' (Griffiths, 1990, p. 235). The New Right also see egalitarianism as distracting attention from what they see as the major raison d'être for a welfare state, that is, the relief of poverty. By giving priority to equality over merit and desert the welfare state also, in the view of the New Right, undermines individual responsibility and the moral standing of government.

Secondly, New Right critics of the welfare state lay great stress on its failure to recognise the importance of choice to individual satisfaction and the promotion of individual growth and respon-sibility. The basic underlying philosophy of the welfare state, the New Right would argue, is that 'the state', that is, the relevant bureaucrats and professionals, knows best. There is, to New Right analysts, an unjustified faith both in their expertise and their altruism.

John Major recently argued for the link between dependency and lack of choice (Major, 1992). We, that is, governments, planners etc., have made people dependent, he said 'not because we provide the welfare and the services, but by denying people the basic human dignity of independent choice in the way they are provided'. He went on to quote Oakeshott, who wrote of 'human beings impelled by an acquired love of making choices for themselves'. The restriction of choice for the New Right both de-nies a fundamental aspect of human dignity and makes for services which lack the innovatory spur of competition.

A third important mistake with which the New Right charge welfare states is that they take a particular, narrow view of welfare. This narrowness has various dimensions. There is what Barry des-cribes as 'the assimilation of welfare to state welfare' (Barry, 1990, p. 116). Welfare states tend to adopt a very statist view of welfare with the state taking a dominating role and 'crowding out' other potential suppliers, for example, the market and the voluntary sector and the family.

Another dimension of this trend to dominance is that welfare states tend to pursue a policy of *state provision of services*. They prefer state provision of services to the provision of cash for those who need services to enable them to purchase what they need in the market place.

For the New Right, all these dimensions of welfare state policies are negative. They value a pluralism of provision, though with minimum state provision, as an approach likely to secure innova-tion and provide choice. They prefer to supply cash rather than the provision of services as that would avoid the creation of powerful bureaucracies and interest groups and provides a quasi-market solution.

Fourthly, the New Right criticise the welfare state for stressing rights rather than responsibilities and obligations. The stress is all on what my country can do for me, rather than on what I can do for my country. This is the essence of Mead's criticism of the welfare system of the United States. The main problem, he writes, is its *permissiveness*, not its size and the government's 'inability to obligate the recipients of its programs, even for their own benefit' (Mead, 1986, pp. ix–x). The United States government does give too much to the poor, he argues, in the sense of benefits given as entitlements, but at the same time it gives too little in the sense of meaningful obligations to go with the benefits (Mead, 1986, p. 3). The message conveyed by rights without obligations is that hard work is no longer required of people.

This New Right concern has a number of strands to it; that is, a concern to ration the seemingly open-ended commitment inherent in ideas of social rights and a concern for social discipline based on the view that it is unhealthy for society and for individuals if they

can get something for nothing. A further argument is that claimants do not, in fact, feel a sense of a right to benefit. If receipt of
benefit brought with it certain obligations then that might, in fact,
strengthen rather than weaken the sense of a right to services.

Finally, virtually all supporters of welfare state policies believe
that the welfare state can be a mechanism for changing society,
that is, making it more equal, reducing or abolishing poverty,
meeting needs, creating a more caring and altruistic ethos. The
New Right challenge this optimism. Willetts argues that 'the welfare state is not a mechanism for changing society but a mirror
reflecting it' (Willetts, 1992, p. 147). It will reflect society's values
and prejudices. What it provides will benefit some groups more
than others and that pattern of distribution will mirror both
society's values and existing inequalities.

By involving government, argues Lord Harris, we do nothing to
transform human conduct or restrain self-interest. All we do is
transfer those self-seeking propensities to the political plane where
their scope for abuse is greater (Harris, 1990, p. 194).

Many of the well-intentioned policies of welfare states do not
change society but instead have negative effects. Policies to help
the poor trap them in their poverty and carefully targeted policies
stigmatise and spoil identity rather than help.

4 The welfare state as a threat to freedom

Freedom, the absence of coercion by others, is the central New
Right value. New Right thinkers see freedom as threatened by the
ideas and operation of the welfare state. Five general threats make
the New Right anxious.

The first threat is posed simply by the expansion of government.
'As government grows', Griffiths writes, speaking for many New
Right supporters, 'both individual freedom and individual respon-
sibility are eroded' (Griffiths, 1982, p. 111). The connection may
seem simple-minded, even simplistic, but it is a real one for New
Right supporters. More government equals less freedom.

Secondly, there is the threat to freedom posed by the vision of
the ideal society expressed by the welfare state. It is not simply the
particular vision expressed in the welfare state which is seen as
threatening but any overarching social vision. For the New Right,

the only truly free society is one without purpose because that will be the only form of society which coerces no one.

The problem with collective goals and social purposes is that it is impossible to ensure that everyone agrees to them. Hayek's view, as summarised by Crowley (Crowley, 1987, p. 48) is that it is immoral for society to seek to enforce any particular pattern of wealth distribution, for example, because not all members of society would accept such a pattern. To be morally defensible, such a scheme would require virtually universal agreement and to secure that is virtually impossible. Gray argues on similar lines in relation to the pursuit of social justice. Because there is no consensus, the pursuit of social justice threatens the transformation of a free society into a totalitarian state (Gray, 1986, pp. 72–3).

Thirdly, there is the very particular threat posed to freedom by egalitarianism. The New Right see egalitarianism as dependent on coercion because redistribution is inevitably coercive. Those affected have not willingly consented to it. The aim may be to promote the rights of others but it is certainly an encroachment on the property rights of those from whom resources are taken. For Hayek, redistribution to provide a basic minimum for all may be acceptable but redistribution for egalitarian purposes is incompatible with the rule of law and the ideals of a free society.

Fourthly, the welfare state is a threat to freedom because of the way it fails to offer people any choice as it is paternalistic and authoritarian. There is little right to choose and usually there is no alternative. New Right supporters argue that the market offers a more effective form of democracy by enabling everyone to make choices. The case for capitalism, Seldon concludes, 'is that the democracy of the market offers the masses more than the democracy of politics' (Seldon, 1990, p. 103). To be deprived of choice is to be deprived of freedom and to be diminished as a person. These are key beliefs for the New Right. They believe that the market can extend choice – it can give service users the power of exit not just 'the precarious power of voice' (Seldon, 1990, p. 107).

Finally, the welfare state is regarded as a threat to freedom because of its basic pattern of organisation. The norm is monopolistic organisations dominated by powerful bureaucracies and influential professional groups. Welfare states entrench producer power whereas, so the New Right would argue, markets give consumers power over producers. Certainly, in welfare states, the dominant forces are producers not consumers. Consumers may have the power of voice but it is the still small voice against the orchestrated professional voice and exit is to the wilderness. There is a clear imbalance of power creating unfreedom. It is a problem, the New Right insist, which is inherent in the nature of welfare states.

5 The welfare state is seen as inefficient and ineffective

As well as more general theoretical and ideological criticisms of the welfare state, the New Right also charge it specifically with inefficiency and ineffectiveness in relation to the services it provides. They see these characteristics as inherent in its nature. Welfare state policies tend to be implemented via large monopolistic programmes. The New Right link size with inefficiency and ineffectiveness and monopolies, by definition, come under the same condemnation. Without the spur of competition, there are no incentives to innovation or greater efficiency.

New Right thinkers are also fiercely critical of the basic instruments of welfare state policies, that is, bureaucracies and professionals. For the New Right they are not the disinterested eunuchs of policy implementation but are strongly interested, and extremely powerful, parties. They have a very clear interest in expansion, and some see them, indeed, as the main beneficiaries of welfare state programmes. Politicians have limited power; consumers have less. Producer power rules. The result is services and systems geared rather to producer interests than to the public interest and the needs of service users. There are no natural corrective mechanisms which ensure service change in response to changing needs or proven deficiencies. Too many powerful people have an interest in perpetuating the status quo.

As the New Right see it, there is little hope of effective control of these welfare bureaucracies. Hayek says 'It is sheer illusion to think that when certain needs of the citizen have become the exclusive concern of a single bureaucratic machine, democratic control of that machine can then effectively guard the liberty of the citizen' (Hayek, 1960, p. 261). In Green's view, 'No system will ever be responsive to customers if producers receive payment whether or not their work is satisfactory' (Green, 1988, p. 71).

The New Right critique of bureaucracies and professionals – particularly of bureaucracies – is a powerful one and has been widely accepted. Deakin sees the general acceptance of the case against large-scale state bureaucracies as 'among the New Right's most striking intellectual achievements' (Deakin, 1987, p. 177).

Another important New Right claim in the inefficiency-ineffectiveness area is that welfare state policies can produce at different times both over-supply of services and insufficient supply. Dunleavy and O'Leary see the over-supply thesis as 'a key New Right claim' (Dunleavy and O'Leary, 1987, p. 117). The reasons are simple. Bureaucracies will always tend to over-supply because growth and expansion are in their interests. In the public sector, there are no built-in restraints which will ensure that production stops at the point where the welfare increment to society exceeds the cost.

It is a commonplace of analysis of the welfare state that there is clear underfunding in some areas, for example, in the National Health Service. Social democratic critics blame government; the New Right blame the system of public financing. A tax-financed service, they argue, will always, and inevitably, be underfunded. Tax financing prevents people from spending what they would spend if such spending was a matter of private decision.

A fourth line of criticism is that in welfare states with universal services, large amounts of expenditure go to those who do not need them – in Gray's vigorous words, 'the British welfare state is a middle class racket without ethical justification or standing' (Gray, 1992, p. 87). The New Right argument is that this is inevitable. Those who have power and influence, who shape and deliver policies, will inevitably do best.

Charles Murray's verdict on anti-poverty policy in the United States is the classic statement of the ineffectiveness of welfare state policies. 'We tried to provide more for the poor', he wrote in *Losing Ground*, 'and produced more poor instead. We tried to remove the barriers to escape from poverty and inadvertently built a trap' (Murray, 1984, p. 9). Clearly, there are likely to be unintended consequences of many policies. The New Right see them as inherent. Barry may well be right that there is no system of welfare, short of the harsh conditions specified by the Poor Law, which will not have counterproductive effects through proving too attractive or through creating anomalies (Barry, 1990, pp. 119–20).

The issue is not whether such perverse effects exist but how extensive they are and how such perversities are to be weighed and balanced against other outcomes.

6 The welfare state is seen as economically damaging

There is space here to do no more than provide a brief sketch of the New Right criticism that the welfare state is generally damaging to the economy. The lines of the argument are clear. What seems to have happened, however, in the late 1980s and early 1990s is that the New Right have laid less stress on the supposed economically damaging effect of welfare state policies and put more emphasis on its socially damaging impact.

The New Right begin their critique of the economic impact of the welfare state from the firm conviction that the free market is the essential force for dynamism and growth. As Gilder puts it, if the politicians want to have central planning and command, they cannot have dynamism and life (Gilder, 1981, p. 237). Every aspect of the welfare state which interferes with the benign forces of the market is therefore actually, or potentially, weakening to the economy.

What gives the market its dynamism is the competition it engenders through offering rewards for the energetic and the successful and punishment and failure for the idle. This simple reward-punishment axis is what creates growth. Anything which reduces the rewards for success or the punishment of failure is therefore economically damaging.

The high rates of taxation demanded by welfare state policies and driven constantly higher by the dangerous heresy of social rights are clearly a tax on enterprise and success. They are, therefore, a disincentive to effort for the wealth creators. There are the high rates of public expenditure which are a burden on the productive elements of the economy. Government provision for old age, illness, unemployment and other contingencies reduces the incentives to individuals to save, leading to too little savings.

The forces making for a dynamic economy are, in the New Right view, reduced by welfare state-type policies. At the same time, the incentives to idleness and lethargy are increased. Gilder pinpoints the upsetting of the balance between risk and security as crucial.

'When too many people know where they are going', he suggests, 'the economy doesn't get very far' (Gilder, 1981, p. 113). In his view, it is impossible to create a system of collective regulation and safety that does not, in the end, deaden the moral sources of the willingness to face danger and fight, which he sees as vital to a dynamic economy. In Mead's view, what undermines the economy is not so much the burden on the private sector from high taxation, as the message government programmes have given that work has become an option for Americans (Mead, 1986, p. 3). Underneath are always the everlasting arms of the state as a safety net.

More specifically, the New Right see social security provision and other forms of labour regulation as damaging competitiveness. Social security benefits increase the cost of labour to employers and become a de facto minimum wage which pushes up the cost of labour.

7 The welfare state is seen as socially damaging

There is a long-standing concern in New Right thinking about the impact of welfare collectivism on the national character and on key social values. For example, in 1944, Hayek believed that 'the progress of collectivism and its inherently centralistic tendencies are progressively destroying' independence, self-reliance, individual initiative and local responsibility (quoted in Willetts, 1992, p. 32). Willetts sees the argument that the welfare state undermines important social values as 'perhaps the most devastating critique of the welfare state' (Willetts, 1992, p. 149).

At the heart of this argument is the belief that the welfare state erodes individual and social responsibility. 'Intervention by the state must never become so great', Mrs Thatcher told the Church of Scotland Assembly in May 1988, 'that it effectively removes personal responsibility' (Thatcher, 1990, p. 336). When she came to power in 1979, she argued 'People had become accustomed to having no responsibility' (*The Guardian*, 22.4.92).

The argument that the welfare state undermines individual and social responsibility has a number of strands to it. First, there is the belief that as government grows so individual responsibility is eroded (Griffiths, 1982, p. 111). People come to believe that they have a right to have their needs met so they feel less responsibility for trying to meet them themselves. Green suggests that perhaps the most damaging effect of the National Health Service's promise of 'free' health care has been 'the way it has undermined the capacity of people for self direction and spread a child-like dependency on the state' (Green, 1988, p. 5).

Second, there is the belief that to protect people from the consequences of their own actions is damaging to individual responsibility. The vital umbilical link between conduct and consequences is severed. Reviewing the years between 1945 and the mid-1980s, Davies argues that the main aim of economic and social policy 'has frequently been to protect individuals and groups from the consequences of their actions. This undermines any idea of responsibility' (Davies, 1991, p. 251). Protecting people from unfortunate consequences, in the New Right view, simply allows them to be the anti-social, irresponsible beings which they are without the crucial disciplines of poverty, unemployment, illness or homelessness.

A third argument is that the welfare state undermines individual responsibility by failing to recognise it. The assumption of social responsibility for the poor and their problems, Mead argues, prevents policy-makers from accepting and recognising individual responsibility (Mead, 1986, p. 46). Society's assumption of responsibility for the needs of the poor prevents any individual responsibility on the part of the poor to get out of that situation.

Fourthly, there is the argument that depriving people of choice attacks a basic characteristic and element in responsible behaviour. To be a fully human, adult person is to have a right of choice in most spheres of life – but not in welfare.

Fifthly, there is the more specific argument that welfare state policies, in general, create a dependency culture and so undermine individual responsibility. It was the welfare state which, in Barnett's view, turned the mass of the British people into a 'subliterate, unskilled, unhealthy and institutionalised proletariat hanging on the nipple of state maternalism' (Barnett, 1986, p. 304). Segalman and Marsland write with ill-concealed relish of 'the culture of serfdom into which we [the British] have gradually sunk since the Second World War', as a result of the welfare state (Segalman and Marsland, 1989, p. 134). 'The only hope we can give to the poor', Keith Joseph concluded, 'is helping them to help themselves; to do the opposite, to create more dependence is to destroy their morality, whilst throwing an unfair burden on society' (quoted in Lowe, 1993, p. 303). The New Right argue that an underclass is created and sustained by the welfare system. Gilder again writes of welfare exerting 'a constant, seductive, erosive pressure on the marriage and work habits of the poor, and over the years in poor communities, it fosters a durable "welfare culture" ' (Gilder, 1981, p. 122).

At the heart of New Right concern about the socially damaging effects of the welfare state is the belief in the moral hazards of social provision, that is, that by providing for certain social contingencies, the welfare state actually promotes the behaviour which leads to the conditions from which it seeks to protect people. Providing benefits for the unemployed increases unemployment. Provision of benefits for single-parent families increases family break-up.

Murray sets out the argument in *Losing Ground* that the extension of benefits for the poor in the United States in the 1960s 'was to make it profitable for the poor to behave in the short term in ways that were destructive in the long term' (Murray, 1984, pp. 8–9). Murray's verdict is that 'social programmes in a democratic society tend to produce net harm in dealing with the most difficult problems' because they have enough of an inducement to produce bad behaviour but not enough of a solution to stimulate good behaviour (Murray, 1984, p. 218).

In addition to this charge of weakening individual responsibility, the New Right also charge the welfare state with damaging individuals' sense of social responsibility. If the state takes over welfare, individuals will come to feel that when they have paid their taxes they have fulfilled all the responsibilities which could properly be required of them. 'If our benign and cooperative relations with our fellow citizens', says Willetts, 'become instead functions of the state, then we are indeed reduced to merely atomistic individuals pursuing our own self interest' (Willetts, 1992, p. 74). People need feel no sense of social responsibility because the state has relieved them of that duty but society is damaged and diminished.

Two other points made by the New Right about the potentially damaging social impact of the welfare state need to be noted. There is the charge that the welfare state destabilises the family. In Britain, the New Right have been concerned about changes in the family such as the increased number of married women working outside the home, the increase in single-parent families and the increase in cohabitation and births taking place outside marriage. They link some of these developments with the influence of the welfare state, for example, encouraging the ending of unsatisfactory marriages by the availability of social security benefits for single parents.

The American critique of welfare and the family is more complex. The availability of cash benefits for fatherless families in the ghetto has, the argument runs, destroyed the father's key role and authority so families break up. Government policy deprives poor families of strong fathers and so dooms them to poverty and damages the economic prospects of the children. 'By making optional the male provider role', says Gilder, 'welfare weakens and estranges the prime mover in upward mobility' (Gilder, 1981, p. 122). The father is reduced to a role of irresponsibility and the family is thus weakened and impoverished. As the worker's family responsibilities are weakened, so is his attachment to the role of worker and provider.

The final socially damaging impact of the welfare state is on 'mediating structures'. Brian Griffiths and David Willetts both make this point. Both argue for the importance of 'mediating structures', that is, organisations coming between the individual and the state, such as the family, the neighbourhood, the voluntary organisation, the church, in the development of civic virtues, as a way for people to identify with the larger society, as a way of empowering people, as a way of reminding people that as citizens we do not fulfil our responsibilities to our fellow citizens simply by paying taxes. Both Griffiths and Willetts see these 'mediating structures' as diminished and threatened by public provision of welfare and the inevitable accompanying centralisation (Griffiths, 1990, pp. 224–5; Willetts, 1992, p. 147).

8 The welfare state is seen as politically damaging

The New Right see welfare state policies as undermining the authority of government and there are two parts to its argument. First, welfare state policies lead to a continuing enlargement of the role and responsibilities of government because of the conviction that every problem has a policy. Governments, therefore, are led to assume responsibilities for policies that cannot succeed such as the abolition of poverty, the improvement of the nation's health, or the equalising of educational opportunity. Failure is inevitable and failure means loss of standing and authority.

The second strand in the argument relates to how welfare state policies lead to the growth of powerful interest groups. The expanded role of government in service provision and making laws creates interest groups which seek to determine government policy. Government becomes a focus for interest group activity such as tenants' groups, claimants' groups, pensioners, women, all seeking government action to remedy alleged wrongs or promote alleged rights. At the same time, government commitments to, for example, improving health services or education mean that it comes to depend on key producer groups to make good its commitments. Government, therefore, loses power and legitimacy. Politics becomes to do with reconciling interest groups. The idea of the common good is submerged in a group politics of envy and self-interest.

Welfare and their ideal society

It scarcely needs saying that there is no one single New Right vision of the ideal welfare system. There are those like Charles Murray who propose the scrapping of the entire US federal and state income support systems for people of working age, so freeing them from the forces that encourage them to remain poor and dependent (Murray, 1984, pp. 227–8, 233). There are others, like John Gray, who argue that a genuinely liberal approach will favour an enabling welfare state with universal entitlement in many areas and targeting and discretion where appropriate (Gray, 1992, pp. 71–2).

It is, however, possible to provide a sketch of the New Right's vision. Markets will play a much larger role; the state a reduced and different role. The New Right favour a larger role for the market for a variety of reasons. Some have emerged in earlier discussion but it is worth drawing them together at this point.

Firstly, there is the argument that the market is the best mechanism for discovering and coordinating dispersed knowledge and preferences. This, rather than its efficiency in generating wealth, is

Hayek's ultimate defence of the market. The market is the best way of finding out what people want and of coordinating knowledge about how best to organise provision. Keith Joseph speaks for all shades of New Right opinion in expressing the judgement that 'the blind, unplanned, uncoordinated wisdom of the market . . . is overwhelmingly superior to the well researched, rational, systematic, well meaning, cooperative, science based, forward looking, respectable plans of government' (Joseph, 1976, p. 57).

Secondly, market provision will provide a wider range of choice than the alternatives. 'The self ordering process', says Hayek, 'will secure for any random member of such a group a better choice over a wide range of opportunities available to all than any rival system could offer' (Hayek, 1988, p. 85). Markets can be, in Gray's words 'enabling devices for human autonomy' (Gray, 1992, p. 26). Choice for the New Right is, as we have seen, a crucial constituent of human dignity.

Thirdly, market systems do not depend for their success on the beneficent motives of service providers. It was Hume who saw and stressed that the market made it possible 'to do a service to another without bearing him a real kindness' (quoted in Hayek, 1988, p. 47). Markets compel providers to be sensitive to the needs of potential users – for the sake of their own survival in business.

Fourthly, market provision reduces the power of providers – the bureaucrats and professionals. It removes that discretionary and uncontrollable power which monopolistic public systems place in the hands of officials.

Fifthly, in market systems, competition benefits the consumer by provision of goods and services at prices which are reduced by the benign forces of competition. Competition keeps prices down and quality up as well as stimulating variety and innovation. It is a mechanism which has a range of benefits to the consumer. The Friedmans' verdict was that 'introducing competition can alone lead to a major improvement in the quality of schooling available to all strata in our society' (Friedman, 1984, p. 163).

Sixthly, market provision fits in better with the fundamental realities of human nature, for example, people's and society's need for individual responsibility and people's essential self- and family-centredness. Nothing depends on the fallible uncertainties of altruism and communal responsibility. 'The market derives its strength', Griffiths states, 'from the instincts and abilities of ordinary people. It works with the grain of human nature' (Griffiths, 1990, p. 233).

Seventh, the New Right also argue that, in general, market provision is more democratic. The New Right have grave doubts about the reality of the supposed democracy of politics. They see politics as much more to do with the struggle between powerful interest groups. They see the barons of welfare bureaucracies as amenable in no realistic sense to public, or political, control. In contrast, in the market everyone counts and the consumer rules. With money in her pocket she is king. As Seldon puts it, 'the case for capitalism is that the democracy of the market offers the masses more than the democracy of politics' (Seldon, 1990, p. 103).

Eighthly, the New Right have great faith in individuals, and little faith in systems and institutions. 'Left to itself', Barry judges, ' "society" generates few problems which individuals cannot solve themselves' (Barry, 1987, p. 192). This belief makes an argument for less reliance on state provision, more reliance on market provision and the support individuals can find in the field of voluntary and informal welfare. It pushes individuals back on their own resources, which is where responsibility *should* rest and where it is good for individuals and society that it *does* rest.

These convictions mean that, for the New Right, markets should play the major role in the provision of social services. This points towards private health insurance, private provision against the needs of old age, encouragement of the private provision of education possibly through voucher or assisted place schemes. In housing, the two major sources of supply should be private landlords and owner occupation, which merits public support because of its social desirability.

The basic direction of New Right thinking is plain: private is better. But after decades of public provision the state has come to be seen by many as the essential provider in many areas. New Right proposals are, therefore, tempered to varying degrees by a sense of this reality and the political and practical difficulties of changing the status quo. The ideal, however, is clear.

Faith in the market has obvious implications for how the role of the state is seen but it does not rule out all state action. Friedman, for example, sets out four areas where, in his view, state action is entirely legitimate and where leaving action to the market would be inadvisable. First, he sees a clear role for the state as 'rule maker and umpire' to create a legal framework for the efficient functioning of the market system. Secondly, Friedman accepts that there are areas of economic activity which can reasonably be regarded as natural monopolies which the state may provide without adverse economic effects on the market system, areas such as the postal system.

Thirdly, Friedman argues that it is reasonable and proper for government to organise free provision of services and facilities where it is simply impracticable or too expensive to organise such provision on a market basis. The example he quotes is city parks where it would be absurd to try to charge everyone who used such a facility and so the market system would never work here.

Fourthly, paternalist provision for those not able to assume full responsibility for themselves is quite proper. Friedman has in mind groups such as the severely mentally ill or people with severe learning difficulties (Friedman, 1962, pp. 28–31).

There is a range of other guiding principles which the New Right assert in relation to the role of government in welfare. Firstly, they are absolutely clear that where the state does get involved in the provision of welfare its role should be limited to the provision of residual, minimal services, that is, safety net provision. That is all that the state can efficiently, legitimately and properly provide.

Secondly, the state must abandon those impossible and destructive goals of equality and social justice. Both are figments of the constructivist rationalist utopianism which has misguided social policy. Neither is desirable or attainable. They simply lead to an ever-expanding role for the state and provoke socially damaging envy and conflict between dissatisfied interests. Charles Murray aptly catches the spirit of the New Right dream. 'Billions for equal opportunity, not one cent for equal outcome' (Murray, 1984, p. 233).

Thirdly, the state's role should be one of enabling rather than providing. It should be enabling in the sense of enabling people to meet their own needs if necessary by vouchers or cash help or enabling voluntary and private providers to meet their needs.

Fourthly, where public provision of services is seen as appropriate, or temporarily at least, inevitable, the state should establish competitive internal markets so that different elements in a service, for example, General Practitioners and hospitals, and different institutions, for example, schools and universities, buy and sell services to and from each other and engage in the beneficent competition from which service users reap the benefits.

Fifthly, the state's role should be competitive and non-monopolistic, working in competition and/or partnership with other providers. In part, this is the twin pillars approach, as set out, for example, in the British Government's proposals for the reform of social security in the 1980s. It can also involve government still providing services but in competition with private or voluntary interests. Hayek, for example, sees no problem with non-monopolistic provision by the state (Hayek, 1960, p. 257).

Sixthly, state provision must be conditional not simply a right. Mead is the great advocate of this approach. Benefits, in his view, must be accompanied by obligations and conditions, for example, employable recipients of social security benefits should be obliged to work in return for benefits. His argument is simply that 'there is good reason to think that recipients subject to such requirements would function better' (Mead, 1986, p. 1). He advocates a policy which combines requiring responsibilities of claimants with support for them in a balance which approximates to what the ordinary person faces when in employment.

Gilder is another advocate of using welfare services to encourage and inculcate socially desired behaviour. He stresses the centrality of marriage and family ties to the work effort of men and therefore to any attempt to take poor families out of the poverty trap (Gilder, 1981, p. 69). Social policy must therefore be deliberately directed to strengthening the male role in families.

As in all schools of thought, New Right supporters range across a lengthy continuum with idealists at one end and the more pragmatic at the other. But the broad lines of the kind of social policies the New Right would like to see are clear enough – more market, less state and a different state.

Assessment

There is no such thing as a value-free assessment. Assessment is always, to a degree, an ideological activity. Bearing that in mind we attempt an assessment of the New Right approach under five headings.

The basic nature of the New Right's approach

First, we need to assess the basic nature of the New Right's approach, the way in which its protagonists approach the issue of the role of the state in welfare. Our judgement would be that, essentially, the New Right proceed by assertion. Their arguments are vigorously put; frequently they strike a resonant chord with the student of social policy but they tend to lack the supporting evidence which the unprejudiced observer would expect. There is argument but a lack of evidence. The welfare state is said to be dominated by egalitarianism. Inequality and low public spending are said to be vital to economic growth. All bureaucrats are self-interested budget maximisers. Welfare creates dependency. These statements may, or may not be true. The New Right propound them – and many more – as if their truth were proven and self-evident. All are contestable and on many there is empirical evidence. The New Right proceed by belief, instinct and assertion rather than a careful examination of often complex evidence.

The philosophical base

A second important area which needs to be explored for an assessment of the New Right is the strength of the philosophical base underpinning the New Right approach.

Three concepts are central to New Right thinking – freedom, justice and individualism. The New Right has a particular view on each of them – a view which is vigorously contested by critics. Essentially, the New Right see freedom as the absence of coercion. Freedom is defined as being *free* to do something, not being *able* to do something. But, if the value of freedom lies in its contribution to autonomy, then surely real freedom must involve positive possibilities. The New Right assert the priority of freedom over all other values but, as Barbara Wootton pointed out, freedom is not one and indivisible. There are many *freedoms* rather than one *freedom* – and some are more important than others. To have a cutting edge, any discussion must be specific about what particular kind of freedom is at issue (Hindess, 1987, p. 161).

As regards justice, the New Right deny the possibility of a valid concept of social justice. The outcomes of economic and social processes cannot be defined as just or unjust, they argue, because they are unintended. For the New Right, only processes and procedures can properly be described as just or unjust. Social outcomes may, indeed, not be intended but, as Plant has pointed out (Plant, 1990, p. 18) they are often predictable and our collective response to them can reasonably be defined as just or unjust.

The New Right's stress on individualism – there is, in Mrs Thatcher's famous words, no such thing as society, only individuals and families – is equally open to criticism. We are all social beings, in part we are what we are, or are not, because of the society in which we live. Like it or not – and the New Right clearly do not – we are all linked to others in patterns and cycles of dependency. We become what we are as individuals largely because of our links and contacts with other people.

The basic philosophical premises from which the New Right start are clearly open to argument and criticism.

The approach to the free market

The third important issue we must explore is the New Right approach to the free market. Faith in the market is at the heart of their approach but how well supported and argued is that faith? Certainly, the market system offers a mechanism of enormous potential value in welfare. Competition *is* a valuable discovery mechanism and it *does* offer choice. The need to compete with other providers or institutions does give providers a powerful incentive to responsiveness to the needs and interests of users and would-be users. Markets may need states; welfare states also need markets, or, at least, some market mechanisms. Barry is surely right in his argument that 'the last decade [the 1980s] has seen the re-establishment of the intellectual respectability of the decentralized market exchange system as a social institution' (Barry, 1991, p. 267). The credit for that belongs to the New Right. The fact that many Democratic Socialist thinkers now accept the value of the market mechanism and that the term 'market socialism' has become part of political discourse is, in part, an implicit tribute to the New Right.

Three criticisms must, however, be made. First, there is a dangerous 'essentialism' about much New Right thinking about the market. Hindess makes this point about Hayek, arguing that

Hayek ignores the fact that markets always operate under specific institutional conditions and those conditions largely shape the way markets function. Markets do not just exist in a vacuum – pure, unchanged and unchanging. They are shaped by the conditions in, and under, which they function. Markets need *locating* if they are to be evaluated sensibly (Hindess, 1987, p. 150).

A second criticism is that the New Right show little appreciation of the significance of inequalities of economic and political power to market outcomes. There is little sense of how structural inequalities of this kind limit the ability to use the market. It is as if the playing field is level when markets begin to operate. John Gray is someone who shows sensitivity to this point. He sees a risk of the invisible hand becoming, in the real world, the invisible boot (Crowley, 1987, p. 58) and suggests that 'redistribution of property holdings may be mandated by the concern for autonomy which is the chief ethical rationale for the market' (Gray, 1990, p. 143). Most New Right thinkers are less sensitive to this issue.

The third criticism is that New Right writings discuss the market in an abstract way with little consideration of the impact a market system might have on society. Harold Macmillan suggested many years ago that if capitalism had actually been conducted as if the theory of private enterprise were a matter of principle and all state intervention therefore had been resisted 'we should have had civil war long ago' (Gilmour, 1978, p. 168). MacPherson in *The Political Theory of Possessive Individualism* argues that a possessive market *economy* will inevitably result in a possessive market *society* and such a society will face acute difficulties in generating a sense of social and political obligation (MacPherson, 1962). Markets need the normative restraints of established and community relationships to restrain a potentially destructive individualism. 'An untempered liberalism', Waltzer concludes, 'would be unendurable' (Kumar, 1983, pp. 156–7). The New Right show no awareness of this issue.

The overall approach to state welfare provision

Central to any assessment of New Right thinking must be an assessment of the New Right's overall approach to state welfare provision. That approach has its strengths but it also has its weaknesses. Among the positive elements would be the forcing on to the agenda of issues of economy, efficiency and effectiveness and the asking of sharp questions about aims and outcomes and costs. For thirty years, these key questions were seldom asked with the proper force and urgency. The New Right put them back where they belong – at the heart of the debate about welfare. Another very important contribution has been to assert the central importance of voluntary and private welfare provision, thus locating state welfare as one method of providing welfare in a system which is essentially pluralist. Also valuable, was the New Right questioning of whether *state responsibility* must necessarily mean *state provision* which is the basic, unquestioned belief of most welfare state policies. The New Right assert the possibilities of an *enabling* state, one that ensures that services are provided, for example, by giving consumers cash or vouchers, or by signing contracts with voluntary or private providers to supply given amounts of service. This approach makes possible a potentially more varied, sensitive and responsive provision of welfare services.

Closely connected with this contribution is the New Right stress on choice and consumer rights. The basic thrust of state welfare has been provision of uniform services, on a take it or leave it basis. Services have often treated service users with scant regard for their individuality or their dignity. Providers have dominated; users have been given little attention, much less than in many parts of the market system.

Set against these valuable insights are other criticisms which are more suspect. First must be the New Right's dismissive approach to the possibilities of politics. They dismiss politics and planning as methods of dealing with social problems or of securing social improvement almost out of hand. They have no faith in humankind's constructive abilities in this area. This lack of confidence in humankind's ability to do anything to construct a 'better' social order than that which evolves from the free play of market forces is a useful corrective to utopian dreaming but it is a denial of historical experience. By taking thought, social ills can be ameliorated and corrected. Governments can and do devise policies which ameliorate, even if they do not solve, social problems. In private industry, firms certainly plan very carefully for the future. They may be devotees of the free market, but they do not reject the possibility of planning to improve their ability to compete.

Central to the New Right's rejection of the possibility of government action to remedy social ills and improve society is the belief that the market is a more successful instrument. The evidence, however, does not support such a view. One obvious example is the New Right argument that economic growth and 'trickle down' are the best ways of tackling poverty. The evidence simply does not support such a view. A rising tide does not raise all boats as some are stuck too firmly in the mud. On the other hand, there is good evidence that government policies can successfully combat poverty, can improve access to health care, and can extend educational opportunities. Government is a proven instrument with a record of considerable success which challenges the New Right rejection of the possibilities of politics. Certainly, there is an issue about the scope and proper areas of state action but the force of the New Right critique of state action almost pushes this – the real issue – to one side.

The New Right critique of the impact of state welfare is also unbalanced. Certainly, state welfare can create dependency. Certainly, there is a moral hazard inherent in social service provision (and of course in all private insurance). Providing for a need may indeed increase the extent of that need. Supplying social security benefits for single parents may actually increase the extent of single parenthood because it allows (mainly) women to escape from unsatisfactory relationships. It would be extremely surprising if the provision of state welfare did not have some negative effects, but those need to be weighed against its positive effects, not addressed in critical isolation. All the evidence, too, suggests that such negative effects are very small and are greatly outweighed by the positive impact.

What the New Right do is to set an idealised market against a partial, worst case assessment of the impact of public provision and that is scarcely satisfactory. What is needed is a coolly balanced assessment of the broad possibilities, effects, costs and benefits of state welfare and a careful weighing of evidence. That we do not get as the New Right are prosecuting, not judging in a cool impartial fashion.

Social analysis

The final area for assessment must be the New Right's general social analysis and its contribution to our understanding of how

social wellbeing can be enhanced. There are certainly positive contributions. The stress on the primary importance of a healthy economy to social welfare is one of these. The priority which the New
Right wish to see given to economic goals and economic growth
over social goals is contestable. The priority they give to the economy as the main engine of welfare rather than welfare state policies is not. Until recently, supporters of welfare state policies in
Britain did not pay sufficient attention to the economy or to the
centrality of work to welfare. The New Right have highlighted
these links and put them on the public agenda.

Another valuable element in New Right social analysis is its
breadth. It was the New Right, effectively, who brought key questions about state welfare to the forefront of public discussion.
What is the impact of state welfare on behaviour? What are the
implications of the extension of social rights without the parallel
extension of obligations? How can state welfare be used to induce
socially desirable behaviour?

Having raised these questions the New Right approach to social
analysis is severely weakened by its strong element of determinism. Economies grow when taxes are low; they stagnate because
of high rates of public expenditure. Benefits create dependency.
Any social planning is impossible because governments can never
know enough to plan intelligently. As always, reality is more complex. No government today can function without some degree of
economic and social planning; in Britain, for example, New Right
governments have devoted enormous attention to planning
changes in public expenditure and to planning the development of
new patterns of social provision. The real issue – perhaps the only
one – is what kind and degree of planning yields positive results.

Our conclusion is that while the New Right have raised a variety
of important questions about the role of the state in welfare and
about welfare state policies their ultimate contribution is no more
than critical. What is offered as an alternative to welfare state
policies is no answer to the complex problems and needs of late
twentieth-century society. If it were put into effect, the New Right
vision of an ideal society would reduce rather than enhance the
freedom and opportunities of most members of society.

CHAPTER 3

THE MIDDLE WAY

The Middle Way perspective on the role of the state in welfare is distinct but ill-defined. It embraces a range of thinkers with differing views but who are united in the conviction that it is both necessary and possible to graft measures of state welfare on to capitalism and soften its rough edges. Traditional Conservatives, for example, Macmillan, Butler and Gilmour in Britain, make up the heart of the Middle Way but non-Conservatives such as Beveridge and Keynes can also, for our purposes, be classified as part of this group. Skidelsky, for example, writes of 'Keynes's philosophy of the Middle Way' (Skidelsky, 1992, p. 229). Burns spoke of Keynes as 'the high priest of Conservative collectivism' and of Beveridge as 'second only to Keynes' as an exponent of this philosophy (Burns, 1963, p. 193, p. 196). It is a perspective which went into political eclipse in Britain in the 1980s and 1990s though strong statements of the position continued to be published (e.g. Gilmour, 1992).

Supporters of the Middle Way share certain clear and common beliefs. They have faith in the free market system as the best way of organising an economy. But they believe it needs managing and that many of its effects need to be controlled and compensated for. They believe that government can manage capitalism and make good many of these unacceptable effects but they have no faith in government's ability to create an ideal society. The attitude of the Middle Way towards the welfare state is one of critical acceptance. This group has few doubts that the state must play a major role in welfare but there is a critical approach to the nature and extent of that role. Certain aims are acceptable, the relief of distress, for example, but others such as the pursuit of greater substantive equality, are not.

The development of the welfare state

The Middle Way approach to explaining the development of the welfare state reflects their critical but endorsing position. It embraces both supportive and critical explanations and together they provide an insight into the thinking of the group.

The Middle Way are keen to emphasise that the welfare state is not the result simply of working-class party efforts but is an all-party creation. Gilmour and Hailsham both stress that the welfare state was not created by the Labour Party in the years after 1945 but has roots which go back deep into English history (Gilmour, 1992, p. 108; Hailsham, 1959, p. 109). Gilmour stresses the importance in its evolution of the great reforming achievements of Neville Chamberlain at the Ministry of Health in the 1920s (Gilmour, 1978, pp. 33–4). The Middle Way would emphasise Addison's judgement that by 1939 the social services in Britain were

> the most advanced in the world . . . and the Social Democrats in Sweden, the Labour Party in New Zealand and the New Deal Democrats in the United States were trying to bring about many of the improvements which Conservatism took for granted. (Addison, 1975, p. 33)

Gilmour also stresses how 'the pattern of British post-war politics was set by Churchill's great wartime coalition, not by Attlee's post-war government' (Gilmour, 1978, p. 18). Hailsham takes the same view (Hailsham, 1959, p. 109). Leading in the House of Commons in the debate on the 1947 Budget, Eden claimed that Labour's scheme of social services originated with the plans of the Coalition and that differences of degree, not principle, divided the parties (Beer, 1982, p. 310). So, for the Middle Way, the welfare state is not to be understood simply as a socialist enterprise. Vincent's judgement is that 'the concept of the welfare state in most European societies owes as much to Conservatism as to other ideologies' (Vincent, 1992, p. 76).

The group also sees the welfare state as a natural product of the relationship which develops between people and the state in a democracy. The state needs loyalty; voters want – and need – benefits and services. Loyalties have to be won; authority has to secure legitimation and respect. There has to be a partnership between state and people because 'If the state is not interested in them, why should they be interested in the state?' (Gilmour, 1978, p. 118).

The developing role of the state in welfare is seen as a pragmatic response to social ills in a democratic society, to the need for health care, to poverty, or to old age. Such ills need to be relieved because they are unpleasant and painful and because their existence threatens the social order. No great principles were involved because supporters of the Middle Way are fundamentally pragmatic people. A problem was diagnosed and defined. Something had to be done. The state was on hand and it was used. 'Tories are bold', says Heseltine, 'in bringing the resources of the state to the rescue of the needy' (Heseltine, 1987, p. 5).

Another approach, which is close to the one just discussed but rather broader, rests on the belief that the welfare state developed as a response to market failures. While sharing a fundamental faith in private enterprise and the free market system, such a faith is constrained by a critical consciousness. The Democratic Socialist critique of the market is a general one. The Middle Way critique is particular and relates to specific problems.

It is a fact of life, for example, that a free market does not provide an acceptable standard of housing for the lower paid in any industrial society (Galbraith and Menshikov, 1989, p. 80). The city economy needs lower paid workers. Governments therefore have to intervene in the housing market and do so in virtually all developed countries. 'Government intervention is required', Gilmour argues, 'not only to make social conditions acceptable, but also to make market economies work. Laissez-faire is not, in practice, a serious option' (Gilmour, 1992, p. 11).

Concern for manifest ills and market failure are further forces for the development of welfare states partly, at least, because they are nourished by a paternalistic sense of responsibility. This has certainly been a powerful force in the development of the welfare state as pursued by the British Conservative Party.

In 1938 Macmillan argued for an extension of the state's role in welfare on the grounds of morality and social responsibility. 'The satisfaction of those needs', he wrote 'is a duty which society owes to its citizens' (O'Gorman, 1986, p. 191). Twenty years later, when speaking of his Cabinet's rejection of the Chancellor of the Exchequer's proposals for cuts of £76m in welfare expenditure, Macmillan spoke of government as having an 'inescapable obligation to large sections of the community, the erosion of which would be both inequitable and unacceptable to public opinion' (Lowe, 1993, p. 81). Beveridge and Keynes would have agreed.

The Middle Way put great emphasis on the need for social stability and order as forces in the development of state welfare. Stability and order are the basis of all social life. It is the state's primary responsibility to secure them. How that is achieved is very secondary – a matter of pragmatism rather than principle.

Concern about the potentially destructive nature of market forces has led many supporters of market principles either to seek to restrain them, or to compensate for the destruction they can wreak. Bismarck and Balfour, for example, both saw social reform as an alternative to revolution and/or socialism. Scruton points out how historically the English Conservative Party saw the market economy as threatening the social order and thus sought to restrain it (Scruton, 1984, p. 95). In Harold Macmillan's judgement, 'If capitalism had been conducted all along as if the theory of private enterprise were a matter of principle we should have had civil war long ago' (quoted in Gilmour, 1978, p. 168). A pragmatic approach to these grim possibilities encouraged an enlargement of the state's role in welfare.

Again, manifest injustice, blatant unmet need and suffering could threaten the moral legitimacy of a social order, and so made legitimate compensating action. This is the concern which inspired Quinton Hogg's famous dictum that 'If you do not give the people social reform, they are going to give you social revolution' (Beer, 1982a, p. 307).

As the Middle Way see it, the very popularity of the welfare state has been a force in its development because it has encouraged parties concerned for power to extend it. In Lowe's view, Conservative support for the welfare state in the 1950s and 1960s was shaped by the manifest support which the new services received from the British public (Lowe, 1993, p. 92). The people had to be given what they wanted. Chris Patten endorses this explanation, seeing public welfare as a response to what 'the electorate has demanded government should carry out' (Patten, 1983, p. 127).

The Middle Way also see the welfare state as growing out of tendencies and crusades of which they disapprove. In the forefront of these is the drive for greater social equality. They see this, not implausibly but in fact incorrectly, as motivating the Labour Party's commitment to the welfare state via the provision of services with egalitarian intentions and through the high levels of taxation which they see as generated by egalitarianism.

This is the unacceptable face of the welfare state. The Middle Way are hostile to egalitarianism as such, and more generally, to the 'utopian' style of politics which that approach represents. But they interpret the belief that social services are the royal road to socialism as a strong impetus to welfare state development.

Underpinning both the drive for equality and the utopian politics which it represents is another set of ideas which the Middle Way see as important. That is the idea that society can be reconstructed and a new social order created through the use of reason, knowledge and will – the underlying ideology of Fabianism. They are profoundly hostile to this 'constructivist rationalism' and what they see as its powerful and malignant influence. They do not see such wholesale reconstruction as necessary, possible or desirable.

Finally, and it is a point of a quite different order, the Middle Way see those who work within the welfare state as an important influence on its growth and development. Heseltine and Patten, for example, both make this point (Heseltine, 1987, p. 43; Patten, 1983, p. 121). What is interesting, and what differentiates this argument from the 'public choice' arguments of the New Right, is that the Middle Way set their point in no theoretical context. For them it is simply a matter of observation. For the New Right it is a part of a theory of economic, and human, behaviour.

The explanations which the Middle Way offer for the development of the welfare state reflect their general stance towards it. It is the product of forces which they endorse and in which they would wish to claim a role. It is also the product of pressures to which they are extremely hostile.

Attitudes towards the welfare state

The attitude of supporters of a Middle Way towards the welfare state is not easy to depict. It is a position between that of the generally critical New Right and the generally supportive Democratic Socialists. It is anti-collectivist but not anti-interventionist. It is both strongly supportive of the idea of the welfare state and profoundly critical of certain policies and certain elements within policies. To capture this ambivalence we look first at the case which this group makes for a major role for the state in welfare, then at the kind of welfare policies which it finds acceptable and then at those policies which it regards as problematic.

The case for a major role for the state in welfare

The starting point of Middle Way thinking is clear. Market systems are not always, in every respect, the best way of organising economic and social life. Government has the capacity, and duty, to make good market imperfections when it can do so. Such a middle way between unregulated capitalism and unrestrained collectivism is possible. Utopianism, in both its left-wing and right-wing varieties, is to be shunned as impossible and dangerous. As the distinguished Conservative thinker Lord Eustace Percy put it more than fifty years ago 'Many of the greatest crimes and the greatest failures of history have been due to the attempt to realise the highest human ideals through political authority' (White, 1950, p. 33).

Supporters of the Middle Way would begin their justification for a major role for the state in welfare from their assessment of the free market system. They believe in capitalism but their faith is not unequivocal. This would be true of Keynes and Beveridge and of Middle Way Conservatives. Norton and Aughey point out that 'fulsome support for the market economy has never been a dominant feature of Conservative politics' (Norton and Aughey, 1981, p. 285). 'We are not the political children of the laissez faire school', Anthony Eden wrote, 'We opposed them decade after decade' (Leach, 1991, p. 108). Chris Patten in his 1983 apologia insisted that 'The Conservative Party is not the political voice of the capitalist system' (Patten, 1983, p. 29). Similarly Gilmour writes of issues 'that could not be left to the market without unacceptable social consequences' (Gilmour, 1992, p. 107).

Secondly, the Middle Way believe that some, at least, of the unacceptable social consequences can be remedied by government action. 'We are not frightened at the use of the State', R A Butler argued, 'A good Tory has never in history been afraid of the use of the state' (Leach, 1991, p. 108). Keynes, says Fitzgibbons, saw no necessary conflict between liberty and a strong state, neither did he think a strong state implied socialism (Fitzgibbons, 1990, p. 163). Keynes set out his goal in 1939. For him, it was an eminently practical one,

> a system where we can act as an organised community for common purposes and to promote social and economic justice whilst respecting and protecting the individual – his freedom of choice, his faith, his mind and its expression, his enterprise and his property. (Moggridge, 1980, p. 47)

Beveridge was equally convinced of the immense potential of state action to make good market failures. Hugo Young concludes of Edward Heath that it never occurred to him 'to be other than a believer in the benign power of government' (*The Guardian*, 6 July 1993).

Thirdly, and as a logical corollary to the first two points, Middle Way supporters want a balance between economic and social policy. They reject the view that with a thriving and competitive economy social policy will take care of itself. 'Social policy', Francis Pym argues, 'should never be subservient to economic policy' (Pym, 1984, p. 113). All societies need social policies. The economy cannot be trusted to meet social needs. The country needs social policies to compensate for the unsatisfactory outcomes of market systems. Social policies, however, have to be paid for and this demands a strong economy.

Fourthly, the state can promote the only kind of equality in which supporters of the Middle Way believe – and that very strongly – equality of opportunity, that is, the opportunity to be unequal after fair and equal opportunities. Given the belief that the state can promote equality of opportunity, the Middle Way believe that it should and must.

Fifthly, one of the strongest continuing strands in Middle Way support for the welfare state is the belief in 'One Nation'. This belief has various strands to it. It runs deep in traditional Disraelian Conservatism. It is expressed in Stanley Baldwin's statement that 'The main ambition of my life is to prevent the class war becoming a reality' (James, 1991, p. 56).

Francis Pym puts 'national unity' as the first of his three objectives for social policy (Pym, 1984, p. 126) and urges the need to use national wealth 'as a means to the improvement of society as a whole' (ibid., p. 112). Gilmour argues that 'There is such a thing as the public good of the country, and no amount of "freedom", "choice", populism or neo-Liberal rhetoric can deny it, or, by themselves, achieve it. The community and society do exist' (Gilmour, 1992, pp. 169–70). Beveridge spoke of want, disease, ignorance, squalor and idleness as common enemies not as enemies with which each individual could seek a private peace (Beveridge, 1944, pp. 254–5). Peter Walker writes of the Middle Way as representing a recognition that 'society is held together only by the moral bond of mutual obligations' and the most fundamental of these is 'the obligation to guarantee to even the humblest the means to live and enjoy a decent life' (Walker, 1987, p. 45).

Finally, there is faith in social improvement, as distinct from a simple compensation for market diswelfares. Though this perspective has little sympathy for what its members see as the naive utopianism of socialists they do believe in the possibility of social improvement, although it will inevitably be slow and slight. Pym puts this as his third aim for social policy after the promotion of national unity and individual responsibility (Pym, 1984, p. 123). 'A sense of hopelessness in the nation', he writes 'is the ultimate failure of statesmanship' (ibid., p. 119). There is the faith that the state can promote such improvement and that it has the responsibility to strive to do so.

When welfare state policies are acceptable

'State provision for welfare', says Ian Gilmour 'is fully in accordance with Conservative principles. The welfare state is a thoroughly Conservative institution, which is why Conservatives did so much to bring it into existence' (Gilmour, 1978, p. 152). Patten expressed the same kind of support. 'There is no case', he argues, 'for dismantling the welfare state; when they function well, its services help to bind the community together and to support rather than weigh down the economic life of the nation' (Patten, 1983, p. 84).

Pym makes the argument rather more specific, arguing for a social policy with three specific objectives – national unity,

individual responsibility and social improvement – and also notes
the limited power of government 'to solve deep-rooted social
problems' (Pym, 1984, p. 126). We begin here to see the outline
of a Middle Way position – approval, even enthusiasm, but conditional on meeting certain criteria. There seem to be a number
which are central.

One characteristic which makes welfare state policies acceptable
to the Middle Way is a pragmatic approach between massive state
provision and non-provision. Supporters want a genuine middle
way between planning and non-planning. They want purpose and
direction accompanied by flexibility and an undogmatic, unprejudiced approach. That kind of purposeful pragmatism is of the
essence of the Middle Way. It leads them to support welfare state
policies when they are a response to real current ills. What is quite
unacceptable are utopian policies driven by ideology and a commitment to overarching ultimate social goals such as the promotion of equality or the creation of a new social order. Such goals, as
the Middle Way see it, are not achievable through welfare state
policies because of the limitations of politics and human nature.

For followers of the Middle Way, the concern is with improving
and making good rather than changing. They follow Burke in distinguishing between reformation (good) and change (bad) (O'Sullivan, 1976, p. 12). 'Work for the elimination of concrete evils
rather than for the realisation of abstract goods', was Popper's
advice, 'Do not aim at establishing happiness by political means.
Rather aim at the elimination of concrete miseries' (Gilmour,
1978, p. 153). This principle, says Gilmour, 'is wholly congenial to
Conservatives' (ibid.).

Oakeshott sees the second function of the politician, after the
prevention of concentrations of power, as being 'to take the initiative in seeking out the current mischiefs and maladjustments in a
society and to set them right' (Waldegrave, 1978, pp. 44–5). Others
are rather more specific in defining what such mischiefs and maladjustments are. Pym writes of the need for, and the legitimacy of
action to compensate for the unfairness of life (Pym, 1984, p. 115).
Prior stresses the need for the state to protect the weak and vulnerable and cites Wages Councils as an example of such a policy
(Prior, 1986, p. 253). Tackling real current ills is a legitimate role
for the state and is underpinned by faith in the state's potential to
remedy such 'mischiefs and maladjustments'.

Another dimension of this pragmatism is support for welfare state policies which promote social objectives defined as desirable. One example would be the extension of owner occupation in housing which is seen as desirable because of the stake it gives people in society and the greater sense of responsibility which it is felt to engender. Another desirable development would be the extension of freedom and security through the social security system. The 'One Nation' group of Conservative MPs, who stood firmly in the tradition of Macmillan's *The Middle Way* (Macmillan, 1938), argued strongly in 1950 for social security benefits as enlarging freedom and security because they provided a guaranteed minimum income (Lowe, 1993, pp. 81–2).

Another desirable social objective is providing support for the family which is seen as the basic social unit. Patten sees support for the family as 'the main objective in social policy' (Patten, 1983, p. 79). He goes on to argue that government does have a role in creating conditions in which the institution of marriage is more likely to thrive because that is seen as the basis of family life (ibid., p. 81) in which society has such a strong interest.

Another dimension of this pragmatism is support for policies which promote individual responsibility. Pym sees this as one of the central aims and functions of social policy. In his view, individual responsibility is best promoted when people can rely on government to do things which they are unable to do for themselves and which underpin the desired individual responsibility. In a free market system without a major role for the state in welfare, individuals are frequently too much at the mercy of circumstances and market forces for them to be able to be responsible individuals. State welfare can – and therefore should – provide the necessary basis for individual responsibility (Pym, 1984, ch. 7). Beveridge argued in similar terms, that if the state provided minimum benefits as of right, people would then see it as worthwhile to top them up with additional voluntary insurance. They would be enabled to be responsible by state provision (Beveridge, 1942, pp. 6–7). But there is a residual concern about the potential of social policies to undermine work incentives and family care.

The Middle Way also strongly endorse policies to promote equality of opportunity. This is the one form of equality of which they are in favour. They believe it can be promoted by welfare state policies, in particular by education. It was because of its potential both for reinforcing social stability and traditional values and, at the same time, providing opportunities for social mobility and social change that David Eccles, a Conservative Minister of Education, spoke of education as 'a service marked out as peculiarly Conservative in purpose' (Lowe, 1993, p. 196).

Another characteristic which makes welfare state policies acceptable to the Middle Way is that they should be part of a genuine mixed economy of welfare. This reflects their willingness to use state action but their desire, as far as possible, to limit it. It also reflects their faith in private and voluntary service provision and their desire to promote them. The Middle Way, therefore, lay great stress on the potential of partnership. All the success stories in the revitalising of the inner cities, Heseltine argues, 'were the product of partnership between the public and the private sectors. . . . There is no other way' (Heseltine, 1987, p. 308). Pym argues along similar lines for a partnership 'working with both individuals and institutions in a practical and sensible way' which is a genuine 'middle way' between interventionism fuelled by a 'Whitehall knows best mentality' and a laissez faire which assumes inactivity by government is a virtue (Pym, 1984, p. 126).

A mixed economy means public encouragement of private provision in, for example, health and education. 'Private health insurance and occupational pension schemes should be encouraged', Patten argues, 'as additional contributions to a welfare state, not attacked as threats to the integrity of the welfare state' (Patten, 1983, p. 84). Gilmour takes the same view. Public welfare on a large scale is necessary but 'More private provision must be encouraged and private competition with public services has economic as well as social advantages' (Gilmour, 1978, p. 152).

There is also a strong belief among this group of thinkers in the value and virtues of the voluntary sector. Beveridge saw the health of the voluntary sector as an index of the general health of society (Beveridge, 1948). In traditional Conservatism, there is equal commitment to the values and virtue of voluntary action. It is an expression of individual and social responsibility and of people's desire to help themselves – all of which are good and merit encouragement.

Another characteristic which the Middle Way see as necessary for an acceptable welfare state policy is that it should direct help to the most needy. Help should not be wasted on those who do not need it. On the other hand, of course, the Middle Way stress on 'One Nation' and the interdependence of all members of society leads them in the direction of support for universal benefits.

Universal benefits can promote the idea of social unity. On the other hand, they can prove very expensive and by giving benefits to all they can fail to give enough help to the most needy. Selectivity and means testing can, in theory at least, focus services on those who need them most but they have the disadvantage of being socially divisive. Pym expresses the dilemma. He wants more cost-effective services but he expresses a distaste for the idea of 'a full-blown means test society' (Pym, 1984, p. 126). What there is here is a basic ambivalence about universalism and selectivity but Middle Way thinking has certainly changed through time to a greater concern, in a more affluent society, about the costs and effectiveness of universalism and to an in-principle belief in selectivity but with doubts about what it might mean if pressed beyond common-sensical limits.

Finally, welfare state policies gain approval when they are appropriately related to economic policies. The New Right see social policy as very much a poor relation of economic policy with economic growth as the main engine of welfare. Democratic Socialists, historically at least, have always tended to put social policy first. Supporters of a Middle Way see neither of these approaches as satisfactory and they seek a genuine balance.

Pym argues that it is 'undesirable for any government to make a hard and fast choice, or to appear to do so, between economic and social policy' (Pym, 1984, p. 113). The choice must, in a sense, be contingent. 'Social policy should never be subservient to economic policy' but 'the reverse should not be the case either' (ibid., p. 113). Too much stress on social policy can overload the economy and 'bring our tax system into disrepute by placing too great a load on it' (Patten, 1983, p. 127). Equally, too much stress on economic policy can put dangerous strains on the bonds which hold society together.

There must be a balance to be determined by circumstances. Having said that, Middle Way supporters would be more enthusiastic about a welfare state which took careful account of other claims on the economy, one which aimed to encourage economic development, which inclined towards what Lowe says Macmillan tried to develop as Prime Minister – an 'opportunity' rather than

simply a 'welfare' state (Lowe, 1993, p. 83) and which was concerned with the functional efficiency rather than the equality of
society. Social policy could contribute to economic development.

In the speeches and writings of those we call advocates of a
Middle Way there is of course a considerable range of views.
Nevertheless, they are united in this strong but conditional approach for a major role for the state in welfare. We now move to
sketch what the group sees as the problematic aspects of welfare
state policies.

When welfare state policies are problematic

The balance between the acceptable and the problematic varies
between individuals and between times and places. Nevertheless it
is possible to pick out ten actual or potentially problematic aspects
of welfare states as seen by advocates of the Middle Way.

First, there is what is seen as their inherent tendency to expand.
This is the product of a range of pressures – from those who work
in welfare state services to advance their own career interests, to
meet the new needs which the provision of any service always
reveals and from the general climate of intervention which government action generates. What the supporters of the Middle Way
find problematic is what they see as inherent tendencies to expand
and the risks of loss of control which they imply.

A second anxiety is that the state's role in welfare tends to
expand at a rate which outstrips the capacity of the economy.
Under governments committed to the welfare state, social policy
tends to dominate economic policy. Social needs tend to be more
prominent than the less obvious, longer-term needs of the economy. The supporters of a Middle Way do not construct any economic theory of democracy to explain this phenomenon. Their
stance is more pragmatic but their anxieties are still real (e.g.
Patten, 1983, p. 127). They see a natural tendency for welfare
states to do more than they can properly afford.

Thirdly, their faith in market forces leaves supporters of the
Middle Way anxious about the efficiency of public provision because it lacks these stimuli. Heseltine can stand as an example of
this anxiety. He sees the state as having a 'natural tendency . . . to
become larger and slacker, to do more and to do it with less

sensitivity and at higher cost' (Heseltine, 1987, p. 58). In his view 'private sector management is always likely to be more efficient than public sector management . . . because of the twin stimulus of the profit and loss account and the workings of competition' (ibid., p. 71). There is little consideration of the possible difficulties of applying market principles to all social policies.

Fourthly, welfare states are seen as having a strong tendency towards monopoly in the provision of particular services. This is one element in the inefficiency and insensitivity with which public services are charged. Monopoly is unpopular with supporters of the Middle Way. It squeezes out private and voluntary provision which are seen as sources of variety and diversity and a stimulus to higher standards in the public sector. It also makes for inefficiency because monopolies have no competitors and it is competition which, above all, is the stimulus to efficiency and responsiveness.

Fifthly, supporters of a Middle Way are generally concerned about the possible, and for some the likely, impact of welfare state policies on other sources of welfare, that is, private, voluntary and family. The Middle Way are concerned about the impact state provision may have because these other sources offer choice and variety, and because voluntary and family welfare are seen both as expressing and encouraging social and individual responsibility and as strengthening social bonds.

Sixth, there is concern about what is seen as the natural drift of welfare states towards centralisation and central planning. The search for equity and uniform standards of service provision leads strongly towards centralisation. Centralisation is seen as problematic in a number of ways. It can be a threat to liberty when policies and services are simply delivered from the centre. It is a threat to local government and local provision which are continuing elements in the Middle Way approach to improving society. It also feeds professional and bureaucratic power. The Middle Way do not share the New Right's fundamental suspicion and distrust of government. Nor do they share the Democratic Socialists' historic enthusiasm for government action. They have faith in the potential of government but share anxieties about the tendency of governments to move beyond what they see as fruitful activity.

Seventhly, those committed to a Middle Way regard the welfare state as very problematic when it moves, as it has seemed to do at certain times, from concern with manifest social ills to an attempt

to construct the ideal society. Supporters of the Middle Way distrust idealism in politics. It tempts people to what are impossibilities because of the radical imperfections of human knowledge and
human nature. 'The Conservative', wrote Quinton Hogg, 'does not
believe that the power of politics to put things right in this world is
unlimited' (Hogg, 1947, p. 11). Such an approach is to misconceive
the purpose of politics which is about reconciling conflicting interests, preserving order and dealing with manifest ills, not pursuing
some ultimate goal. Pym rejects the very notion of the ideal society
as incompatible with his belief that society is simply the sum total
of the individuals composing it (Pym, 1984, p. 114).

The problem, however, as the supporters of the Middle Way see
it, is that welfare states are constantly tempted to struggle to develop the ideal society. It is embedded in their very nature and
gives Middle Way supporters continual anxiety because of what
they see as the risks attending such a pursuit and because of their
judgement that the attempt is bound to fail.

Eighthly, advocates of the Middle Way are concerned about the
impact of welfare state policies on individual responsibility and
individual self-reliance. There is always, of course, a risk that public provision will undermine individuals' willingness and ultimately
their capacity to provide for themselves and for their families. The
absence of evidence that this has happened, or is happening, does
not reduce the anxiety. It is one of those fears which is rooted in
instinct and a scepticism about the moral capacity of the individual, and the belief that in an ideal world individuals would not
have to rely on services provided by the state.

Chris Patten expresses one aspect of this anxiety when he quotes
with approval Angus Maude's defence of selection in education.
Maude's defence is based on selection as part of the essential, that
is, desirable, toughness in education. 'A society which abandons all
toughness in its educational system', he writes, 'will in the end
become soft itself' (Patten, 1983, p. 99).

Ninth in this catalogue of problematic elements in the welfare
state is anxiety about the ideas of rights embedded in the welfare
state. The whole Middle Way approach is based implicitly on an
idea of what is owed to people as citizens above and beyond what is
owed to them as reward for their productivity in the market system.
But there is anxiety about the idea of social rights if expressed too
strongly and taken too seriously. This anxiety has a number of

elements. First, there is concern that the ideas of rights is capable of virtually indefinite expansion. It therefore fuels welfare state expansion beyond what might be considered desirable on social or financial grounds. Secondly, there is anxiety that it feeds a false notion of the relationship between the individual and the state, that is, that the state is a body on which the individual can make limitless claims when the state is in fact simply other citizens. Thirdly, there is the anxiety that the idea of rights leads to too much of a focus on individuals and leads to too little attention being paid to the society which alone makes rights possible. Fourthly, a concentration on rights, which is a natural if not inevitable focus of attention in welfare states, leads to an ignoring of the vital and complementary concept of obligations. A society which focuses on rights at the expense of obligations is an endangered species.

Finally, members of the Middle Way tendency are anxious that welfare states drift, or are consciously driven, from a concern with welfare to a preoccupation with redistribution and the promotion of equality. This concern is both general and specific. It is general because such a concern is just one example of the dangerous preoccupation with the promotion of particular ideals via welfare state policies. It is particular because supporters of the Middle Way have specific fears about equality and redistributive policies. These fears embrace the economic damage which can result (e.g. Gilmour, 1978, pp. 181–2; Patten, 1983, p. 174); the damage to social harmony generated by such policies because of their perceived unfairness; and the impossibility of success which is to be welcomed because the goal is misconceived and to be regretted because of the way the standing of government is damaged by failure.

For the New Right, the problematic elements of welfare state policies loom much larger than they do for the supporters of the Middle Way. For the advocates of the Middle Way, the case for a major role for the state in welfare is much stronger. They are committed to such a major role because they believe state action can make good many of the mischiefs and malfunctions of market systems without significantly damaging the wealth-generating capacities of such systems or their social stability. They are 'market people' rather than 'welfare state people' but they accept a major role for the state in welfare as inevitable, appropriate, rich in possibilities but requiring continuous scrutiny and review.

Welfare and their ideal society

Supporters of the Middle Way would strongly endorse what Keynes described as his aim, that is, 'a regime which deliberately aims at controlling and directing economic forces in the interests of social justice and social stability' (Boothby, 1962, pp. 111–12). Their fundamental orientation, however, means that they focus on dealing with manifest ills rather than generalised ideas. Having said that, the principles which the Middle Way believe should determine the state's role in welfare in their ideal society are very clear.

Pragmatism

Firstly, it must be pragmatic and undogmatic, driven by no particular ideals and guided by no particular theories. The aim is simply to improve the social condition of the people. 'The answer to the question "what kind of society do we want to build?" ', wrote Francis Pym, 'is therefore vague – "a better one" ' (Pym, 1984, p. 117). But it is the only answer a doctrineless, dogma-free follower of the Middle Way can properly give. The aim is the simple one, in one sense, of improving the world, not changing human nature or the direction of human evolution. For followers of the Middle Way, as Gilmour put it, 'society is not a laboratory for social experiments' (Gilmour, 1978, p. 159).

This pragmatism comes out very strongly in the Middle Way attitude to government. Each age, Keynes argued in *The End of Laissez-Faire* needs to distinguish the appropriate sphere of individual and state action. It is not something which can be settled on abstract grounds (Skidelsky, 1992, pp. 225–6). For the Middle Way 'there is no fixed frontier for the activities of the state' (Gilmour, 1983, p. 179). Pym argues along similar lines.

> We have no fixed notion of the role of government. We do not believe that government intervention is always good or always bad. It depends on circumstances. If the government can usefully intervene to improve life for people it should do so, but it should never do more than it needs to. (Pym, 1984, p. 174)

Embedded deep in Middle Way thinking is a deep hostility to systems, to political blueprints and to utopianism. 'We do not', says

Pym, 'start with the blueprint for an ideal world, but with an understanding of the real one and a desire to improve it however we can' (Pym, 1984, p. 172). The main enemies in that pilgrimage are seen as ideology and dogma. The great Middle Way belief is that there are always alternatives. The Middle Way supporters do not lack principles but 'Principles are guiding lights, not chains' (Heseltine, 1987, p. 299). Keynes put it in a slightly different way when he argued that the doctrines of liberalism should properly be seen as *means* not *principles* (Fitzgibbons, 1990, p. 165). The guiding lights are essentially pragmatic. 'If we can only get our people to think about realities instead of dogmas and theories . . . we might achieve something' Macmillan wrote in 1985 as he surveyed the dogma-dominated debacles of Thatcherism (quoted in James, 1991, p. 447).

A focus on manifest ills

Secondly, the ideal role for the state in welfare for this group is a focus on manifest ills, unfairness and injustice – a commitment which grows directly out of the pragmatism we discussed above. Government is to be reactive when dealing with conditions defined as problematic such as poverty, bad housing, or ill health. The goal is the removal of acknowledged ills and diswelfares. Government must also be involved in the remedying of unfairness and injustice. Market outcomes are not necessarily fair or just, they must be tested against the yardstick of pragmatic common sense. When they are deemed unacceptable, compensation or action by government must be provided. This pragmatic response to injustice is fuelled by the belief that markets, and indeed life itself, are often unfair but that governments can, and therefore should, help to compensate for such social injustices (Pym, 1984, p. 115).

It was this belief which led Beveridge to his crusade against the five giants barring the road to social reconstruction. Want, disease, ignorance, squalor and idleness were gross and damaging ills which blighted people's lives and deprived them of the basic freedom and security to which all citizens had a right. Government must therefore tackle them. Galbraith has adopted a similar view that the task of government is not to seek to develop an alternative economic system or to build a new society. Rather, our concern must be 'with making more effective and more tolerant and equitable the economic system we have'. We should be aiming at 'a socially better performance by the existing system'. This should be our approach, Galbraith argues, because 'We are for what works best' (*The Guardian*, 25 November 1992).

Where the market fails to provide socially desirable or necessary goods such as health care according to need, adequate housing at prices people can afford, or education to maximise the abilities of the poorest, then government must step in. Equally, the weakest bidders in the labour market need protection against exploitation and 'it is the government's task to perform this role' (Prior, 1986, p. 253).

This concern with manifest ills and injustices grows out of a pragmatic approach to government, a faith in its capacity, a concern for people before systems and theories and a particular view of the nature of society and social order, that is, that it needs constant social maintenance if the free market engine of growth is to function efficiently and acceptably, as it needs to for social improvement.

A commitment to balance

A third element in Middle Way social policy is a commitment to balance. It is part of the distrust of dogma, part of the distrust of simple, single-track solutions, part of how supporters of the Middle Way perceive the world. A commitment to balance leads to pragmatism and pragmatism grows out of a belief in balance. Mrs Thatcher's dismissive view expressed to Jim Prior as he escaped from a 'more ferocious than usual' argument with her to attend the relaunch of Harold Macmillan's *The Middle Way* was that 'Standing in the middle of the road is very dangerous, you get knocked down by the traffic from both sides' (Prior, 1986, p. 106). Supporters of the Middle Way see the middle of the road as the safest place to stand.

The commitment to balance expresses itself in various different ways. There is the strong commitment to market capitalism, the belief, as Waldegrave put it that 'Liberalism is very nearly true' (Waldegrave, 1978, p. 59). But this faith is balanced by a sense of the weaknesses and limitations of markets and a conviction that faith in markets cannot override every other consideration. 'Adam Smith's "invisible hand" can get up to a great deal of mischief on its own', said Patten, 'and must occasionally be handcuffed or directed towards some new and different task' (Patten, 1983, p. 105). So markets must be harnessed and balanced by government action to remedy their malfunctions and injustices and so capitalise on their strengths.

In the running of social services there must, for advocates of this approach, be a balance between a search for the kind of efficiency which markets can generate and a safeguarding of the fundamental values and aims of those services. Patten spoke of the requirement to balance the needs and interests of the community and the collective with the potential of market mechanisms to generate greater efficiency in the production and delivery of those services. The issue, as he saw it, was how to get market efficiency gains 'without appearing in the process to devalue those services' (Patten and Marquand, 1991, p. 20). The search was for balance – a search implied by a recognition of the virtues of markets and the value of public services.

Patten also expressed the desire and need for another kind of balance when he stressed:

> [the] need to be more explicit about the social responsibilities that should go with successful individualism. The first must be accompanied by the second; each must be balanced by the other if a necessary and more general balance is to be achieved.

The Middle Way approach to equality and inequality expresses this same ideal. It has never sought to promote a general equality but at the same time it has been sensitive to the potential dangers of what might be seen as excessive inequality to a sense of 'One Nation'. What it has sought to do is to make inequality tolerable by portraying it as inevitable and desirable, by promoting an ideal of equality of opportunity and by making provision for the poorest. One of Macleod's well-used phrases expressed the aim of extending to young people 'more equal opportunities of proving themselves unequal' (Fisher, 1973, p. 16). The aim was to balance equality and inequality.

We have already discussed another area of balance emphasised by this approach, that is, the balance between economic and social policy. For the New Right, to exaggerate hopefully forgivably, economic policy is the only real social policy. For the Democratic Socialist, traditionally at least, social policy has been the primary concern. Neither of these simplicities is acceptable to supporters of the Middle Way, as there must be a balance. Social policy cannot be 'subservient to economic policy' (Pym, 1984, p. 113) but, equally, social policy must not be overemphasised. No government, Pym judges, can make a hard and fast choice (ibid., p. 112). The priority to be given to either must depend on circumstances and needs but the guiding aim must be balance.

Promoting values

A fourth central concern is that the role of the state in welfare must be value-oriented. It cannot and must not be value-neutral. This may seem at odds with the Middle Way rejection of policies aimed at promoting the ideal society, and to some extent it is, but its primary concern is with individual character and behaviour rather than with the shape of the economic and social order. The aim must be social policies which promote the values and modes of behaviour which advocates of the Middle Way see as central to their idea of a good society.

Pym, for example, sees acceptance of individual responsibility as crucial to the healthy society. To rely too much on government is to abdicate responsibilities which are important to our lives as individuals and to social wellbeing. Heseltine makes the same point: 'the more that people are enabled to take responsibility for arranging their lives, the more likely they are to better themselves and their communities' (Heseltine, 1987, p. 305). Middle Way social policies seek to promote individual responsibility. This does not mean that they will promote the idea of obligations at the expense of rights but rather that they will seek a balance between them – between the New Right emphasis on obligations and the Democratic Socialist stress on rights.

Middle Way social policies are concerned to promote opportunity. Boyle describes Macleod as stressing opportunity rather than equality as a principle as a desirable aim of government (Boyle, 1973, p. 16). The same idea is expressed in Beveridge's belief that the primary responsibility of the state was to provide work for the unemployed, not doles. Again, it is the opportunity offered, in theory at least, by the education system which led Sir David Eccles to describe it as a particularly Conservative policy area.

'Not equality but fairness' is a constant theme of Middle Way policies. This belief means that high degrees of inequality are intolerable. It means that there should be public protection for the victims of certain market unfairnesses. It means that everyone must have an equal right to a good education but we should not confuse that, Patten believes, 'with the claim that everyone has a right to an equal education. That is unfair . . .' (Patten, 1983, p. 90). Acceptance of progressive taxation and hostility to the deliberate promotion of inequality which characterised the 1980s are all fuelled by this commitment to fairness.

Property is one of the strongest Middle Way values. Scruton writes of 'man's (sic) absolute and ineradicable need of private property' because 'Through property man imbues his world with will, and begins therein to discover himself as a social being' (Scruton, 1984, p. 99). O'Gorman writes of the Conservative view that a property owning democracy is 'the only form of democracy which can survive' (O'Gorman, 1986, p. 3).

For the Middle Way property is much more than possessions. It represents a stake in society and even, as in rights to social security, a kind of contract between the individual and government. It gives security and an opportunity for the expression of individuality. As Anthony Eden, the coiner of the phrase 'property owning democracy' put it, 'upon the institution of property depends the fulfilment of individual personality and the maintenance of individual liberty' (James, 1987, p. 327). Middle Way policies will therefore be concerned, for example, to promote home ownership and share ownership.

Supporters of the Middle Way are not afraid of state action but they do, as we saw earlier on in this chapter, have some nagging doubts about it. One is that state action can enfeeble people and erode individual will and individual responsibility. Given their view that life is hard, competitive and unfair, this is potentially problematic. It leads, for example, to approve of selection in education because that represents the selection for success and non-success which is a feature of human life. It is the kind of concern which leads Heseltine to argue that payment of unemployment benefit should be conditional on doing something for the

community (Heseltine, 1987, p. 310). Something for nothing encourages a false view of reality which is unhelpful to those temporarily enjoying it and to society.

A mixed economy

The fifth plank in a Middle Way ideal social policy is commitment
to a mixed economy of welfare, a partnership between the state
and other sources of welfare provision. Advocates of a Middle
Way believe in the value and virtues of private welfare as a source
of variety and choice, as setting targets for public provision and as
an additional contribution to the welfare state. Supporters firmly
believe in the individual's right to spend money on buying education or health care if she or he so wishes. There is comparable
enthusiasm for voluntary welfare both as a valuable contribution
to overall welfare and as part of the pattern of intermediate institutions which traditional Conservatives and Liberals such as Beveridge have always seen as part of the good society.

The New Right belief in the mixed economy of welfare is driven,
in large part certainly, by a dislike of state provision. The Middle
Way enthusiasm is driven by rather different beliefs – by a faith in
a public-private partnership as the ideal mode of provision, by a
genuine belief in voluntary organisations as part of the fabric of
the good society, by a keen sense of the ultimate responsibility of
the state for social welfare and at the same time of its uneven
capacity to meet the varieties of human need.

Underpinning the idea of the mixed economy of welfare is an
underlying belief in partnership as a basic principle of social life.
Gilmour, for example, speaks of the individual and the state as
mutually dependent and mutually sustaining (Gilmour, 1978, p.
148). Pym, in rejecting both laissez faire and interventionism says
he prefers 'to think of the government's role in terms of a partnership – working with both individuals and institutions in a practical and sensible way, in order to achieve national objectives' (Pym,
1984, pp. 126–7). The partnership could be of various kinds such as
government finance for voluntary agencies, or to enable individuals to purchase in the private market.

The Middle Way commitment to a mixed economy is an active
one, an expression of a particular approach to public responsibility

rather than an attempt at abdication. Patten, for example, shows a keen awareness of how a successful mixed economy depends on public policy. If stress on the centrality of the family to welfare is to be more than rhetoric, the government must provide the financial support which mothers need to enable them to stay at home and care for young children. If government wishes to encourage community care then 'Stronger support for the family is the lynch pin of any policy for encouraging community care' (Patten, 1983, p. 83). The aim of the Middle Way is a less statist, more pluralist, welfare state with greater variety and diversity which is actively promoted and sustained by government activity. The boundaries between the various forms of provision will be ill-defined because they are the result of pragmatic judgements rather than principles.

One nation

Finally, Middle Way social policy is driven by a commitment to order, community, solidarity and the 'One Nation' tradition. It is sustained and directed by a powerful sense of society, by the need to sustain it through active government policies and by the importance of the nature and cohesiveness of society to the lives of individuals.

The commitment is rooted in the belief that human beings are social animals and that the individual can, as Patten puts it, 'attain his full stature, only in groupings greater than himself' (Patten, 1983, p. 7). Pym sets out a similar view in his argument about interdependence as representing a basic fact of life. Interdependence, for him, must be rooted in individuality but, equally, without a sense of interdependence true individuality cannot exist (Pym, 1984, p. 109). Keynes, great individualist though he was, was very critical of liberalism for, as he saw it, placing the individual at the centre and failing to define a satisfactory relationship between the individual and society (Fitzgibbons, 1990, p. 165). He was fiercely critical of laissez faire. In a famous passage he drew out and contested its key principles. 'The world', he insisted, 'is **not** so governed from above that private and social interest always coincide.' He continued:

> We cannot therefore settle on abstract grounds but must handle on
> its merits in detail what Burke termed 'one of the finest problems in

legislation, namely to determine what the State ought to take upon itself to direct by the public wisdom, and what it ought to leave, with as little interference as possible, to individual exertion. (Keynes, 1927, p. 39)

The Middle Way have a strong sense of the importance of society to the individual. This sense of the importance of order and stability and the fact of interdependence of people and society lead to a concern in Prior's words 'to plane down the causes of conflict' (Prior, 1986, p. 260) because conflicts threaten the order which is the basis of welfare. It is so important because only in a context of order and stability can individuals and communities grow and develop.

Concern for order and community must lead to a concern for poverty and inequality because they challenge the assertion of 'One Nation' and threaten conflict. People in cities, Heseltine insisted, must be able to see 'that the government's interest is in the welfare of the poorest families and not solely in the fortunes of the entrepreneurs whom we need to attract' (Heseltine, 1987, p. 307). The needs of the poorest must be balanced against society's need for order and growth. Gilmour's main concern about schools opting out of local education authority control is the social divisiveness which he thinks will result as LEAs are left with a rump of underfunded schools 'largely confined to the poorer classes' (Gilmour, 1992, pp. 170–1).

Advocates of a Middle Way see a clear and significant role for welfare state policies. They are sceptical about their ability to create a new society but convinced about their utility in ameliorating manifest ills, promoting desirable values and maintaining social cohesion. To achieve these desirable and possible ends social policies must be pragmatic, balanced and seek a partnership between a wide range of institutions and interests.

Assessment

The Middle Way start from three basic assumptions. The first is that, in Keynes's words, 'Capitalism, wisely managed, can probably be made more efficient for attaining economic ends than any alternative system yet in sight' (Keynes, 1927, pp. 52–3). It is seen as the best system in its capacity to generate economic growth, to give scope to individuals to realise their capacities and to create the kind of society which Middle Way supporters wish to see.

The second assumption is that, whatever its virtues, capitalism creates problems. 'In itself', as Keynes put it, 'it is in many ways extremely objectionable' (ibid., p. 53). It creates poverty, un-acceptable inequalities, and unemployment. It blights lives and communities. These are problems which are inherent in the very nature of the free market system. They are systemic and they will not be solved simply by economic growth.

The third belief is that government action can solve, or at least ease, many or most of these problems. It can ease the problem of poverty, it can reduce unacceptable inequalities, and it can main-tain full employment.

Making an assessment of the Middle Way perspective depends on how one judges these key assumptions – and such judgements are going inevitably to be value judgements.

The New Right, obviously, would endorse the Middle Way sup-port for capitalism, though they would do so with enthusiasm rather than with any reluctance. The Left, in contrast, would argue that capitalism is an inefficient economic system, that co-operation is a far more effective engine of growth than competition, that capitalism inevitably creates a polarised society, driven by short-term considerations of profit which are ultimately destructive.

The Left would enthusiastically endorse the Middle Way judge-ment that capitalism creates destructive problems. That judgement lies at the heart of their hostility to capitalism as an economic system. The New Right, on the other hand, would deny that cap-italism produces problems. They see what the Middle Way define as problems as facts – inescapable results of a capitalist system, the small price which has to be paid for the many blessings which capitalism brings, a price which should not be overestimated but must be kept in proportion by setting it against the many and manifest blessings of the free market.

On the question of the potential of government to make good these ills, commentators will differ widely. It is perhaps the vital issue because it is on the validity of Middle Way beliefs in the possibilities of reform through politics that the viability of their whole approach rests. Skidelsky writes of Keynes's scepticism about the benefits of large-scale social change being 'matched by an extraordinary optimism about the possibility of intelligent management of short run problems' (Skidelsky, 1992, p. 224). That judgement could be extended generally to supporters of the Middle Way. They have little faith in government's ability to reconstruct society but great confidence in its ability to ameliorate manifest ills. Is that confidence justified?

There are two main lines of criticism. The first, from the New Right, is that advocates of a Middle Way fail to understand the nature of capitalism. They do not grasp that capitalism is a system, that it cannot be tinkered with without upsetting its fundamental self-balancing nature. Hayek, of course, emphasises both the crucial nature of the spontaneous market order and its fragility. In spite of their supposed rejection of constructivist rationalism, the New Right see the Middle Way as sinking into that very trap of believing that they can reconstruct capitalism. Removing, or limiting, punishment for failure and reward for success, for example, may seem socially desirable but to do so is to damage key economic mechanisms.

The other line of criticism from the Left and the New Right is that the Middle Way fail to grasp the limited possibilities of government. The two groups agree on this judgement but they reach it by very different routes. The Left argue that the Middle Way fail to grasp the limited scope for government action of the kind they advocate in a capitalist society. In a capitalist society, they argue, all government can offer is small-scale reactive amelioration, much less than the Middle Way require to achieve their goals of economic and social stability, equality of opportunity, and helping the most needy.

The New Right argument is of a different kind. It stresses the impossibility of carrying through the kind of programmes which the Middle Way want to see. They are impossible because governments, that is, people, will always lack the knowledge and the capacity to design and implement the kind of programmes needed to achieve Middle Way goals.

The essential charge is that Middle Way pragmatism blinds its supporters to the essential nature of capitalism and the realities of government. The New Right argument would be that Middle Way proposals threaten the economic health of the system on which the Middle Way rely to fund their policies. The Left would argue that the Middle Way fail to grasp the fact that the ills which they seek to ameliorate are endemic in the very nature of capitalism and that the distribution of power and dominant values doom their ideas to ultimate failure. For both groups the pragmatism of the Middle Way reflects a critical failure of economic and social analysis.

The Middle Way response would be to contest the premises of their critics and to argue that it is precisely that kind of theoretical approach which the New Right and the Left bring to the issue which blinds them to practical possibilities. Theories are aids to understanding not statements of truth. The Middle Way dispute that they can fully illuminate reality in all its complexity.

The Middle Way would also point to history and experience, to the successes of Middle Way policies in Britain, West Germany and the United States in various periods between 1950 and the late 1970s. Those policies did promote economic prosperity, raise standards of living, extend educational opportunities, promote owner-occupied housing, and maintain economic and social stability and other desirable ends. The New Right response would be that, in all those countries where they were adopted, Middle Way policies in the end created economic crises and social dislocation. The Left would argue that they failed to change capitalism or to correct its fundamental instabilities.

Few would quarrel with Middle Way goals. The crucial question is whether or not they are attainable in the real world and, more particularly, whether they are achievable by the policies put forward by advocates of the Middle Way.

CHAPTER 4

DEMOCRATIC SOCIALISM

Democratic Socialists disagree on many issues but they share the fundamental belief that their ideal society, Democratic Socialism, is a superior system to capitalism. For them, the welfare state is a significant staging post in the transition from laissez-faire capitalism to socialism. At times, they may have been very critical of its many failings but they have always insisted that it constitutes a very important step forward in human civilisation from the laissez-faire capitalism of the nineteenth and early twentieth century. They have always understood and accepted that this transition to Democratic Socialism would be both gradual and slow for they have consistently rejected any other form of transition but the parliamentary process for both pragmatic and ethical reasons. Social policy plays a very special role in this gradual transition to socialism for it 'represents the way to build, step-by-step, and policy-by-policy, the just society' (Wicks, 1987, p. 253).

The development of the welfare state

There is no one fully developed and coherent theory of the development of the welfare state that commands universal support in this group. The theory that comes closest to this is what might be called the working-class power model. The welfare state is the outcome of a long process of working-class struggle against entrenched opposition from the capitalist class and its allies. This process began during the early days of industrialisation with the formation of trade unions and working-class political parties and it has continued to the present day in different forms. It is evidence that progress can be achieved through peaceful parliamentary means provided a favourable balance of political power exists in the country.

This view of the development of the welfare state is in direct contrast to those views which see this development as the inevitable result of non-political factors such as demography, economic growth, industrialisation, or bureaucracy, or simply as the offspring of the demands of the capitalist system. It overlaps with both the pluralist view which relies heavily on the belief in the role of pressure groups and of great individuals in reforms and with that brand of Marxism which accepts that working-class organisations can override opposition and improve their living conditions through the parliamentary process. The significance of pressure groups is acknowledged but it is not usually given primacy; rather, it is seen as an auxiliary force particularly in those areas of policy where dominant economic interests are not involved in a direct and important way. It also differs from 'parliamentary Marxism' not only in terms of conceptualisation but in the genuine belief that reforms are useful and of benefit to the working class and that further progress is possible before the achievement of a socialist society.

Writing in the early 1930s, Tawney saw the development of the welfare state as 'the natural consequence of the simultaneous development of an industrial civilization and of political democracy' (Tawney, 1931, p. 125). Industrialisation created not only unprecedented national wealth and massive social problems but also the political forces necessary to press for the necessary reforms. In a political democracy, however, reform movements stand a better chance of success if public awareness and sympathy are developed through the publication of empirical evidence. Thus persuasion as well as pressurisation is needed for the creation of the welfare state and ultimately of socialism.

This was a fundamental tenet of the Fabian Society set up at the end of the last century. One of the aims of the Society, according to one of its earliest leaders, George Bernard Shaw, was 'the collection and publication of authentic and impartial statistical tracts' with the express intention of making 'the public conscious of the evil conditions of society under the present system' (Shaw, 1896,

p. 7). That the upper classes would oppose such reform movements was to be expected for they saw them as a threat to their long-established social and economic privileges.

Writing in the mid-1950s, Crosland and Titmuss advanced rather similar explanations of the development of the welfare state. When discussing the influence of wars on the development of social policy, Titmuss concluded that the upper class would concede social reforms if it felt that the support of the working class was necessary to winning the war. It is an argument for the indirect rather than the direct influence of working-class power.

> The aims and content of social policy, both in peace and in war, are thus determined – at least to a substantial extent – by how far the co-operation of the masses is essential to the successful prosecution of war. If this co-operation is thought to be essential, then inequalities must be reduced and the pyramid of social stratification must be flattened. (Titmuss, 1958, p. 86)

The parenthesis in the above quotation is significant for elsewhere Titmuss gives additional reasons for the growth of state welfare. He refers to the demand for social justice and social integration, particularly during and in the aftermath of wars; the influence of professional groups; the effects of industrialisation and the influences of technology, particularly in the case of health care services. As Wilding points out, Titmuss was a practically-minded student of social policy and in view of the complexity of social services his multi-causal approach was a healthy corrective to grand theorising in this area (Wilding, 1976, p. 151).

Writing at about the same time and referring to the pre-war situation, Crosland took up a similar but more theoretical position. He maintained that in the period before the Second World War, economic and political power were concentrated and, as a consequence, the whole society 'was effectively controlled by a capitalist ruling-class which held all or most of the important levers of power' (Crosland, 1956, p. 5). The result was that, despite the mass unemployment and poverty of the 1930s, government refused to intervene thus providing 'striking evidence of the continued subservience of the political authority to the interests of business' (ibid., pp. 6–7). This was just one illustration of the ability of the capitalist class to thwart social reforms. Moreover, when governments did intervene in economic affairs, the purpose 'was not to limit the economic power of private enterprise, but, on the contrary, to give additional sanction or support to its policies' (ibid., p. 17).

It needed the landslide victory of the Labour Party at the end of the war, according to Crosland, to change the whole balance of power in society and hence the prospects of social reform in the country. The capitalist class lost its dominance in society as a result of three main changes in British society: the social and economic policies introduced by the post-war Labour Government; the growth in trade union power in an economy with full employment; and the rise of the managerial class whose interests were served not simply by maximising profit, as was the case when industry was owned and managed by the same class, but also by being good employers to their workers and their communities. As a result of these changes, the balance of power had come to rest with the forces of the Left. In his opinion, this 'national shift to the Left, with all its implications for the balance of power, may be accepted as permanent' (ibid., p. 9). By the 1950s, Britain had ceased to be a class society and governments could no longer be dictated to by the upper classes. Indeed, governments of the Left now possessed enough political and economic power to introduce the kind of reforms that they wanted. In brief, not only did the forces of the Left establish the welfare state but, by doing so, they changed the whole balance of power in society for good, thus making the road to socialism not only possible but relatively easy.

Many Democratic Socialists then, and most probably all today, disagree with Crosland's views on the distribution of power in post-war Britain. The dominance of the New Right ideology, the rise in unemployment and the restrictive trade union legislation of the 1980s are living evidence of the ephemeral nature of Crosland's analysis. All Democratic Socialists, however, share his view that the development of the welfare state has been primarily the result of constant and determined effort by the forces of the Left.

All the references so far have been to British authors whose views were based on the experience of Britain. Several social scientists, however, have found support in comparative research for the working-class power model of the development of the welfare state. In a study of seventeen industrial democratic countries in the 1970s, Stephens found that what he called socialist rule, that is, government of the Left, was 'a very important determinant of the level of welfare spending' (Stephens, 1980, p. 99) and of the existence of progressive forms of direct taxation and hence of income equalisation. This enabled him to conclude that 'the growth of the welfare state is a product of the growing strength of labour in civil society and that it represents a step toward socialism' (ibid., p. 89). Several other studies in the 1970s came up with similar, though not as strongly convincing, results.

Such findings were in direct contradiction to the earlier findings by Wilensky that the nature of political ideology and of political parties is irrelevant to the development of the welfare state. What really matters, he argued, is the level of 'economic growth and its demographic and bureaucratic outcomes' (Wilensky, 1975, p. xiii). The majority conclusion of comparative studies of the 1970s was that politics does matter though there were differences of opinion concerning the degree of association and on whether the determining factor was working-class strength or, as Castles claimed, the weaknesses of parties of the Right (Castles, 1978).

Many comparative studies of the 1980s onwards continued to lend support to this thesis but in a more sophisticated and restrained way. Korpi's later work, though supportive of this thesis, acknowledges that other factors are also important and that the working-class power model should not be seen as a 'one-factor theory claiming to explain welfare state development more or less exclusively in terms of working class or Left strength' (Korpi, 1989, p. 312). Using a broader definition of the welfare state, Esping-Andersen concludes that 'The hope of finding one single powerful causal force' for the development of the welfare state 'must be abandoned'. Instead, he uses three factors: 'the nature of class mobilization (especially of the working class); class-political coalition structures; and the historical legacy of regime institutionalization' (Esping-Andersen, 1990, p. 29). Using these three factors, he classifies the 18 countries in his sample into three groups, adopting as the criterion of classification not simply the volume of public expenditure but a 'de-commodification' factor, that is, the extent to which the state frees the individual from dependence on the market by providing high quality benefits and services to all as a matter of right. This led him to the important conclusion that there were three worlds of welfare or three types of welfare states. First, the liberal residual welfare states which limit the provision of benefits and services as of right and which tend to rely on selective benefits. Second, the corporatist conservative states which provide a comprehensive range of benefits and services but where class and status determine the allocation with the result that 'the redistributive impact is negligible' (ibid., p. 27). Third, the social democratic welfare states where universal benefits and services of a high standard are provided to all as of right with the result that redistribution through welfare is high. What decides the nature of the welfare state is a complex list of factors directly and indirectly related to the relative position of the working class in the power structure of society. More recent work seems to suggest that working-class power is important not so much for the level of social expenditure but for the quality or level of benefits. Kingas' study of sickness benefit expenditure in 18 OECD countries for the period 1960–85 concluded: 'When analysing benefit levels, we find that politics matter, whereas power constellations appear to have negligible influence on spending levels' (Kingas, 1991, p. 41).

Similarly, Vaisanen's analysis of all social insurance expenditure in 18 OECD countries for the period 1930–85 concluded that 'improvements in the level or quality of social rights, in this case income replacement ratios' seem to require Left party participation in government (Vaisanen, 1992, p. 323).

Clearly, the development of the welfare state is and will remain a hotly contested issue for both methodological and ideological reasons. Definition of what constitutes working-class power varies from one study to another; definition of social expenditure ranges from the very broad to the very narrow; and the number of countries as well as the period covered by the various comparative studies also varies. Moreover, theories and ideologies of welfare often influence each other, with the result that explanations of the development of the welfare state inevitably reflect in varying ways and degrees the investigator's views. It is for this reason that Democratic Socialists have attributed so much emphasis to the labour movement as the driving force behind welfare provision and ultimately of socialism.

We will be examining the strengths and weaknesses of the class conflict model in some detail in the next chapter. Suffice it here to say that, on the credit side, it is a model which actively involves the political process of a country and it can be put to some sort of empirical test. On the debit side, a mono-causal explanation for the development of the welfare state is insufficient; it glosses over the conflict of interests within the working class; and it tends to conceal the fact that many reforms were introduced by the upper classes for their own interests. As Lloyd George said in the 'national efficiency' debate in Britain at the beginning of this century, you 'cannot maintain an A–1 empire with a C–3 population'. (Gilbert, 1970, p. 15). Also, many Conservative politicians from Balfour in Britain to Bismarck in Germany acknowledged that social reforms were necessary not to promote the cause of socialism but to thwart it. Hence, it was the duty of intelligent Conservative governments to introduce such legislation where necessary. Thus, for both positive and negative reasons, the upper classes do have a stake in the development of the welfare state.

Attitudes towards the welfare state

The unreserved support of the welfare state by this group is so well known that we need only summarise it and devote more space to the kind of social services that it supports. Tawney set the scene in the early 1930s when he dismissed criticisms by Marxists that the social services were mere palliatives propping up a bankrupt capitalist system as 'a piece of "clap-trap" ' (Tawney, 1931, p. 120) and went on to defend the emerging welfare state despite its weaknesses. Over the years, this has remained an article of faith for this group. Seven reasons have been given in defence of the welfare state.

The first and primary justification for the welfare state is the elimination of suffering and want in society – a justification that is very similar to that offered by the previous group we discussed. Crosland voiced this more clearly than others when he argued that the ultimate goal of the social services is not social equality but 'the relief of social distress and hardship and the correction of social need' in society (Crosland, 1956, p. 148). There has been no change on this over the years though it is recognised that the welfare state has delivered less than it promised. The work of many Democratic Socialists, but Townsend's in particular, has shown that though the extent of poverty would have been higher without the welfare services, a great deal more needs to be done before poverty can be abolished (Townsend, 1979). What distinguishes them from Marxists is their confidence that this can be achieved within the realm of a developed welfare state.

Second, Democratic Socialists have joined forces with many others who see some social services as a stimulus to the economy and hence an investment in the country's economic prosperity. Education is the best example of this belief in social service expenditure as an investment in human capital: it improves the quality of labour and thus raises the prospects of productivity and economic growth in society. Relying heavily on Keynes, they see social security expenditure not only as a means to alleviate poverty but also as a way of putting money in the hands of people who will spend it and thus stimulate consumption, demand and production. In these and other ways, expenditure on the social services can facilitate and encourage economic growth. It is only since the mid-1970s that they have also accepted the claim that too high levels of public expenditure may have deleterious effects on economic growth.

Third, their support for education goes beyond national economics to include the fulfilment of the abilities of all children, irrespective of their social backgrounds, both as a desirable end in itself and as a means of creating a more egalitarian society. It is for this reason that writers from Tawney in the 1930s to Crosland in the 1950s and to Meacher in the 1990s have paid so much attention to education. Tawney's forthright condemnation of the class nature of the educational system and his call for radical reforms are well known. 'The hereditary curse upon English education is its organisation upon lines of social class' (Tawney, 1931, p. 142), he wrote in 1931, and proceeded to argue that in the same way that wise parents desire the best education for their children so, too, 'a nation, in so far as it is wise, must desire for all children' (ibid., p. 146). Twenty-five years later, Crosland repeated the charge and the call to reform. 'The school system in Britain', he wrote, 'remains the most divisive, unjust, and wasteful of all the aspects of social inequality' (Crosland, 1956, p. 188). A great deal needed to be done to rectify the situation but the least that should be done is for the state to ensure that state schools are as good as independent schools. Another twenty-five years on and Meacher proclaimed that 'a radical transformation of British education and training systems – in coverage, quality and form – is perhaps the single biggest prerequisite' (Meacher, 1992, p. 35) for a truly free and egalitarian society and proceeded to make a list of reforms, some of which we shall be discussing later in the chapter.

Fourth and fifth, the welfare state, or rather the social services, can promote altruism and social integration in society. It is Titmuss's writings that bring out so passionately and vividly these two justifications. Like all the other writers in this group, it is universal social services that Titmuss sees as worthy of support. Such services promote social integration because they are provided to all without discriminating for or against any one ethnic group or any one socio-economic group in society; unlike private services, they reach the hard-to-reach groups in society; and they provide institutional opportunities for citizens to show their altruistic support for one another. Titmuss believed that people were neither altruistic nor egoistic by nature but 'the ways in which society organises and structures its social institutions – and particularly its health and welfare systems – can encourage or discourage the altruistic man; such systems can foster integration or alienation' (Titmuss 1970, p. 225). It is for this reason that he was so enthusiastic about the ideological basis of the National Health Service despite his many criticisms of many of its operational aspects. 'I regard the National Health Service Act', he wrote, 'as one of the most unsordid and civilised actions in the history of health and welfare policy' (Titmuss, 1968, p. 208). The Act promised to provide medical care to all in need, free at the point of consumption without regard to any other personal criteria. Similarly, using the giving of blood without payment in Britain, as compared to the commercial basis on which it is transacted in the United States, Titmuss was able to argue not only for the ethical but also the practical superiority of the British system. The commercialisation of blood-giving and receiving 'represses the expression of altruism, erodes the sense of community, lowers scientific standards', and leads to all sorts of undesirable consequences in both health care and society in general (Titmuss, 1970, p. 277). It is this congruence between the ethical and the practical that made state social provision superior to market provision for Titmuss. In recent years, however, several Democratic Socialists have come to accept that social services do not always act as agents of socialist change but as a means of social control, particularly when they are provided under strict eligibility rules.

To these five justifications of social service provision – the abolition of poverty, promoting economic growth, fulfilment of individual abilities, promoting social integration and encouraging altruism in society – Titmuss added a sixth which was his unique contribution: compensating for diswelfares in society. In industrial societies, technological change is both necessary and inevitable if economic growth is to be maintained. But it has to be acknowledged, he argued, that every factor 'contributing to economic growth is also a factor contributing to social need' (Titmuss, 1958, p. 107). It is therefore fair and just that those who lose their jobs should be compensated, for they are, after all, 'the social pathologies of other people's progress' (Titmuss, 1968, p. 157).

Finally, many of the early Democratic Socialists believed that the welfare state would reduce both horizontal and vertical inequalities. Since they were reluctant to attempt this through the wages system, they hoped that the provision of social services would reduce the differences in living standards between the sick and the healthy, the employed and the unemployed, the young and the elderly and other such horizontal inequalities. On this they have not been as disappointed as in the case of vertical or socioeconomic inequalities. Research in the 1970s and 1980s has shown that the middle and upper classes benefit as much from state welfare as working-class groups. Le Grand sums up his findings on this issue in the early 1980s as follows: 'Public expenditure on the social services has not achieved equality in any of its interpretations. Public expenditure on health care, education, housing and transport systematically favours the better off, and thereby contributes to inequality in final outcome' (Le Grand, 1982, p. 137). We will return to this issue in the final section of the chapter.

These are the main reasons for the support of the interventionist welfare state and the rejection of the idea that the market can meet the needs of all groups in society. But, as must have become apparent by now, the social services that Democratic Socialists have in mind are different from those of the Right. Again Titmuss provides the answer when he writes that 'socialist social policies are totally different in their purposes, philosophy and attitudes to people from conservative social policies. They are (or should be) pre-eminently about equality, freedom and social integration' (Titmuss, 1968, p. 116). To achieve these objectives, social services must be provided primarily on a universal, that is, free to all at the point of consumption, rather than on a means-tested basis. Though there is general agreement on the principle, there are differences of opinion as to how this is best achieved. But before we explore these differences it is worth emphasising the point that no one in this group argues for the total elimination of means-tested or selective services. Titmuss concedes this point in a much quoted paragraph:

> The challenge that faces us is not the choice between universalist and selective services. The real challenge resides in the question: what particular infrastructure of universalist services is needed in order to provide a framework of values and opportunity bases within and around which can be developed acceptable selective services provided, as social rights, on criteria of the *needs* of specific categories, groups and territorial areas and not dependent on *individual tests of means*? (Titmuss, 1968, p. 122; emphases in original)

Titmuss's distinction between selective and means-tested benefits or services is an important one but it has not been taken up by others in this group with the result that the debate has been between means-tested and universal services. The definition of 'universal' used by this group refers simply to the way services are provided, that is, whether they are free to all at the point of consumption. It does not take into account either the way they are financed or the extent of use made of the services by different groups in society, for under such a definition there are no universal services. The opposition to means-tested services or benefits is based on seven inter-related reasons, some of which are objections of principle while others are of a more practical nature.

First, and foremost, means tests are stigmatising since their major purpose 'is to keep people out; not to let them in. They must, therefore, be treated as applicants or supplicants; not beneficiaries or consumers' (Titmuss, 1968, p. 134). There is a great deal of evidence in support of this objection to means tests not only from the days of the Poor Law but from more recent times and even nowadays (Dean and Taylor-Gooby, 1992; Page, 1984; Ritchie, 1990). It is true, as Pinker points out, that those who feel stigmatised by means-tested benefits and services 'do so after having been stigmatised by adverse experiences in the economic market' (Pinker, 1979, p. 168). This, however, strengthens rather than weakens the argument for non-discriminatory forms of social provision.

Second, many Democratic Socialists fear that means-tested services designed only for the poor gradually but inevitably degenerate into second-class services. As Titmuss reminded his readers, the weight of historical evidence of the Poor Law in this and in other countries showed that 'separate discriminatory services for poor people have always tended to be poor quality services' (Titmuss, 1968, p. 134). Evidence from those countries today where a state service is provided for the poor only, such as state health care for the uninsured in the United States, leads to the same conclusion.

Third, means-tested benefits or services result in low take-up rates. There are genuine differences of opinion as to why this is the case and whether the situation can be improved through administrative methods but there cannot be any doubt that the criticism is correct. In 1987, for example, the take-up rates for the three means-tested benefits of income support, family credit and housing benefit were 81 per cent, 51 per cent and 80 per cent respectively whereas for retirement pension and child benefit the take-up was total (DSS, 1992, p. 349).

Fourth, the administrative costs of means-tested benefits are of necessity higher for they involve individual testing and sometimes personal interviews as well. Thus, they cost twice or three times as much to deliver as universal or insurance benefits, depending on which benefits are compared.

Fifth, there is the troublesome issue of where to draw the dividing line below which people receive benefits or services and above which they do not or have to pay for the services. It is a crucial issue not only for individuals but for governments as well. If the line is drawn at too low a level, government expenditure will be reduced substantially but many people will be disqualified. The opposite is the case if the dividing line is drawn too high. Inevitably, feelings of grievance will run high among those individuals whose income is above the qualifying line by a few pounds only. To cope with some of these problems the idea of a band rather than a line has been suggested. This will certainly reduce some of the problems but it will make the system even more complicated, and hence more costly to administer and more difficult for the public to understand.

Sixth, there is the problem of incentives and poverty traps. Means-tested benefits and services always create poverty trap situations but the more services and benefits that are means-tested, the greater the depth and steepness of poverty traps. Indeed, the force of this argument is acknowledged by many writers of the Right and there is substantial evidence to support the claim (McLaughlin, 1991).

Seventh, it has been argued that social services which are being used by everyone stand a better chance of survival against the welfare reductionist tendencies of Right-wing governments than other services. This is an extension of the second argument and it surfaced during the Thatcherite years. The claim was that 'if the middle classes benefit from programmes, then they will use their not inconsiderable political skills to obtain more resources for those programmes or to defend them in periods of decline' (Le Grand, 1989, p. 210).

There has been some support in this group for a limited role for means-testing but it has always been very much a minority opinion. Crosland, for example, argued that so long as the service or benefit was not essential to the individual, income-testing was acceptable. Even then, however, the qualifying income line for free services should be set as high as possible because if it were so low that only the low-paid did not have to pay 'there is more danger of inferior feeling arising than if only surtax payers are compelled to pay' (Crosland, 1956, p. 87). Moreover, income-testing was to be used to decide whether to pay or not to pay for services which were available to all. He felt that 'while social equality of course requires universal *availability* of the public service, it does not always require universal *free* availability' (ibid., p. 87; emphases in original). Crosland's views have not been taken up by others so far and they remain very much a minority position in this group.

This general adherence to universality has remained an article of faith in this group despite the convincing empirical evidence, referred to earlier, that universal provision does not reduce income inequalities in society. The basic reason for this 'is that the issue about universality versus selectivity is not a technical one, although it has technical aspects, but one which draws upon moral and political values which are not easily reconciled' (Plant, 1993, p. 13).

Democratic Socialists recognise that universal social services are more costly to the state than means-tested services and they acknowledge that the feasibility of universal provision depends a great deal on high rates of economic growth. As far back as 1976, Crosland warned that though high rates of economic growth do not by themselves create a socialist society, 'low or zero growth wholly excludes the possibility' (Crosland, 1976, p. 74). Some, however, believe that the economic factor has been exaggerated. Hattersley, for example, argues that the reason for the underfunding of the National Health Service in Britain is not because 'we cannot afford it in the way that the pre-war poor were unable to pay a doctor's bill. It is because either consciously or unconsciously society chooses to spend less on health care and more on something else' (Hattersley, 1987, p. 90). Herein lies a troublesome issue for Democratic Socialists: consumerism seems to dominate people's way of life and seems to reduce their willingness to pay the necessary taxes to finance high-cost social services.

It comes as no surprise that private social services are viewed with either suspicion or hostility by most members of this group. But this antipathy has been confined mainly to health and education and never covered housing, the personal social services or even social security. They have raised three main objections to private provision. As long as there is a flourishing private sector, governments will tend to neglect state provision for, if for no other reason, pressure from the middle and upper classes to improve state services will be missing. Secondly, private services inevitably increase existing inequalities in society and by doing so they also undermine social integration. Thirdly, private provision is far less accountable to the public than state services despite the rhetoric to the contrary. The large insurance companies, for example, that dominate private provision in social security and health are answerable, at most, to their shareholders and to no public body.

Where Democratic Socialists have differed is on the solution to the problem. Crosland's answer was not to abolish private provision but to make state provision so good that not many people would want to use private services. Titmuss's condemnation of private services was far more sweeping because he was far more convinced that they created two nations, undermined social integration and had an adverse effect on state social provision. However they are justified by their supporters. Titmuss believed that in effect 'their whole tendency at present is to divide loyalties, to nourish privilege and to narrow the social conscience' (Titmuss, 1958, p. 55). His solution was not only to improve the state social services but to abolish private provision as well. Thirty years later, Hattersley adopts a very similar position. Having argued for an improvement in the state systems of education and health, he still feels that the abolition of private education and medicine would 'by any sensible analysis, increase the *sum* of liberties' in society and, therefore, for any socialist government to shrink 'from the assault on private medicine and private education is either to lack courage or to neglect a real chance to extend the totality of freedom' (Hattersley, 1987, p. 147; emphasis in original). Whatever the divisions of opinion among theorists, there is no doubt whatsoever that political parties of the Left prefer to concentrate on the improvement of the state services for it is the only politically viable policy.

Despite their steadfast commitment to universality and their opposition to private social services, most Democratic Socialists have recently abandoned their support of centralised, bureaucratically-run, uniform social services. A sea change has taken place in the attitude of this group regarding the best way of running the services and particularly on the role of public participation and consumer choice. Whereas neither Titmuss nor Crosland nor others from the 1950s down to the 1980s considered the usefulness of public participation and consumer choice, it has now become an essential part of a socialist system of social service provision. It is a move away from the socialism of the Webbs and Morrison to the socialism of Morris and Cole. We will examine this new approach to social provision later in the chapter. Suffice it to say here that there appears to be a tension between the traditional aim of socialist social policies 'to achieve greater social equality' (Abel-Smith, 1984, p. 169) through state social services which are provided in a uniform way up and down the country and which are also universalist in nature, and the more recent emphasis on consumer empowerment and choice.

It is this tension that Plant refers to as the communitarian and the libertarian socialist approaches to the enforcement of social rights. Whilst the communitarian will emphasise the legal enforcement of rights through uniform services for all, the libertarian will stress the placing of 'more power by way of strict entitlements into the hands of the consumers' (Plant, 1988, p. 13). The second approach implies not only a reduction of professional power but also a certain amount of shopping around by the service users. Both approaches envisage improvements in the standards of social provision and reductions of inequalities but they set about achieving their objectives differently. As Plant astutely observes, the communitarian approach 'will not meet the mood of the times' (ibid., p. 13) for in affluent and consumer-oriented societies, consumer choice exerts a powerful public appeal that political parties of the

Left neglect to their electoral peril. It is a good illustration of the argument that people's experiences in the private market influence their attitudes to state services. If this diagnosis is correct, the libertarian approach will triumph for Democratic Socialists are fundamentally political realists. It is, however, an approach which runs the risk of exacerbating inequalities for the middle class are more adept in exercising their right of participation and choice than the working class.

Welfare and their ideal society

The central and unifying feature of the type of socialism that this group aspires to is its gradualist and democratic nature. This sets them apart from the followers of other types of socialism. One of socialism's great weaknesses over the years has been its diverse and often conflicting varieties. As Wright put it: 'The history of socialism is the history of socialisms. Moreover, it is a history not of fraternal plurality, but of rivalry and antagonism' (Wright, 1987, p. 1). Despite the wide range of socialisms spawned during the nineteenth century, only two survived into political possibilities: the democratic gradual type discussed here and the authoritarian revolutionary discussed in the next chapter.

The roots of Democratic Socialism are to be found in Owenism, Fabianism and Christianity rather than in Marxism. From Owenism came the co-operative strand, from Fabianism the technocratic and gradualist influence and from Christianity the ethical and egalitarian tradition. The main influence of Marxism on Democratic Socialism has been the acceptance of a modified version of the class analysis of society. It accepted the notion of conflict in society but rejected the conclusion that this conflict could only be resolved in violent revolutionary ways. From its very early days, Fabianism was unashamedly gradual and parliamentary and not only did it never waver from this position but it also greatly influenced socialist movements abroad. An early Fabian, Annie Besant, attacked the then revolutionary Social Democratic Federation in Britain and insisted that socialism could only be achieved 'by a slow process of evolution, not by revolution and bloodshed' (Hattersley, 1987, p. 7). Thus, building socialism has always been seen as a long-term process involving changes not only in legislation but in people's values and attitudes.

This belief in gradualism and democracy has been vindicated by the course of history, for today all socialist parties in advanced industrial societies are adherents to the parliamentary road to socialism. Even the Communist parties of Europe which once advocated the revolutionary road abandoned that approach in favour of the parliamentary process. Gradualism, however, has its weaknesses, too, for it can result in timid reformism that leads to nowhere.

The perception of the welfare state as a staging post to socialism indicates not only approval by Democratic Socialists but also a recognition that it is different from socialism for a variety of reasons. Tawney's strong support for social policy measures was coupled with the warning that they can go so far in promoting social equality but 'till a radical change has been effected in the balance of economic power' the road to social equality will remain blocked (Tawney, 1931, p. 120). Thus, for Tawney, the main weakness of welfare reforms is that they do not greatly affect the distribution of economic power and wealth and they thus cannot by themselves lead to the creation of a socialist society. In the mid-1950s, Cole reached the same conclusion when he insisted that 'the welfare state is, all the same, not socialism . . . it is at most only socialistic – if even that' (Cole, 1954, p. 319). A similar view was subsequently taken by Titmuss, Crosland, Townsend, Abel-Smith and others in the 1960s but with the added criticism that many of the social services benefited the middle and upper classes more than the working class.

Writing from an American perspective, Harrington, too, feels that the welfare state is not a socialist society and it cannot solve the current economic and social problems for three reasons:

> the class nature of capitalist societies vitiates, or subverts, almost every effort towards social justice; private corporate power cannot tolerate the comprehensive and democratic planning we desperately need; and even if these two obstacles were overcome, the system still has an inherent tendency to make affluence self-destructive. (Harrington, 1972, pp. 332–3)

These criticisms are accepted by most writers in this group. Where they differ is on the solution to the problem and particularly on the acceptable role of the market in a socialist society.

Democratic Socialists have, on the whole, accepted that the market has an important role to play but it must be both limited and regulated to rectify its defects. The notion of an unregulated market is incompatible with Democratic Socialism for the former stresses the centrality of individualism in social and economic affairs while the latter emphasises the spirit of fraternity and fellowship. In more concrete terms, Plant lists the following as market defects:

- the free market leads to concentration of wealth and power;
- the market prefers long-term to short-term returns;
- despite embodying individual choices, markets may lead to outcomes which might not have been chosen had they been foreseen;
- the external effects of markets on the environment;
- the ways in which markets undercut any appeal to the public good on which their own operation may well depend'. (Plant, 1988, p. 17)

Over the decades, three main positions have emerged in Democratic Socialist thinking in relation to the role of the market in a socialist society: bureaucratic centralism, social democracy and market socialism. We begin with bureaucratic centralism for it dominated the approaches of parties of the Left for decades. It stems from the work of the early Fabians who saw capitalism as both exploitative and anarchic and who, therefore, felt that in a socialist society the means of production and distribution must be owned by the government and that the economy must be planned centrally. The first part of the programme would abolish exploitation and reduce inequality while the second would do away with the waste engendered by anarchic capitalism. Despite competing paradigms, it was this Fabian vision of socialism that became the official programme of the Labour Party at the end of the First World War and gradually came to dominate the policies of other European socialist parties, particularly after the consolidation of the Soviet Revolution.

In democratic societies, it was for the first time adopted by the Labour Government in Britain at the end of the Second World War. Not only were the social services expanded but many utilities were nationalised – coal, gas, electricity, telephones, transport –

and administered centrally. Many on the left of the Labour Party were disappointed that the government did not go further to nationalise the insurance companies, the banks and other enterprises. Socialism became synonymous with state collectivism and central planning. The post-war experience in Britain demonstrated that, as a group, nationalised industries were neither more efficient nor more concerned with the welfare of their workers or their clients than private industries. This, and the pressure on governments to reduce their financial responsibilities, has led to the virtual abandonment of this model of socialism among Democratic Socialists.

The second model of Democratic Socialism is closely associated with the work of Crosland. As we saw earlier, he argued that the post-war reforms changed the face of British capitalism beyond recognition for good and there was, therefore, no case for further nationalisation measures on any significant scale. Indeed, post-war experience showed that 'public-monopoly nationalisation, despite considerable achievements in certain exceptionally difficult industries, no longer seems the panacea that it used to be' (Crosland, 1956, p. 320). The mixed economy was a sufficient economic base for governments of the Left to introduce further measures that would equalise opportunities in society – the hallmark of a socialist society. For those who argued that there was a case for nationalised industries not on economic grounds but because they increased the power of governments of the Left, he maintained that the government 'has all the economic power it needs – the only question is whether it chooses to use it; and from this point of view the mere change in ownership did not always make a decisive difference' (ibid., p. 318). Crosland's conclusion on the power of governments will be disputed by many but his conclusion that no further widespread measures of nationalisation were needed would be accepted by most Democratic Socialists. Many of these, however, will be arguing that there is another form of ownership apart from private and nationalised, an argument that takes us to the third socialist approach to the market, market socialism. In brief, the social democratic model sees socialism as very similar to a fully developed welfare state with a few added fiscal programmes to reduce inequalities of income and wealth. Its main objective is to humanise, not to abolish, capitalism in terms of private ownership.

Market socialism appears to be the favourite model today (Forbes, 1986; Le Grand and Erstin, 1989; Miller, 1989). It is an attempt to steer a middle course between bureaucratic centralism and social democracy. Its central claim is that the economic system of Democratic Socialism is plural in nature: some enterprises should be owned by the state, others privately, others co-operatively, others jointly between capital and labour *but* the emphasis should be on workers' co-operatives and workers' participation. Thus, according to Meacher:

> a feasible socialist market economy should be pluralistic. There should be a large co-operative sector, a sector in which capital-labour partnerships were formed in varying proportions around a 50:50 norm, a sector of worker buy-outs of larger firms, as well as a sector taking conventional capitalist form. In addition, basic industries requiring massive levels of investment – such as oil, coal, electricity, telecommunications – would be state-managed or at least very closely state-regulated, even though subject to (mainly international) market competition. (Meacher, 1992, p. 133)

The wide support of market socialism stems from the realisation that, on one hand, nationalised industries cannot deal sufficiently well with consumer goods as the experience of centrally planned economies in Eastern Europe showed (Nove, 1983) and, on the other, that governments cannot humanise a capitalist system that is dominated by private enterprise, as the experience of Western European countries has so far shown.

Critics of market socialism come from both Marxism and the New Right. Many Marxists tend to see market socialism as either unworkable or marking the abandonment of one of the fundamental socialist principles, that is, that if industry and enterprise are to operate for the public good rather than for the benefit of the few, they must be owned by the state. Thus most Marxists do not see any difference of substance between market socialism and a social democratic economy where the state plays an important role in economic affairs. Both forms of economic organisation are essentially capitalist.

Writing from a New Right perspective, De Jasay is critical of both the very idea of market socialism and its workings. For him, the market is an integral part of capitalism and it only functions well when it is free from government interference and regulations.

Thus the attempt to combine the market with socialism which is based on the notion of government intervention in the market is a contradiction in terms. He also raises questions about such practical matters as the commercial viability of co-operatives, the source of funds to set up co-operatives and the practicability of workers' participation – issues which have been raised by others who are positively disposed towards market socialism. His overall conclusion is that market socialism is a confused notion constructed by well-meaning but misguided people who believe that 'everything men of good will would like to do to society is feasible and painless' (De Jasay, 1990, p. 33).

There is no doubt that market socialism does raise some very difficult questions about finance, administration and commercial viability in today's competitive world of international capitalism. Who will provide the funds for workers' co-operatives? Will co-operatives respond quickly enough to technological changes and consumer demand? How and who will decide which enterprises will be run privately or otherwise? Will elected managers be able to take unpopular decisions? Will work incentives not inevitably suffer? (Gray, 1992) Weisskopf assesses ten such objections to market socialism and finds them either unsubstantiated or marginally relevant. He does, however, conclude that 'as models of market socialism have been refined over the years, the distinction between market socialism and social democracy has been somewhat blurred' (Weisskopf, 1992, p. 258). What is generally agreed is that any move towards market socialism will have to be cautious, experimental and gradual if it is not to lead to the same disappointment as bureaucratic centralism.

The notion of market socialism fits in well with the new approach to the provision and delivery of social services that we referred to earlier. In both the economy and the welfare sector, participation and empowerment are the dominant themes. To illustrate how different the new thinking is compared to the previous Titmussian approach, we will refer to the work of two contemporary writers on the issue.

Wicks notes that so far the strongest tradition among the Left has been to favour strong government and acknowledges that it has had some good results. But he argues that the time has now come to develop the other socialist tradition of empowering people in a direct way. This calls for the democratisation of social policy; for the need 'to develop more accountable and democratic relationships' (Wicks, 1987, p. 181); for a new social strategy which realistically involves policies 'that delegate power and responsibility and which also encourage those initiatives which have developed over the last decade in many local communities' (ibid., p. 182).

Meacher takes the argument for public participation in social policy a lot further. His central proposal is not so much public participation but empowerment of the individual user of the services whether public or private. He finds the present system of accountability in the social services blunt and ineffective and he calls for a new approach. 'A new model of service delivery is therefore needed. It should discriminate neither for nor against either the public or the private sectors, but use whichever maximises accountability for the individual, without regard to income, and for all equally' (Meacher, 1992, p. 91).

He applies this principle to the various social services and makes a list of suggestions. In housing, 'municipal tenants should have the right to self-management' (ibid., p. 91). In the health service, there should be a patients' charter; general practitioners should be required 'to issue a practice statement' of the services they provide; and there should be elected health authorities rather than appointed as at present. In social security, the management board of local offices should be made up 'of at least 50 per cent claimants or their representatives' (ibid., p. 92). In education, parents should have more say in their children's schools and one way of achieving this is that elected parents should form 'three-quarters of the membership of the board of governors' (ibid., p. 93) running each school. In order to further reduce the power of administrators, he proposes that they should be appointed for a limited term, assessed at the end of the period and re-appointed only if found satisfactory. There should be a streamlined system of appeals and ombudspeople in all social services with adequate staff issuing annual reports of their work. To ensure that senior managers and administrators do not become detached from their services, they should 'spend time doing front-line jobs, like delivering meals-on-wheels or working on reception desks' (ibid., p. 99). To ensure minimum standards and to promote best quality, residents should be issued with detailed customer contracts and there should be a quality commission to oversee all this. These are the main proposals but there are many others all designed 'to put power directly into the hands of the public over the service controllers, but which do not depend on the vagaries of income and are not limited by the tendency of markets to cream off the most lucrative consumers' (ibid., p. 102). This emphasis on empowering the individual user of the service is not instead of, but rather within, the framework of universal social service provision. It is a different approach from that of previous decades which appealed to the professional ethic of the providers of the service in the very difficult task of improving the quality and delivery of services. It is clearly an attempt to marry the best features of state provision with the strengths of the market. It has some superficial similarities with the approach of the New Right but in essence it differs fundamentally because of its attachment to state social services that are adequately funded.

Closely related to the notion of empowerment is the notion of consumer choice. It is true that Titmuss made the case for choice within the state social services but this was of a limited nature and it was confined to the state sector. He did not believe that in such services as education, medical care, social work or social assistance people could shop around 'to the same extent as they can for shoes or cabbages in the private market' (Titmuss, 1968, pp. 67–8). Properly trained administrators rather than consumer choice was the way to improve the quality of social provision. In his words, 'if social services are to be delivered effectively, equitably and humanely, more and better educated administrators are required' (Titmuss, 1974, p. 55). Today, however, several influential writers in this group are making consumer choice a central plank of their arguments for a socialist form of social service provision.

We have already referred to the positions of Meacher and Wicks in relation to consumer empowerment which come very close to maximum feasible consumer choice. Meacher argues for the abandonment of homogeneous provision in several areas of social policy. Instead, 'equivalent funding should be put at the disposal of the consumer/claimant who would then have the opportunity to buy in whatever service, or combination of services, suited their particular needs' (Meacher, 1992, p. 102). The idea of vouchers, strongly advocated by the New Right, has come to be accepted by many Democratic Socialists because they see it as, among other things, enhancing consumer choice. Le Grand, for example, argues that there is nothing unsocialist in the idea of vouchers. Using education as an example, he argues that if 'all schools were state owned' and if there was no other way of purchasing education, that is, 'no private fee-paying schools, and no possibility of topping-up the education voucher by paying more to the school', then vouchers would increase consumer choice, raise educational standards and help to reduce educational inequalities (Le Grand, 1989, pp. 199–200).

We now turn to the ethical value base of Democratic Socialism. On this, as on its social welfare aspects, there is substantial agreement. Equality, liberty and fraternity have been its underlying values though different writers have emphasised them differently. Beginning with equality, no one in this group has ever defined it as sameness or uniformity, that is, that everyone should wear the same clothes, drive the same cars, live in the same houses or even be paid the same wage or salary. What the notion of equality has meant for this group is that excessive inequalities are unjustified and they should be reduced. Thus the Democratic Socialist society would be one, according to Hattersley:

> which is organised in a way which diminishes rather than accentuates the differences in prospects that flow from sex, origin and income; one which is committed to a reduction in those disparities of wealth and power which are the product of entrenched privilege; and one which is more concerned with liberty than the neo-libertarianism of the far right could possibly be. (Hattersley, 1987, p. 25)

Such a society will not only ensure that no one lives below a certain standard but it will also attempt to increase equality of opportunity for all, and particularly for those with disadvantages so as to reduce overall inequalities. This implies a range of policies including those of positive discrimination in support of weaker groups in society.

There are understandable differences of opinion as to what constitutes acceptable or unacceptable inequality. Taking wealth and income as examples, there is no agreement on the dividing line between the acceptable and the unacceptable face of inequality. These are matters to be decided not a priori but in the democratic process of politics. There are, however, some agreed policy guidelines: a minimum income for all; a minimum wage and perhaps a maximum wage; and redistributive taxation policies. Using medical care as an example, the emphasis will be on a national health care system, free to all at the point of use, adequately funded to provide treatment speedily and effectively. Though there are differences of opinion on the acceptability of private medical care, no one in this group envisages a major role for it. Thus, the value of equality has very important practical implications for both economic and social policy for it implies a substantial role for governments in public affairs and a justification of inequalities rather than taking them as natural, beneficial and inevitable.

The definition of liberty is very similar to that of Beveridge discussed in the previous chapter. It is a two-dimensional concept: freedom from the arbitrary actions of government and freedom from material deprivation. For this group, a person who is in dire poverty, or who is illegally detained by the police, or who is homeless, or whose telephone is tapped by the secret services will experience a curtailment of his or her freedom. All this stems from the fundamental belief that people have social as well as political and legal rights and the infringement of any kind of right is an infringement of liberty. They reject the claim by the New Right that there is a substantive difference between social rights and other rights (Plant, 1992). For this reason, government services are crucial to the fulfilment of rights; without them, all types of rights will suffer and hence liberty will suffer. Tawney's conclusion in 1949 that, 'The increase in the freedom of ordinary men and women during the last two generations has taken place, not in spite of the action of governments, but because of it . . . The mother of liberty has, in fact, been law' holds as true today as it did then (Tawney, 1964, p. 169).

Democratic Socialists, however, agree that if equality were to be defined as total equalisation, then the degree of government intervention needed to achieve it would be so substantial that individual freedom would suffer. It is one of the reasons why they have rejected total equality – the other being that it is in itself undesirable morally and economically – and they have opted for the notion of partial equality. Despite this, they have recently come under intense political criticism from the New Right that their policies on equality would destroy freedom. To combat this New Right criticism, Hattersley has elevated liberty above equality in the value base of socialists. 'Liberty is our aim. Equality is the way in which it can truly be achieved' (Hattersley, 1987, p. 23). Though not all socialists will agree with this, they will share the sentiment behind it.

The value of fellowship is more difficult to define than the other two but it is no less important. It dominates the writings of both Tawney and Titmuss particularly in relation to social policy. The acquisitive society that Tawney castigated with such venom was no different from the society where blood is sold for money that Titmuss rejected so passionately. Fellowship implies love for one's neighbour; a free gift for a stranger; altruism as well as self-interest; the good of the community as well as individual interest. It is a very demanding, and some might say impossible, value in its policy implications. Yet it is essential to the idea of socialism for without it socialism loses its communitarian appeal that distinguishes it so clearly from capitalism. It is equally important to the provision of universal social services for without it the whole edifice degenerates into an exercise of the calculus of individual interest. Taken to extremes, however, the application of fellowship can be stifling to the expression of individuality which is also essential to socialism as well as to individual liberty. Crick aptly sums up all this as follows: 'Fraternity without liberty is a nightmare, liberty without fraternity is competitive cruelty, but fraternity with liberty is humanity's greatest dream' (Crick, 1984, p. 23).

Though values are broad, vague and flexible concepts which can be interpreted differently at the margins, they are a useful indicator to practice, particularly when seen as clusters rather than individually. They do identify different political positions in relation to welfare and other issues in society. No one can deny that the value cluster of Democratic Socialists implies a different society from that of the value cluster of the New Right.

Assessment

Democratic Socialists have always been the strongest advocates of a universalist welfare state. This has become even more apparent in recent years with the rise of the New Right theory and ideology and the election of governments anxious to 'roll back the frontiers of the state'. Yet the fragmentation of the working class, the recent prolonged economic recession in most advanced industrial societies, the expansion of social needs, the rising tide of public expectations, the unmistakable public demand for choice and participation in the provision of social services and the unwillingness of many groups to pay high rates of direct taxes, some of it actively fostered, have forced Democratic Socialists to rethink their attitudes in relation to both the welfare state and Democratic Socialism.

As far as the welfare state is concerned, there is now greater reluctance to promise substantial improvements in either the scope or the levels of services or benefits. This is noticeable not only in the case of politicians in this group but also of writers. Wicks, for example, accepts that in the current economic climate some 'cherished reforms' may have to be delayed (Wicks, 1987, p. 177). The general acceptance of economic or rather fiscal constraints on the scope and generosity of government provision has narrowed the vision of the socialist agenda for a universalist welfare state. The methods proposed by Democratic Socialist parties for 'squaring the welfare circle' are not too dissimilar to those adopted by Right-wing parties and governments (George and Miller, 1993, Ch. 1).

In the case of their ideal society, the standard response has been that it is both necessary and legitimate to change the *means* but to retain the *ends* of Democratic Socialism. Until recently, most Democratic Socialists agreed that the minimum ends of their socialism were the abolition of poverty, the reduction of class and other inequalities and the improvement of living standards including welfare provisions. They would also have agreed that the means necessary to achieve these ends were an economic system where most of the means of production and distribution were owned and run by the state; full employment was ensured by governments; social services of a universalist type were run by trained professionals and administrators; and progressive forms of taxation for both income and wealth were used to finance government activities.

Nowadays most socialists will still support the same minimum ends but with more emphasis on the reduction of power inequalities between individuals than on the reduction of economic inequalities. Moreover, the means considered necessary to achieve these ends have changed considerably. We have already seen that the preferred economic system is market socialism where most of the means of production are not owned and run by the state but by co-operatives. Bearing in mind the globalisation of industry and trade, it is difficult to see how co-operative enterprises will compete successfully with multinationals. Thus, market socialism will most probably reduce power inequalities in the workplace but will it increase economic growth or maintain full employment which are so necessary for the improvement in living standards and welfare provision? Similarly, the greater emphasis placed today on participation and consumer satisfaction at the expense of professionalism in welfare services will probably create a less inegalitarian ethos in the provision and receipt of services. But doubts must remain as to whether this will reduce socio-economic inequalities in the use of services since everyone knows that working-class clients of services are less skilful in participating and in exercising their right of choice than the middle and upper classes.

There is a logical inconsistency in the contemporary Democratic Socialist approach of retaining the same ends but changing the means. The contemporary version of Democratic Socialism can certainly provide greater democracy in society such as at work, in the social services and elsewhere. It can not, however, seriously promise that it can meet the other minimum ends of socialism. In the past, Democratic Socialism emphasised its egalitarian rather than its democratic aspirations; nowadays, the emphasis is on the second rather than the first word of the creed. This is a very different kind of socialism from the socialism of the past in terms of both means and ends. Socialists may have changed capitalism in some minor ways over the years but capitalism has changed them and their creed even more. Indeed, it is doubtful whether the new brand of market socialism that so many Democratic Socialists aspire to today poses any real threat to capitalism. The socialism of the future will contain more elements of capitalism than past brands of socialism did. Capcialism rather than socialism is a more apt description of this emerging ideology.

CHAPTER 5

MARXISM

Marxism's great attraction for those interested in debates on the welfare state is that it seeks to explain the welfare state through a series of inter-related theoretical premises first enunciated by Marx and Engels and subsequently developed by Marxist writers. There is thus a body of theory which can be assessed, modified, accepted or rejected. As we shall see, however, this body of theory is not as tightly knit as Marxists sometimes claim. In its classical form, it is often ambiguously or inadequately articulated with the result that it is open to more than one interpretation.

For many Marxists the term 'welfare state' is a form of mystification because it misleadingly presents a caring face of capitalism and thus distorts the real functions of state welfare in society. The 'welfare state' is neither a wholly malevolent nor benevolent institution, as the previous ideologies discussed in this book portray it, but a form of capitalism. For Gough the welfare state is nothing more but 'a constituent feature of modern *capitalist* societies' (Gough, 1979, p. 3; emphasis in original); for Ginsburg the welfare state 'remains part of a *capitalist* state which is fundamentally concerned with the maintenance and reproduction of capitalist social relations' (Ginsburg, 1979, p. 2; emphasis in original); and for Offe 'The welfare state in no way represents a *structural change* in capitalist society' (Offe, 1972, p. 481; emphasis in original). For all these reasons, the term welfare capitalism is, to many Marxists, preferable, for it reflects more accurately the functions of state welfare activities in advanced industrial societies.

The development of the welfare state

Marxist explanations of the development of the welfare state are rooted in the Marxist analysis of how capitalism as an economic system functions. At the heart of this is the thesis that the capitalist mode of production is both exploitative and conflict-ridden. It is exploitative because the means of production are owned by a small minority which naturally tries to maximise for itself the profit generated by the production system. It is conflict-ridden because the equally understandable attempt by the workforce to improve its wages and working conditions comes up against the opposition of the owners of enterprises. Thus class conflict and exploitation are the *natural and inevitable* results of the private ownership of the means of production that is the essential feature of a capitalist economic system. The degree and nature of exploitation and conflict may vary from time to time and from country to country but it cannot be abolished under capitalism.

This same class conflict has also a positive side for it is the driving force behind political change in society, bringing about the eventual overthrow of the capitalist system and the ultimate creation of a socialist society by a politically aware and organised working class. Marx and Engels acknowledged that there were other forms of conflict in society, such as of religion, nationality, gender or other sectional interests, but these were resolvable within capitalism and they were, in the last analysis, better understood as variants of the class conflict.

The economic base, or structure, of society influences and eventually determines the nature of other institutions in society that form its superstructure. The nature of the political system, the dominant ideology, the family, the social services and other such institutions are largely, though not wholly, determined by the way the production system is organised and by the level of its performance. Marx and Engels acknowledged that the institutions of the superstructure can exert some influence on the nature of the production system but, on the whole, their materialistic theory of change gave a determining weight to the latter. What they did not do is to specify the conditions within which economic factors allow non-economic factors a degree of freedom. It is for this reason that they have rightly been criticised that they wanted ' "to have it both ways" to assert both determination and autonomy, to claim both dependence and independence' (Hunt, 1992, p. 53).

They also acknowledged that human beings can help to shape the course of history but such an influence must be seen within the context of their materialistic theory of change. In Marx's words: 'Men make their own history, but they do not make it as they please; they do not make it under circumstances chosen by themselves but under circumstances directly encountered, given and transmitted from the past' (Marx, 1963, p. 225).

The logic of a capitalist system, in Marxist analysis, is to maximise production and private profit. In the process, however, it creates problems and crises for itself through overproduction, inflation, under-investment or excessive unemployment. It is, therefore, in need of constant support, regulation and protection if it is to survive and thrive. These functions are performed by the state whose nature depends on the balance of political forces in society. In capitalist societies where the power of the capitalist class clearly overwhelms the working class, the state can act blatantly as merely 'a committee for managing the common affairs of the whole bourgeoisie' (Marx, 1973, p. 69). In capitalist societies, however, where the working class cannot be so easily dominated by the power of the capitalist class, the state has to act with greater caution and tact, even conceding or pre-empting some of the demands of the working class. Either way, the state has a certain degree of autonomy so that it can perform its functions satisfactorily even in the face of opposition from certain quarters of the capitalist class. Above all, 'the intervention of the state is always and necessarily partisan: as a class state, it always intervenes for the purpose of maintaining the existing system of domination, even where it intervenes to mitigate the harshness of that system of domination' (Miliband, 1977, p. 91).

This brief account of the classical Marxist analysis of how a capitalist system works indicates that the development of the welfare state could be seen as the result of three inter-related reasons: state action to promote the needs or requirements of capital; a response to class conflict; and state pre-emptive action, in a Bismarckian sort of way, to undermine the radicalism of the working class. These are ideal types for, in practice, the same reform measure may contain elements of all three. It is also crucial to distinguish between the motives behind a reform measure and its consequences for the two do not necessarily coincide. A piece of social legislation passed in order to pacify the working class may not necessarily achieve that result; a reform measure resulting from class struggle and designed to benefit the working class may benefit other groups in society just as much, if not more.

Of these three reasons for social reform, the first is the central part of the logic of Marx's analysis of capitalism; the second is always implied; and it is only the third that is explicitly, even if briefly, discussed. Marx's general view that the capitalist system, with some exceptions, could only be replaced through working-class revolutions inevitably marginalised his discussions on reform. Thus, there is no discussion in his writings on the educational, Poor Law or health reforms of the nineteenth century but some attention is given to the factory legislation in Britain, perhaps because it is an issue close to the production system.

For Marx, the factory legislation which reduced the hours of work was 'the result of centuries of struggle between the capitalist and the worker' (Marx, 1976, p. 381). It was a hard fought and limited working-class victory which would also, in the long run, benefit capital through the ensuing improvements in workers' health even though employers never saw it that way. This janus nature of social reform – limited short-term benefit to the working class and long-term benefit to the capitalist class – was one of the reasons that dissuaded Marx from championing the reform road to socialism.

It is probably true to say that until the 1960s, most Marxist writers emphasised either the class struggle or the Bismarckian explanation of social reform. Laski in the 1930s saw social legislation as 'a body of concessions offered to avert a decisive challenge' to the supremacy of the capitalist class (Laski, 1934, p. 270). Thirty years later, Miliband described the extension of the social services at the end of the Second World War as 'part of the "ransom" the working class has been able to extract from their rulers in the course of a hundred years' (Miliband, 1969, pp. 109–10). A notable exception to this was Saville who as early as 1957 saw the development of the welfare state as the result of all three factors outlined above (Saville, 1957/58).

As Marxist scholarship began to seriously analyse the nature of the state in advanced capitalist societies, there was a tendency, at first, to overstress the significance of the 'needs of capital' explanation before an uneasy consensus was reached on the necessity for a dual explanation involving elements of both the 'needs of capital' and the 'class struggle' while relegating the 'Bismarckian' element to an appendix of the other two. Gough, for example, summarises his discussion on the development of the welfare state as follows:

> We have discerned two factors of importance in explaining the growth of the welfare state: the degree of class conflict, and, especially, the strength and form of working-class struggle, and the ability of the capitalist state to formulate and implement policies to secure the long-term reproduction of capitalist social relations. (Gough, 1979, p. 64)

Any assessment of the validity of the Marxist explanation for the development of the welfare state must examine closely the notions of class, class struggle, capitalist state and class state action. Beginning with class, most commentators would concede the point that at the time when Marx was writing there may well have existed in Britain two main classes, the working class and the capitalist class, but subsequent economic, technological, management and financial changes have at least modified or even changed completely this dichotomous class division.

We referred in the previous chapter to Crosland's view that by the mid-1950s Britain had ceased to be a capitalist country: the capitalist class, as a result of the managerial revolution, lost its power while the working class, as a result of rising economic affluence and the expansion of the social services, had lost its cohesion and was fractured into a series of socio-economic groups pursuing economistic struggles through their individual trade unions, often at loggerheads with one another. Similar views on the changing nature of class have since been expressed by several writers of different political persuasions and academic disciplines. Skidelsky, writing at the end of the 1970s, claimed that contrary to Marx's expectations, 'the further progress of the division of labour produces not a Marxist simplification into proletarians and capitalists, but increasing occupational diversity leading to growing conflicts of interests, values, understandings and life-styles' (Skidelsky, 1979, p. 79). Writing from a Left perspective, Gorz argued that the massive technological changes in industrial production have led to widespread de-skilling with the result that skilled workers have all but disappeared from the industrial and political scene.

'The age of the skilled workers, with their powers in the factory and their anarcho-syndicalist projects, has now to be seen as an interlude which Taylorism, scientific work organisation, and, finally, computers, and robots have brought to a close' (Gorz, 1982, p. 28). These and other such views maintain that the working class, as defined by Marx, has ceased to exist in both an objective and a political sense.

Marxists will have no difficulty in refuting several of the strands of this vaguely defined post-industrial school. History has already proved it wrong on two counts. The claim that managers are less likely to pursue profit than owners not only lacks logical credibility since managers are also owners as shareholders, but the recent management zeal for profitability at all costs including the job security of the workforce speaks volumes. As for the aspiration that technology will liberate the world from heavy toil and from want and that the problem of the future will be how to manage our increased leisure in our post-industrial societies, one only has to look at the depths of economic recession and the high rates of unemployment in almost all industrial societies today to realise the emptiness of this forecast.

The criticism, however, that the working class is fractured and that it has lost its Left-wing radicalism cannot be dismissed so easily, if at all. Though Marx acknowledged the subdivisions within the two main classes, he, nevertheless, treated them in monolithic terms in his analysis of capitalism. The only major exception to this was his acknowledgement that the state attempts to protect the interests of the capitalist class as a whole even though this may occasionally be against the interests of some of its sections. What is more, his primary concern with the respectable industrial working class, his neglect of other groupings and his stigmatisation of the 'lumpenproletariat', left a legacy which distorted Marxist studies of the growth of the welfare state (Mann, 1986).

Most Marxists today accept that the whole issue of class and class struggle is much more complicated than Marx envisaged. There are legitimate questions about the boundaries between the two main classes, about the differences between state and private employees and about working-class desire for or rejection of socialism. Everyday industrial conflicts also show quite clearly that there are subdivisions within the working class and that its members can often find themselves in situations where their interests do not coincide and may well be in conflict. The general conclusion of a study of class formation in Britain by Westergaard and Resler is typical of the findings of other studies in this field: 'The labour market is in effect a patchwork of markets where skilled and un-skilled blue-collar and white-collar employees, men and women, workers in this industry and that, one region and another, sell their labour on different terms' (Westergaard and Resler, 1975, p. 347).

More recently, several Marxist scholars have openly accepted the fact that in the current situation it is best to define classes in terms of the unequal ownership of assets rather than simply in terms of their structural position in production. Wright, for example, abandoned his early structural approach to class with the result that his new analysis proposes twelve classes depending on the possession of assets in the means of production, in skills and in organisation (Wright, 1985).

Despite all this, however, many Marxists will still agree with Miliband's assessment that these divisions do not 'create an un-bridgeable gulf between different groups of workers' (Miliband, 1991, p. 47); that there are plenty of examples of contemporary working-class solidaristic struggles; and though Marx's prediction of increasing socialist radicalism among the working class has not so far been vindicated, it would be 'very rash' to conclude that this will never happen. The future can only be unpredictable for everything 'now as always before, depends on the many different factors which determine the nature, terms, purposes and out-comes of the struggle' (Miliband, 1991, pp. 450–1). The future is, of course, always unpredictable but the evidence so far is not at all encouraging for future working-class socialist radicalism. We will return to this issue in the last section of the chapter. Suffice it to say here that the classical Marxist notion of class is in severe difficulties.

Marx's subordination of other conflicts in society to that of class was generally accepted by generations of Marxists until the recent upsurge of anti-racism and feminism. Many of the leaders of these two social movements have raised the stakes by insisting that divisions and discriminations by race and gender cannot be either explained or remedied through class struggle.

Others, while still adhering to the class line, maintain that it is only through a combination of class and either race or gender that such discriminations can best be understood. As we shall show in the following chapter, these divisions of opinion run deep within the feminist movement. Recent empirical evidence shows the importance of all three factors in the distribution of life chances in society. In the United States, for example, the full-time, full-year earnings of black men with higher education are inferior to those of white men with equivalent education; the earnings of women are inferior to those of men even when education and race are taken into account; and the earnings of white women are superior to those of black women with equal years of education (Finnie, 1988).

A certain degree of misunderstanding has crept into these debates. What many feminists question is not so much that social policy legislation was the result of class struggle but rather that it benefited all sections of the working class. Wilson makes the point that in the case of Britain such legislation as the Factory Acts and the post-war Social Security Acts 'could certainly not be said to have operated in the interest of women who were in both cases defined as home-bound individuals dependent on a male bread-winner' (Wilson, 1980, p. 87). Similarly, Williams notes that Gough's

> generalised concept of class struggle and the implicit unitariness of the working class obscures a view suggested by feminist history that what were seen as gains for some sections of the working class (often the male white skilled sections) can also be seen as losses for other sections – women, the poor, Black people. (Williams, 1989, p. 139)

This is not a mere quibble about history but a political statement that women's problems have to be addressed directly and not simply through the class struggle.

Marxists are divided between those who insist on the absolute superiority of class and others who are more accommodating to the significance of gender and race. Miliband, while very critical of those on the Left who are dismissive of the contribution that such social movements can make to the cause of socialism, still concludes that class is paramount. These social movements have their special contribution to make but

> [it] must be said that labour movements will remain at the core of the struggle for radical reform and revolutionary change in advanced capitalist societies. New social movements may doubt this,

or deny it. But all conservative forces in their societies do not doubt it. For them, the main protagonist, as always, remains organised labour and the socialist Left: it is they who must above all be contained, repelled, and, if need be, crushed. (Miliband, 1991, p. 114)

In brief, Marxists still insist on the primacy of the class struggle above all other struggles, just as Marx did, simply because it is the mode of production that is the basic feature of a capitalist society.

In the last chapter we examined the comparative evidence in relation to the role of class conflict in the development of the welfare state. Here we look at the historical evidence, some of which lends support to the class struggle thesis of welfare growth but, as always, other evidence does not. We will examine the supporting evidence here and return to the contradictory evidence in the last section of this chapter. Supporting evidence inevitably comes from periods when working-class radicalism and discontent were high. Such a period was the 1920s in Britain when men and women returned to civilian life to find that there were not enough jobs for them, the social services were grossly inadequate, and the working classes were organised in trade unions and had a political party to champion their causes. Gilbert's detailed study of government papers and other documents led him to the conclusion that in the 1920s governments were faced: 'Not with the request for charity for the helpless but with an intractable demand for work or maintenance from society's most dangerous and violent element, the unemployed adult male. Beside the threat of revolution, nothing else was important' (Gilbert, 1970, p. viii). He was referring to the various government policies directly or indirectly concerned with unemployment. Deacon's examination of the development of unemployment insurance benefits during this period led him to a very similar conclusion. Using government documents, he concluded that 'the unemployment insurance scheme was extended in the early 1920s because Ministers were convinced that such a concession was essential if a serious threat to political stability was to be avoided' (Deacon, 1977, p. 10).

The class conflict model of the growth of welfare is action-based, it involves actors in the development of the welfare state and it is therefore amenable to some kind of empirical verification. The needs of capital approach, both as regards social control and social investment, is 'functionalist' not only in the sense that it sees welfare as performing specific functions to satisfy the needs of capital, but also because it sees the growth of welfare as an automatic response to these needs of capital. It is not amenable to any serious historical verification. Its acceptance or rejection depends on the view one forms about the validity of the notion of the state on which it relies. It is a somewhat 'mysterious', as well as a troublesome and controversial notion even though in the Marxist analysis of politics in advanced industrial societies 'there is no other institution which is nearly as important as the state' (Miliband, 1977, p. 66).

Marx wrote very little on the notion of the state and what he did write was often unclear. It is, therefore, not surprising that his ideas on the state have been variously interpreted. The state, according to some Marxists, is made up of such ideological and repressive apparatuses as the central and local government, the police, the army, the judiciary and a range of semi-public bodies. Others define it more widely to include the church, the family, the school and so on. The broader the definition, the more powerful the state potentially can be. Whatever definition is used, the fact remains that it is difficult for the state as a whole to plan the economic and the social life of a country in ways that are beneficial to capital. Therefore, 'a class-conscious political directorate is needed to co-ordinate the activities of nominally independent government agencies' in order to ensure that government policies are supportive of the capitalist class (O'Connor, 1973, p. 67).

Marxists are anxious to point out that their notion of the state and the way it functions is not a conspiracy theory but depicts a pretty natural process for three main reasons. First, the top personnel of the various state apparatuses consist of individuals with a common social, educational and economic background. It is, therefore, to be expected that their decisions will favour the capitalist class for by doing so they promote their own interests as well. Second, the capitalist class has such immense economic power, particularly with the advent of the multi-national corporation, that it can influence or even dictate government decisions on issues that relate to its position in society. This influence can be exerted either directly or indirectly through the electorate by using its stranglehold on the mass media. Third, there is a strong structural reason arising from the fact that a capitalist system has its own rationality of what is and is not desirable, of what should or should not be done in the economic sphere that inevitably influences government decisions in favour of capital. As Miliband puts it: 'A capitalist economy has its own "rationality" to which any government or state must sooner or later submit, and usually sooner' (Miliband, 1977, p. 72).

What is at issue here is not the correctness of these three propositions, for there is enough evidence in support of them. What can be questioned is the conclusion drawn from this, that is, that class power is translated into state power and that the capitalist class becomes, in essence, the ruling class. Let us examine each of these propositions separately before considering the conclusion.

There is enough evidence to show that in Britain the majority of the top personnel in the constituent agencies of the state have a similar family and educational background as the leadership of industry, commerce and finance: they come from higher class family backgrounds and they were educated in one of the exclusive private schools or at the universities of Oxford and Cambridge. Though there is no evidence that the political views of the members of the state agencies necessarily coincide with those of the top echelons of the capitalist class, it can reasonably be inferred from their voting patterns that such a correspondence does exist, in the main. Moreover, even though there are some in the top positions of the state agencies who do not come from the same family and educational backgrounds as members of the capitalist class, again it can reasonably be inferred that many of them are co-opted into the capitalist class culture.

There is also no doubt that the various sections of the capitalist class, jointly and separately, can exert a great deal of influence on governments. A decision by a large company to invest, to close down a factory, or to transfer its business abroad exerts strong pressure which no government can afford to ignore. The control of the mass media, barring some exceptions, by members of the capitalist class enables it not only to exert continual influence in public affairs but also to influence, at times most decisively, the outcome of general elections. There is also considerable evidence that such international bodies as the World Bank and the International Monetary Fund use their economic power almost to dictate to governments loan terms which are, in the main, designed to reduce expenditure on welfare and to boost business profitability. All in all, the capitalist class is not one pressure group among many but a very special one with more power and potentially greater influence on governments than any of the other pressure groups, with the possible exception of labour at specific moments in the history of an industrial country.

Most Marxists consider the third reason why the state serves the interests of the capitalist class as the most important of the three. This is particularly important today with the globalisation of private capital because if the government of a particular country decides to act in ways that are fundamentally contrary to the basic ideas of capitalist production and distribution, it 'would invite the flight of capital to other, more inviting, centres of accumulation. This is one major reason why the nation state, short of a revolutionary change, will not contravene the long-term imperatives of capital accumulation' (Gough, 1979, p. 43). This assumes that the public is, on the whole, supportive of the basic capitalist ideology of the superiority of the private market over all other forms of production and distribution. It is here, Marxists claim, that even a weak type of Gramsci's notion of hegemony becomes a useful explanatory tool. As Miliband points out, the capitalist class does not need to persuade the rest of society

> that the existing social order is splendid, but rather that whatever may be wrong with it is remediable without any need for any major structural change, and that any radical alternative that may be proposed – meaning in effect a socialist alternative – is in any case bound to be worse, indeed catastrophically worse. (Miliband, 1991, p. 140)

There is, however, a quantum leap between the evidence showing that the capitalist class is capable of exerting very considerable influence on public affairs and the conclusion drawn from this evidence that the capitalist class is the ruling class in advanced industrial societies irrespective of (a) which political party is governing, (b) the state of public opinion and (c) the issue under consideration. Possibilities are turned into certainties and tendencies into inevitabilities in the relationship between capital power and state power. It involves a gross underestimation of the significance of Left-wing politics and an unjustifiable exaggeration of the dominance of the capitalist class.

The result is the creation of a notion of an omnipotent and omnipresent state that effectively blocks all paths to socialist change. Miliband's attempt to overcome this criticism by suggesting that 'while the state does act *on behalf of* the "ruling class", it does not for the most part act at its *behest*' (Miliband, 1977, p. 75; emphases in original) merely complicates the issue by attributing to the state a more astute guardianship role. Whether one accepts the Miliband or the more functionalist Marxist perspective on the state, the important point is that social reforms are introduced in order to strengthen rather than weaken the capitalist system. Over the years, the state 'has acted as the "conscience of the rich", and taken upon itself the responsibility of protecting the dominant class from its own short-sightedness' and by doing so it may have prevented the emergence of 'much greater strife and turmoil than has in fact occurred in advanced capitalist countries' (Miliband, 1991, p. 133).

Miliband is here emphasising the social control rather than the social investment function of welfare reforms. Convincing empirical evidence is hard to come by though Pierson summarises what can best be described as circumstantial evidence that lends support to this thesis. There is, first, the evidence that welfare measures within the Poor Law system were coercive; second, payment of benefits to the unemployed is often conditional on a range of rules designed to protect work discipline; third, 'the administration of benefits by the state has placed considerable discretionary, investigative and directive powers in the hands of (middle class) state officials' (Pierson, 1991, p. 53); and the fact that trade unions and other working-class organisations were against state welfare measures when they were first introduced. Despite all this, however, his conclusion is that 'it is difficult to sustain the argument that the growth of the welfare state was exclusively or even predominantly in the interests of the capitalist class' (ibid., p. 54).

Attitudes towards the welfare state

Marxist explanations of the development of the welfare state insist that the welfare state is a contradictory social formation. It involves concessions to the working class and hence it is to be welcomed; but it also involves protection and support for the capitalist class and hence it is unacceptable. It is perhaps true to say that during the post-war period down to the mid-1970s, most Marxists saw the welfare state as, on balance, favouring private capital despite the fact that it may have come about partly as a result of class conflict and the benefits conferred on the working class.

Ginsburg's detailed analysis of the social security system in Britain conveys this message most clearly. His general conclusion is that 'the social security system is concerned with the reproduction of capitalist social relations' (Ginsburg, 1979, p. 47). It attempts to do this in several ways. First, by fixing the level of benefits at a low level, it tends to pull down the level of wages; second, it tries to make sure that the able-bodied unemployed are readily available for employment if and when they are needed; thirdly, it seeks to do the same with married women and pensioners as cheap labour; and fourth, the social security rules and regulations are designed to maintain and strengthen industrial discipline (ibid., pp. 47–8). He applies a very similar analysis to social security and women as well as to government involvement in the provision and finance of housing.

During the 1970s, however, several Marxists began to discuss not only the functions but the 'disfunctions' of large-scale welfare provision to capital profitability. O'Connor's work is by far the most important in this for it influenced the work of other Marxists in both the United States and in Britain.

O'Connor's first premise is that 'the capitalist state must try to fulfil two basic and often mutually contradictory functions – *accumulation* and *legitimation*' (O'Connor, 1973, p. 6; emphases in original). In other words, the state must provide services and benefits which improve private capital profitability and which also strengthen the social acceptability of the capitalist system. He points out that 'few state outlays can be classified unambiguously' with the result that the same service may well perform both functions even though it emphasises one of them (ibid., p. 7). No state can afford to neglect either of these two functions for obvious reasons. If it neglects its accumulation function then profitability and economic growth suffer; if it ignores its legitimation function then it will ultimately have to resort to coercive measures and this will undermine its public image and its legitimacy. Thus, social services are an integral part of the capitalist system: they grow out of it and they are essential to its economic and political survival.

All this is generally accepted among Marxists and even other writers. The main weakness of this typology is that it divorces economic growth from political legitimacy. In fact, it can be argued that what has made capitalism socially acceptable is not so much that it has provided social services, even though these are import- ant, but because it has raised economic growth rates and general living standards. This may help to explain why the general public has continued to support capitalism throughout the Reaganite and Thatcherite years of the 1980s.

O'Connor's distinctive contribution, however, is his second pre- mise: the fiscal crisis of the state, that is, 'the tendency for govern- ment expenditure to outrace revenues' (O'Connor, 1973, p. 2). This fiscal crisis is the result of the structural tendencies contained in the first premise rather than the outcome of incompetent or profligate government. More specifically, however, the fiscal crisis is the result of the public demand, on one hand, for more and better government services and, on the other, the public unwilling- ness to pay the necessary rates of taxation.

> Every economic and social class and group wants government to spend more and more money on more and more things. But no one wants to pay new taxes or higher rates on old taxes. Indeed, nearly everyone wants lower taxes, and many groups have agitated suc- cessfully for tax relief. Society's demands on local and state budgets seemingly are unlimited, but people's willingness and capacity to pay for these demands appear to be narrowly limited. (O'Connor, 1973, p. 1)

Three interesting points emerge from this. First, the notion of public tax aversion or revolt which comes straight from the New Right approach to welfare that was so skilfully publicised by Fried- man. Second, O'Connor abandons the traditional Marxist mono- lithic approach to class and adopts a fractured approach that refers to different interest groups in society. Third, he refers to group demands as the driving force behind government expenditure rather than the 'needs' of capital on which his thesis is based. As Mishra very rightly points out, O'Connor's thesis, though in theory based on Marxist principles, was in reality 'a long way from the schematic interpretations of Marxist theory, functional necessities of capital or a bipolar class struggle' (Mishra, 1984, p. 76). Be this as it may, O'Connor's contribution remains important for it high- lighted the 'dysfunctional' nature of public expenditure to capital accumulation. The welfare state was not simply a trusted guardian but also a structural adversary of capitalism. Where O'Connor differed from the New Right was primarily on the solutions to the fiscal crisis of the state which he proposed.

Other Marxists began to raise more fundamental questions about the role of public expenditure to capital profitability. While O'Connor stressed the fiscal disfunction, Gamble and Walton discussed the economic disfunction of public expenditure to profitability. Their argument was again very similar to the emerging New Right claim that high levels of public expenditure were responsible for the decline in profitability, best exemplified in the Bacon and Eltis de-industrialisation thesis (Bacon and Eltis, 1976). Gamble and Walton show that Keynesian policies were responsible for the resolution of the economic crisis of the 1930s to the advantage of private capital. In the post-war period, state involvement continued to benefit capital until such time when full employment, trade union strength and international competition made it impossible for private capital to use the unemployment weapon in order to reduce costs and thus increase profitability (Gamble and Walton, 1976).

Though Gough takes a more balanced position in this debate, he reaches the same conclusion. He tries to show that social service expenditure can both improve and depress economic growth and profitability, depending on which social service one is referring to and whether the financial burden for the provision of services falls mainly on the workers or on the capitalists. Bearing in mind all this and the balance of industrial power in Britain during the post-war period, he, too, concluded that high rates of public expenditure contributed to the worsening of both inflation and economic growth rates in Britain (Gough, 1979, pp. 126–7).

Similarly, Offe examined what he considered to be the two main arguments by the New Right against the welfare state, that is, that it reduces incentives to invest and to work, and found them both valid. Nevertheless, his rather comfortable conclusion was that 'while capitalism cannot coexist *with* the welfare state, neither can it exist *without* the welfare state' (Offe, 1982, p. 11; emphases in original). The welfare state provided benefits to the working class but at a considerable cost to them. It did not reduce inequalities, it dealt with the symptoms rather than the causes of social problems. It provided benefits under strict eligibility and behaviour tests and it conditioned 'a false ideological understanding of social and political reality within the working class' (ibid., p. 12).

The success of Reaganism and Thatcherism in the 1980s brought about a multitude of conflicting responses from Marxist writers. They were taken aback by the success of the New Right and the passivity of ordinary people, as distinct from the official trade union response, towards welfare cuts, 'rationalisations', privatisations, and marketisation. It became clear that the decline of the welfare state 'engendered so far not a tougher-minded general militancy of the Left, but a politics of retrenchment and narrow self-interest' (Rustin, 1980, p. 72). Some Marxists attributed it all to the highly bureaucratic nature of welfare services that alienated its users. Thus, Corrigan concludes that this 'has turned significant sections of the population away from the welfare state as a progressive set of institutions' (Corrigan, 1979, p. 15). Others felt that the payment of benefits, whilst welcome to working-class interests in one respect, also 'contributed in large measure to the considerable acquiescence of the Labour movement in the capital restructuring process' (Ginsburg, 1979, p. 78).

Both of these reasons may well have had something to do with the success of the New Right but equally, and perhaps even more important was the fact that certain sections of the working class preferred tax cuts to benefits which was the central electoral offer of New Right governments. Also, many sections of the working class were convinced by the New Right message that welfare cuts were necessary for the preservation of jobs and wage standards. Now, as always, the working class is divided into numerous groups whose welfare interests are often in conflict and whose political allegiances are, as a result, different.

The anti-welfare programmes of the New Right governments during the 1980s also brought about a new appreciation of the attitude of private capital towards social policies. Whereas in the past, Marxist writers saw capitalist opposition to welfare provision as not only misguided but also unusual, some Marxists now came to see it as quite normal and widespread. Miliband sees the state as being pressurised against social reforms by the capitalist class and counter-pressurised by the working class. Under this pressure 'provision has to be made, and it is made; but it is made grudgingly' (Miliband, 1991, p. 132). He also finds capital's opposition to social policies understandable not only because of possible financial considerations but also because social services 'raise expectations; they enhance the notion of state responsibility and social rights against the notion of individual competition and striving' (ibid., p. 133). In other words, social services and benefits undermine the capitalist ethos and value system. This is a far cry from the tranquillising effects that social services were said to have on the working class.

Amidst all this variety of reactions to the New Right successes, Marxists have become divided between those who see the welfare state as an enduring institution and those who question its long-term survival, at least in its post-war structures. Therborn and Roebroek optimistically concluded their analysis of the growth of the welfare state as follows:

> the welfare state is an irreversible major institution of advanced capitalist countries. Or, to be more precise, it is irreversible by democratic means. The size of the population benefiting from the welfare state ensures that as long as democracy accompanies advanced capitalism, the core of the welfare state is safe. (Therborn and Roebroek, 1986, p. 332)

Interestingly enough, their view is not based on the notion of working-class solidarity for the welfare state but on the number of different groups (the elderly, unemployed, single parents and so on) benefiting from welfare provision.

Writing at about the same time, Offe reaches the opposite conclusion on the future of the welfare state. He is convinced that the economic, industrial and employment changes of recent years have led to the 'virtual evaporation' of classes and other groups who were the main supporters of traditional collectivist values and welfare state provisions. The result is that the 'welfare state as we know it as a major accomplishment of postwar Western European societies is rapidly losing its political support' (Offe, 1987, p. 528). What will follow is a minimalist welfare state for the poor as the well-paid and the affluent groups are allowed and encouraged to opt out of state provision into private insurance programmes. In a period of five years, Offe's position on the durability of the welfare state changed quite considerably.

To conclude this section: Marxists have always seen the welfare state as a contradictory social system, being both 'good' and 'bad'; both furthering and limiting the interests of the working class; protecting and undermining the survival of the capitalist system; worth supporting and justifiably attacking. The emphasis given to these conflicting features of the welfare state has always varied between one school of Marxism and another as well as according to the configuration of social, political and economic conditions prevalent at any one time.

Welfare and their ideal society

Marxism is primarily a theoretical analysis and critique of capitalism and only secondarily a detailed exposition of socialism and communism – the ideal societies that would follow on from capitalism. This is largely due to the reluctance of Marx and Engels to embark in any big way on what they called 'utopian' thinking. As Engels put it in relation to the housing question: 'To speculate as to how a future society would organise the distribution . . . of dwellings leads directly to utopia' (Engels, 1936, p. 98). Decisions on the details of policy could only be taken by individual socialist governments in the light of the social, economic and political conditions that prevailed in their particular country at the collapse of capitalism. Though there is an element of truth in this argument, it is equally correct, if not more so, that a fairly clear picture of the good society must be painted if it is to attract popular support. On balance this reluctance by Marx and Engels has proved a serious mistake for it has led to all sorts of speculation and differences of opinion among their followers on both the structure and the details of Marxist socialism, let alone communism. This should not be taken to mean that they said nothing about their ideal society. They made enough references which, taken together, provide an outline of the main broad features of their socialist and communist society.

To begin with, they both insisted that their ideal society could not come about until capitalism reached its developed technological stage with the concomitant material abundance and the political awareness and sophistication of the working class.

> No social order ever perishes before all the productive forces for which there is room in it have developed; and new, higher relations of production never appear before the material conditions of their existence have matured in the womb of the old society itself. (Marx, 1970, p. 504)

Revolutions in economically undeveloped or developing societies could not lead to the establishment of socialism for, apart
from the risk that this would simply create a dictatorial system, the
absence of material abundance would mean that 'only *want* is
made general, and with *want* the struggle for necessities and all the
filthy business would necessarily be introduced' (Marx, 1947, p. 24;
emphases in original). These and other references make it abund-
antly clear that Marx and Engels would not have considered the
Soviet Union a socialist country. The same comment applies to all
the other ex-East European countries for, in addition, they both
argued that a socialist society could not be imposed from outside;
it could only be created by the country's own working class. Their
ideal society would come about through either working-class,
peaceful parliamentary methods or through working-class revolution, depending on the balance of political forces in society. It
needs to be borne in mind that Marx and Engels were writing at a
time when the right to vote was either non-existent or limited to a
small privileged minority. It is, therefore, not surprising that they
put more emphasis on the revolutionary than the parliamentary
road to their ideal society. They acknowledged, however, that
where there was a strong working-class movement, the parliamentary road was both possible and preferable. Having stressed the
general necessity of force, they acknowledged that 'there are countries, such as America, England and I would add Holland . . .
where the working people achieve their goal by peaceful means'
(Marx, 1964, p. 293).

Despite this qualified acceptance of the parliamentary road to
socialism, there can be no doubt that their approval of force as a
political means has proved very damaging to political parties at-
tempting to implement Marxist ideas, and it is no surprise that it
has been renounced by most Marxist writers and by all the communist parties in advanced industrial societies.

The parliamentary reformist struggle is now the accepted means
despite all the problems that this raises. What chances, however,
does a reform programme that threatens the very existence of
capitalism stand of being implemented by a Left-wing government? Miliband speaks for most Marxists when he says that such a
programme will be strongly resisted by the capitalist class with all
the means at its disposal, political, economic and even coercive,
but the solution for the government is 'to move very fast and very

far in radical directions: the inescapable choice confronting it would be radicalisation or retreat' (Miliband, 1991, p. 230). This type of desperate political thinking is yet another example of the problems created by the Marxist insistence on an omnipotent and omnipresent capitalist state.

Though Marx and Engels did not leave a detailed blueprint of their ideal society, they sketched out its outline in numerous references in several of their works. They envisaged that capitalism would be followed by socialism and then by communism. The very fact that socialism would follow on the footsteps of advanced capitalism meant that it will inevitably be 'still stamped with birth marks of the old society from whose womb it emerges' (Marx, 1970, p. 324). In such a society, the income distribution principle will, therefore, be 'from each according to his ability, to each according to his work'. No guidance is provided as to how this principle will be implemented in practice, for in theory it can be argued that this is exactly what happens under capitalism, apart from the payment of profits to a small minority.

Numerous steps, however, will be taken to destroy the class system and to lay the foundations for the egalitarian communist society. These steps range from the socialisation of the means of production and distribution to the provision of a range of social services that would be available to everyone. Neither Marx nor Engels envisaged a centralised, nationalised system of ownership of the type that emerged in the Soviet Union. Rather, they had in mind a 'co-operative society based on common ownership of the means of production' (Marx, 1970, p. 323), a society 'composed of associations of free and equal producers' (Marx, 1964, p. 290). This emphasis on co-operatives and workers' participation rather than on nationalisation and bureaucratic decision-making was in line with their general idea that work in a socialist society should be satisfying and non-alienating.

During the socialist stage economic growth would rise and economic abundance would be achieved; the antithesis between mental and physical labour would be reduced; the difference between town and country would decline; work would become rewarding and satisfying; social services would be developed on socialist lines; and citizens would become increasingly communitarian in spirit and outlook. Thus the foundations will be laid for the classless communist society which can then 'inscribe on its banners: From each according to his abilities, to each according to his needs!' (Marx, 1970, p. 325). Again, no clear guidance is provided as to what needs are to be satisfied, at what level, or who will decide on such matters. Implied in all this is the belief that people will be prepared to work hard but will not be anxious to demand too much for themselves to the detriment of the needs or demands of their fellow citizens.

In a communist society, the state will gradually wither away and the division of labour will disappear. People will be competent to perform several jobs adequately to their own satisfaction and without any loss to the economy. Thus, in contrast to the capitalist society, life will be different in a communist society

> where nobody has one exclusive sphere of activity but each can become accomplished in any branch he wishes, society regulates the general production and thus makes it possible for me to do one thing today and another tomorrow, to hunt in the morning, fish in the afternoon, raise cattle in the evening, criticize after dinner, just as I have a mind, without ever becoming a hunter, fisherman, shepherd or critic. (Marx, 1947, p. 22)

As many commentators have remarked, Marx and Engels accused others of being romantics and utopian but their general view of life in a communist society is the apotheosis of romanticism and uto-pianism (Lee and Raban, 1988, p. 120)

Having outlined the classical Marxist position in terms of both theory and political practice, we now move on to look briefly at the main divisions of opinion that have recently emerged within Marxism. Chilcote and Chilcote identify three such divisions: the 'post Marxists', the 'analytical Marxists' and the 'new structural Marxists'. We have already made reference to the post Marxists for, despite their differences, their unifying claim is that

> the primacy of class should be repudiated because, according to their view, the working class in capitalist countries has failed to live up to its revolutionary expectations and the model of struggle should now incorporate a multitude of interests emanating from various strata, groups, and social movements. (Chilcote and Chilcote, 1992, p. 90)

Several writers belong to this school (Bowles and Gintis, 1986; Gorz, 1982; Laclau and Mouffe, 1985) but, in many ways, their ideas have their origins in the change of policies of European communist parties in the 1970s and the adoption of what came to be known as 'Eurocommunism' (Carrillo, 1978). It follows that if the struggle for socialism is to be waged by a plurality of groups, the beneficiaries of socialist change must also be seen in this broader perspective.

Analytical Marxism coheres around four themes that set it apart from classical Marxism: 'rational decision-making, unequal endowment of assets, problems of collective action, and theory of history' (Chilcote and Chilcote, 1992, p. 93). Individuals make rational, mainly self-interested, choices and, therefore, all social issues can be explained by such individual actions. Class action is nothing more but the aggregate of individual actions (Carling, 1986; Elster, 1985; Roemer, 1982). The rational actions of individuals are based on the assets that they possess and these, in the case of Wright already referred to, range from the possession of wealth in terms of stocks and shares to the possession of skills and educational qualifications, and to organisation assets depending on the person's position in the enterprise. As a result of this unequal possession of assets, society is made up of classes, the number of which varies from one writer to another but all are different from the classical Marxist position. Finally, and despite their adherence to individual rational action, analytical Marxists adhere to a materialist conception of history. Overall, their differences from classical Marxism are so fundamental that they amount to almost 'a general repudiation of Marxism in theory and in practice' (Meikseens Wood, 1989, p. 87).

The new structural Marxists are in agreement with the classical Marxist view that human beings must be seen primarily as the products of their environment rather than as isolated individuals making rational choices. They differ, however, from classical Marxism in several ways particularly on the notion of class. Human beings are shaped by many structural processes, activities and identities of which class, in the traditional Marxist sense, is only one. Thus conflicts of gender, ethnicity, and ecology must be seen for what they are rather than be subsumed under class conflict (Isaac, 1987).

Bearing in mind these and other divisions within contemporary Marxism, what is the vision of a socialist society that commands support among most Marxists?

First and foremost, there is now universal agreement among Marxists that a socialist society will be democratic along the lines of contemporary parliamentary democracy. A common comment in these debates now is that socialism has to be democratic or it will not come about at all.

Second, it is generally accepted that the path to socialism will be through the ballot box and the parliamentary process for, if for no other reason, there is no public support for any other approach. Most Marxists are mensheviks now!

Third, a socialist society will be an industrial society with the usual division of labour and laying stress on economic growth. Several prominent individuals with deep Green ideas, Bahro being the most notable of these, have parted company with Marxism because of this issue.

Fourth, very few, if any, Marxists now adhere to the classical Marxist view that in a socialist or communist society the market will disappear altogether and the state will provide for all human needs. As Hobsbawm put it: 'I am not, of course, denying that socialists in the past, including Marx, dreamed of an entirely non-market, perhaps even non-monetary, communist society; they did, but that utopia cannot be maintained any longer, and it is not' (Hobsbawm, 1992, p. 61).

In this kind of democratic industrial society, Miliband puts forward the view that socialism will have three basic features: the socialisation of the major means of production and distribution; the reduction of inequalities; and the partnership between state power and popular power. To these, he could have added a fourth, the satisfaction of basic human needs, and a fifth, universal social services, for they are implied throughout his writings.

Fifth, Marxists consider the socialisation of the major means of production and distribution as an absolute must for several reasons: it will reduce wealth concentration and, to a lesser extent, income inequalities; it will facilitate better co-ordination and planning of national priorities; it will reduce human exploitation at work; and it will encourage a better system of workplace relations that could be conducive to higher rates of productivity. They are also agreed that this does not mean centralised, bureaucratic nationalisation but, rather, a mixed system of co-operatives and nationalised enterprises with maximum workers' participation and public accountability. Most of them will also exclude the socialisation of very small businesses, individual shopkeepers and such like enterprises. Though this may sound like the mixed economy found in many capitalist societies, it is argued that it is in fact very different because: 'the "mix" would be the reverse of the one prevailing in all advanced capitalist countries: instead of the public sector being relatively small and marginal, and a junior partner to the private sector, it would be predominant' (Miliband, 1991, p. 232).

Sixth, the reduction of wealth inequalities and, to a lesser extent, income inequalities will follow from the abolition of large-scale private enterprise. Salary differentials must be kept low and the salaries and occupational benefits of managers must be open to public scrutiny. The purpose of such measures 'is not perfect equality, which is an absurd notion, but a striving for rough equality, which is a very different thing' (Miliband, 1991, p. 232). Policies for equality must extend beyond the market place and they must include gender, race, religious and other such forms of association.

The satisfaction of basic human needs is the seventh feature of the current Marxist vision of an ideal society. Like writers in the other groups, they find the notion of needs difficult to pin down for policy purposes but there is general support for the notion of a hierarchy of needs. Mandel uses the concept of 'relative intensity of needs' in order to distinguish between fundamental needs which have to be satisfied; secondary needs which must be satisfied as far as possible; and luxury, or marginal, needs which must be left to the individual. Fundamental needs include not only food, clothing and housing but also 'education, and health provision; guaranteed transport to and from the workplace; and the minimum of recreation and leisure'. Secondary needs include 'most of the sophisticated foods, drinks, clothes and household appliances (excepting the fanciest ones), the more elaborate "cultural" and "leisure" goods and services, and private motor vehicles' (Mandel, 1986, p. 11). All other goods and services belong to the luxury category. He acknowledges that there are demarcation problems and also that, as Marx argued, the nature of needs changes over time. For this reason, he makes the point that the socialist goal 'is one of a gradual satisfaction of more and more needs, not of a restriction to basic requirements alone' (ibid., p. 20). Similarly, Doyal and Gough maintain that 'a concept of human needs is an essential component in formulating a feasible socialist vision of what the future could be like' (Doyal and Gough, 1984, p. 6). The notion of need is as troublesome as the notion of ideology we discussed in the first chapter and general agreement on the principle of need satisfaction does not necessarily mean agreement on its policy implications (Hewitt, 1992, ch. 10).

The eighth aspect of a Marxist socialist society concerns the relationship between the state and the various classes and groups in society. It is acknowledged that the state will not, as Marx and Engels claimed, wither away and that it will continue to exist for as long as one can see in the future but its nature and functions will be different. It will now be staffed and run by persons who are supportive of socialism and its function will be to maintain and promote socialist policies and ideals, in the same way that the capitalist state promoted capitalism. Miliband echoes the views of many Marxists that to safeguard socialist policies from the attacks of the capitalist class, an alliance between the new state and all radical, Left-wing groupings in society – not just the working class – will be necessary. This alliance, however, must be a two-way process for 'just as society would check state power, so too would the state, democratically invested with the capacity to do so, constitute a check on the power of popular institutions and agencies' (Miliband, 1991, p. 233). In other words, the state should not be allowed to act in dictatorial ways and none of the various groups or agencies in society should be allowed to frustrate the general will as expressed through government policies. In this, there is a clear acceptance that socialism has to be democratic and participatory but also an awareness that the process will be a rough and chequered one, for in a democratic society government policies can be reversed.

Finally, a socialist society will provide social services which appear to be of the same nature as those advocated by Democratic Socialists: they will be universalist, redistributive, participatory and, wherever possible, preventive. Marxists, however, are less tolerant of the role of private social services and would argue for their abolition.

This brief outline of the ideal society envisaged by contemporary Marxism shows, first, how far contemporary Marxism has travelled from its classical origins and, second, how similar it has become to Democratic Socialism in terms of prescription if not of theoretical analysis. Marxists have come to realise, perhaps too late, that if they want to continue influencing academic debates and to begin to shape political events they need to abandon many of the classical Marxist ideas and to formulate their utopia in ways that make sense in today's world.

Assessment

Despite its many weaknesses, Marxism remains the most satisfactory model among all the 'isms' discussed in this book in explaining the development of the welfare state. It suffers, however, from several weaknesses, some of which have already been mentioned. First, the treatment of the working class as a unitary force conceals many divisions and conflicts of interest within it. As Wetherly put it, ' "working class pressure" is really an abstraction, for the class or the labour movement as such does not enter into struggle – class struggle almost always involves particular sections of the working class' (Wetherly, 1988, p. 35). Second, the claim of Marxism that all structural conflicts in society can be subsumed under the banner of class grossly underestimates the importance of gender, race, religion, or nationalism in the development of the welfare state. Third, as we have argued elsewhere, the relevance of the Marxist explanation can be substantiated by empirical evidence and by logic in areas of policy with strong economic implications but not in other areas of social and public policy. It is logical that the capitalist class will oppose such policies as the taxation of wealth pursued by a Left-wing government with the support of the working class. It is less clear, however, why the same should apply to such measures as the adoption of children, traffic offences or cruelty to animals (George and Wilding, 1976, p. 20).

Fourth, like all other explanations, it treats the development of policy as a single stage process. Parker has classified the growth of public policy into three stages: innovation, that is, the creation of a new policy; development which refers to the substantial alteration of existing policies; and reform, that is, minor modifications of existing policies (Parker, 1975, p. 19). Marxist explanations have more to say in relation to the first than the second stage and more for the second than the third.

Fifth, Marxist explanations, particularly of the 'needs of capital' type, occasionally fail to distinguish between the causes and the functions of policy. Causes and functions may be and often are related but there are many instances when they are not. The fact, for example, that a state health service helps to improve the health of the workforce does not necessarily mean that the latter was the cause for the creation of the service in the first place.

As regards the functions of the welfare state, Marxism had, until recently, overemphasised the integrative contribution of welfare to capitalism. It is only in the last twenty years that a more balanced approach has emerged which also recognises the disfunctional nature of some types and degrees of welfare to capitalism. Thus high levels of public expenditure, when financed out of direct taxation, may well make profitability more difficult; similarly, when services or benefits are provided as of right, they may well undermine the ethos of the private market.

The major weakness of classical Marxism has been the nature of its ideal society and the means required to achieve it. We have shown that its ideal society is not only utopian in the extreme but it also contains severe contradictions which make it an unworkable model. It stresses, on one hand, technological advance, material overabundance and high labour productivity while on the other it asks for altruism, a leisurely approach to work and a disinclination to high levels of consumption. Its acceptance of the use of force to achieve political ends has made it unacceptable in advanced industrial societies. Contemporary Marxists have abandoned many of the features of classical Marxism but the negative public image of their message has so far stubbornly persisted. It is this that has forced most of the communist parties of Europe to change their name long after they changed most of their policies but whether this will have much effect on public support remains doubtful. The long association of academic Marxism with communist parties in Europe and elsewhere and the close links of many of these parties with the now-extinct Soviet-style regimes account for the current decline of Marxism and does not augur at all well for it as an ideology in the foreseeable future. If and when it emerges from its current decline, it will most probably be a more pluralistic ideology in terms of both theoretical analysis and political prescription.

CHAPTER 6

FEMINISM

'Throughout the social sciences', says Giddens, '. . . feminist authors have forced a rethinking of pre-established notions and theories' (Mayo and Weir, 1993, p. 35). That is certainly true of the analysis of welfare states. Feminist analysis has four essential starting points. It starts from the argument that to a very large extent the activities of the British welfare state over the past century have focused on women. It moves on, secondly, to argue that, if those actions are to be understood, it is vital to use a form and method of analysis which focuses on 'putting women into a picture that has largely been drawn by men' (Pascall, 1986, p. 6). If the welfare state is essentially a women's state, analysis needs to focus very strongly on what that state means for women in terms of assumptions, impact and outcomes. The third starting point is that 'an analysis of the position of women is not marginal but central to a true understanding of the nature of the Welfare State' (Wilson, 1977, p. 39) because, 'only an analysis of the Welfare State that bases itself on a correct understanding of the position of women in modern society can reveal the full meaning of modern welfarism' (Wilson, 1977, p. 59). Sapiro argues in exactly the same way about the United States, that 'it is not possible to understand the underlying principles, structure and effects of our social welfare systems and policies without understanding their relation to gender roles and gender ideology' (Sapiro, 1990, p. 37). Feminist analysis does not just illuminate the position of women; it throws light on the very nature of welfare states. The fourth point underpinning the feminist analysis is that women's position in society, that is, women's subordination, must be understood as *systemic* and as having deep structural roots which make change extremely difficult. The welfare state needs, therefore, to be understood in the context of women's overall position in society.

Strands of feminism

All social and political movements, and indeed all ideologies, contain different strands and groupings and feminism is no exception. Although all the strands within the feminist movement are united by certain common concerns, they are fundamentally divided in their analysis of the reasons for women's unequal position and the strategies they propose for correcting it. They also differ on the question of the extent and nature of women's subordination.

It is possible to subdivide feminism into a large number of groupings; Williams, for example, uses six categories (Williams, 1989, pp. 83–4). Our concern, however, is primarily with what unites feminists rather than with what divides them so precise discrimination is not crucial to our analysis. We therefore restrict our analysis to three groupings – what we describe as liberal, socialist and radical feminism.

Liberal feminism

Liberal feminism has a long history. Its concern is with equal rights for women – in education, in every kind of occupation, in key positions in society. Liberal feminists have, therefore, campaigned on issues such as the removal of discrimination in education, the ending of quotas restricting the access of women to medical schools, the ending of direct and indirect discrimination in recruitment to jobs, wages, pensions and in the granting of mortgages. The focus of liberal feminist activity is the state which is seen as a neutral, disinterested arbiter open to the influence of sweet reason and political pressure.

There are a number of criticisms made of the liberal feminist approach by other feminist groups. First, it takes a view of the state which is simplistic and naive. The state is capitalist (the socialist feminist view) and male-dominated (the radical view). To expect disinterested action by the state to benefit women is therefore naive. Secondly, liberal feminism fails to see that the status quo, which disadvantages women, is very much in the interests of men. Reform is not simply a matter of winning an argument. There are many individuals and groupings who gain from things as they are. Thirdly, liberal feminists restrict their analysis of women's unequal position to the public sphere. Simply to pursue the extension of opportunities in the public sphere, the critics argue, is to ignore a crucial part of women's lives. That the personal is political is perhaps the key insight of the feminist movement. Unless, and until, that insight is absorbed, attempts to extend women's opportunities in the public sphere will bear little fruit. Fourthly, liberal feminists see the answer to women's inequality as lying in securing equality of opportunity in male terms. Such equality fails to take account of female difference. Women are simply not in a position, in many areas, to compete on equal terms with men because of the domestic division of labour and assumptions about their caring role. Fifthly, liberal strategies are criticised as primarily benefiting certain groups of women, that is, white, highly educated middle-class women. To its critics, liberal feminism is a middle-class strategy.

Socialist feminism

Socialist feminism attempts to place an analysis of the position of women in society within the context of a conventional socialist analysis of capitalism but it concludes that women's position cannot simply be understood as a dimension of capitalism. It is an element in a particular form of capitalism – patriarchal capitalism.

In a capitalist society, according to socialist feminists, women play a particular role in biological and social reproduction. Their unwaged labour in the home is a subsidy to capitalism because it reduces the cost of reproducing the next generation of workers and servicing male breadwinners. Women's assumed dependence in the family and on a male breadwinner depresses their own earning capacity because employers do not need to pay them the full costs of reproducing their own labour power. Their low pay reinforces women's dependency within marriage and on marriage – they need a share of a man's earnings (V. Bryson, 1992, p. 240).

A symbiotic relationship therefore exists between capitalism and the family.

Socialist feminism sees the welfare state as a social system which both colludes with this system of exploitation and sustains it through policies designed to support the family. Socialist feminists, too, point out that, like men, women experience capitalism in different ways. Although all women suffer in a patriarchal system, some can break through to economic success into a prefigurative capitalist feminism (Kenny, 1993).

The strength of socialist feminism lies in its location of women's subordination in the nature of economic and gender relations in a capitalist society. Its weakness is the strand of determinism which runs through the analysis. All capitalist societies can be deemed to exploit women but some much more clearly and extensively than others. So, clearly, there is some scope for reform and amelioration.

Socialist feminists accept the possibility of reform and seek to work through a classic policy of permeation – in Left-wing political groupings and in local and central government. They have clear policy demands, for example, that women should have access to social security benefits as individuals not simply as dependents of men and that there should be a major collective commitment to the provision of public child care services.

Radical feminism

Radical feminism's approach to the position of women in society is to see women as a group oppressed by men as a group. This oppression has its roots in male and female biology. Although the basic thrust of radical feminism is in terms of biological explanations there are radicals who offer a materialist explanation of what they see as the fundamental conflict between men and women (e.g., Delphy, 1984) seeing men and women in marriage as members of opposing classes – the woman as employee, the man as employer.

Radical feminism's contribution to a feminist social analysis has essentially been fourfold. Firstly, it has drawn attention to problems which have not been central concerns of other feminist groups, for example, rape and domestic violence. Secondly, given their fundamental hostility to men, radicals have proceeded, quite logically, to argue for separate services provided for women by women, for example, Well Women Clinics, self-help groups, women-only counselling services. Thirdly, radical feminism has provided a powerful corrective to the simplistic tendencies of Marxist explanations of women's subordination – that it is all the product of capitalism. Radicals criticise such explanations for failing to grasp the complex nature of social and gender inequality. Finally, radical feminism, whatever the rights or wrongs of its analysis, has powerfully reinforced the central thrust of the feminist argument that the personal is ultimately political, that women's position can only be understood in the light of their domestic relations, in this case their sexual relationship with men.

Radical feminism has been the subject of wide-ranging criticisms. Firstly, radical feminists seem to assume a commonality of interests and position between women which is at odds with reality. Secondly, radical feminism assumes a false universalism in its arguments about relations between men and women. Critics question whether relations between men and women are always and inevitably relations of conflict. Thirdly, critics accuse radical feminists of biological reductionism, of reducing the complex issue of women's unequal position in society to a simple single explanation – biology. All feminists would accept the significance of biological differences but would shy away from such a single factor and therefore in their view, simplistic, analysis.

Finally, there is the pragmatic criticism that, even if it were true, radical feminism leads women and men nowhere, except into the wilderness. It offers no practical possibilities or hopes. It simply describes and explains a reality which is by its very definition unchangeable because it is rooted in biology, unless lesbian relationships and new methods of artificial reproduction become possible and generally acceptable. Separate services may provide interesting insights and models but they can offer no more than that.

An analysis of the different groupings within feminism emphasises difference rather than similarity. It does not capture the compromises which characterise the realities of real life. That there are common threads linking the different strands within feminism is clear and that justifies an analysis based on what unites rather than on what divides.

The development of the welfare state

Feminist analysis has added new insights to our understanding of the development of welfare states. To the idea that their development in Western Europe is to be understood as a compromise in the struggle between capital and labour, feminism adds the insight that it should be regarded also as the outcome of gendered political forces.

Feminists also stress women's contribution to the development of welfare states. In Lewis's view, for example, the role of women in bringing about the British Labour Party's commitment to the welfare state in the 1930s and 1940s has been underestimated (Lewis, 1991, p. 93). She sees women in and around the Labour Party as having 'played an important part in the construction of the social policies which made up the post Second World War welfare state' (ibid., p. 115).

Between the wars, feminists concentrated on the needs of mothers because their needs were seen as the most important. What this did, however, in Dale and Foster's view, was to reinforce the equation that woman equals mother. In turn, this serves to underpin the idea that women should, therefore, be seen as economically dependent on men. This is the view which is enshrined in the Beveridge Report (e.g., Beveridge, 1942, p. 49) and so in post-1945 legislation in Britain and which has led to Beveridge's unenviable position as 'the arch-villain in most feminist writing' (Williams, 1989, p. 123).

Feminists were always divided on which developments would be of most benefit to women. Before 1945 socialist and working-class feminists pressed for the development of maternity and child welfare services rather than for the introduction of Family Allowances because of the fear that such allowances might undermine male wage bargaining so hitting workers and their dependents. Fabian women wanted Family Allowances to give women a measure of economic independence and to free them from the need to look for paid work which would distract them from the primary task of caring for children. Other groups supported Family Allowances as a way of undermining the concept of the family wage and so, hopefully, of marking a move along the road to equal pay (Ungerson, 1985, p. 4).

Feminists interpret the development of the welfare state in very different ways. The division is between those who see the state as a male state consciously aiming to maintain men in a position of dominance and privilege and those who see the state as operating with, and from, dominant assumptions which have the effect, but not the explicit intention, of maintaining male superiority and women's inferiority.

Views have also changed over time. In the early post-war years, before feminism's 'second wave', there was more enthusiasm for, and less criticism of, the British welfare state. Vera Brittain, for example, viewed it in uncritical fashion, as 'a product of the women's revolution' and as a system which 'embodied the change in social values which that revolution accomplished' (Pugh, 1992, p. 285).

Socialist feminists see the welfare state as very clearly adopting policies designed to support a model of the family, and a pattern of gender relations, functional to capitalism. The welfare state is also seen, however, as functional to male comfort, power and privilege. State social policy is seen as sustaining this model of the family and as designed to do so.

Radical feminists see the welfare state as developing, above all, to preserve a model of gender relations which ensures male dominance. Their focus is male-female relations with less regard for the economic and social context. They see men and women as groups with fundamentally antagonistic interests. Men are seen as dominant. The state is therefore male-dominated and the welfare state becomes a mechanism for maintaining male supremacy.

Liberal feminists see the welfare state as an approach to organising economic and social relations which can be, and has been, used by women to reduce inequalities and contribute to the development of a more sympathetic public opinion. They see the development of equal pay and sex discrimination legislation and of a social security system marginally more sensitive to women's needs as a sign that the political system can respond to women's needs. The welfare state offers both a possibility and a place for the extension of women's economic and social rights.

Black feminists see the development of the welfare state as being driven by racist ideology – by assumptions about the inferior intellectual ability of black children, the unsuitability of black men and women for positions of responsibility, and as a way of institutionalising a division of labour which confines black people to low paid and unskilled work. They see the development of the welfare state as part of the social and gender control apparatus of a male, racist state.

Attitudes towards the welfare state

Different feminist groups have different attitudes towards the achievements of the welfare state and its potential as a mechanism for helping women. Nevertheless, it is possible to distinguish certain common themes in the feminist analysis.

As we shall see, the basic feminist stance is a highly critical one. Most feminists accept the potential of welfare state services to improve women's lives and opportunities but they are deeply critical of much of the service provision. They stress the great importance of such policies to women because they intervene at key points and stages in women's lives such as birth or child-rearing and because they can extend women's opportunities. At the same time, feminists are critical of the values and assumptions which underpin much policy. They see social policies as providing massive reinforcement for particular constructions of women's role in society and as providing a powerful prescription of what women's consciousness should be (Wilson, 1977, p. 7). They also conclude that 'The welfare state has rarely prioritised *women's* welfare' (Lewis, 1991, p. 112). There has been much concern historically about class inequalities, runs the argument, and relatively little about inequalities of gender.

The ambivalence of the welfare state

Ambivalence characterises the feminist approach to the welfare state. There is stress on the ambivalent nature of the welfare state and its outcomes and this then becomes an element in feminist ambivalent attitudes towards it.

There is ambivalence about the welfare state's impact. Yvonne Hirdman, the Swedish historian, describes the impact of the development of the welfare state in Sweden as amounting to no more than a 'modernization of the gender system'. Hernes, on the other hand, describes the Scandinavian welfare states as on the way to becoming 'women friendly' states (Siim, 1993, p. 26).

Support for the family is a basic element in many welfare state policies. The nature of state support for the family can, however, have very important wider implications. Siim contrasts the outcome of 'family policies' in Denmark and Britain. In Denmark, the aim has been to help facilitate the integration of women into the public sphere. In Britain, in contrast, the state has used its social policies to support the home-making role of women and 'in this way the state in Britain became a major obstacle to the integration of women in the public sphere' (Siim, 1990, p. 95). Leira's argument based on the Norwegian situation is that 'the relationship of the [Scandinavian] welfare states to mothers is ambivalent, shaped by contradictions as well as mutual dependence' (Leira, 1990, p. 135).

Support for the family, almost inevitably becomes support for the predominant family form. Different, minority forms therefore do not fare as well. Dominelli points out in a cross-national review of family policy, subtitled 'The Reinforcement of Patriarchal Conjugality', that the feminist view would be that family policy must provide support for a variety of family forms (Dominelli, 1991, p. 200). Public support for one form can only generate ambivalent attitudes in feminists towards such policies.

Feminists are also ambivalent about the state's intentions in family policy. Is the intention support for the family or is it support for family responsibility to avoid state responsibility? While the state may provide direct support for families as part of community care policy, feminists would endorse Walker's judgement that its main concern in community care has been 'to ensure the continuance of the prime responsibility of the family for the support and care of its own members' (Walker, 1983, p. 121). Feminists see the state's concern to support a particular family form as snarply constrained by fear of undermining women's commitment to caring work (Pascall, 1986, p. 96).

The ambivalent nature of the welfare state has other dimensions. Feminists criticise it for reinforcing women's dependency on men because of the way in which entitlement to social security benefits depends on a husband's contributions. At the same time, the work opportunities provided by the welfare state have given many women a new independence (Gordon, 1990, p. 187). This expansion of the social welfare industry, from which many women have greatly benefited as workers, has, at the same time, exacerbated the growth of a segregated labour marker, an issue we discuss more fully later.

The welfare state can be of enormous benefit to women but it can, equally, reinforce patterns of dependency and particular gender roles. It can, as Langan and Ostner suggest has happened in

Sweden, simply mean a shift from personal dependency to state dependency (Langan and Ostner, 1991, p. 135). It can liberate and also trap. Its approach to women and women's rights remains profoundly ambivalent. In Britain, government has at the same time promoted women's freedom to do paid work and increased the burden of unpaid caring work (Lewis, 1993, p. 5). The inevitable result is a profound ambivalence among feminists towards the welfare state.

Failure to take account of women's particular needs

Another line of feminist criticisms of the welfare state is that it has failed to take account of women's particular needs. The argument has a number of strands. First, feminists criticise the welfare state for its failure to guarantee women an adequate independent income. Pronouncing judgement on the social security systems of the United States, Canada, Great Britain, Sweden, the Soviet Union and China, Dominelli concludes that 'The feminist objectives of breaking the connection between work and income so that all individuals receive an income independent of their family situation . . . remains to be fulfilled in each of these countries' (Dominelli, 1991, p. 120).

The evidence that the welfare state fails to take seriously women's basic needs is the increased risk of poverty which women face in many countries. The 'feminization of poverty' is striking evidence of the failure of welfare states. Pateman emphasises the increased risk of poverty which women face in the United States and Australia (Pateman, 1988, p. 233). Millar and Glendinning argue that in Britain 'Government policies in the 1980s have exacerbated women's vulnerability to poverty' (Millar and Glendinning, 1992, p. 4). The fact that in so many countries women tend to be dependent on social assistance rather than social insurance benefits is evidence of the failure of social security schemes to take account of their special needs.

Secondly, feminists criticise the welfare state for its failure to take account of women's special needs in relation to balancing home and work. Most women are in paid work; most women with children are in paid work. In some countries, Australia, Britain and the United States, for example, the state continues to see providing adequate child care as a private matter. It is as if policy is still guided by the ideology of the female homemaker-male bread-winner family model even though that represents myth and nostalgia rather than reality. Public provision for child care in Britain remains way behind levels of provision in most of Europe (e.g., Harman, 1993, p. 93). This helps to explain why in Britain married women with small children have the lowest economic activity rates in Europe (Siim, 1990, p. 92). In turn, this helps to explain the extent of poverty among women and children as work is a main route out of poverty. Not all countries, of course, have been so unresponsive. In France, policy-makers began to address the implications of the increase in married women's employment in the early 1970s. In the Scandinavian countries there has been much more generous provision of public child care and of parental leave. The contrast between countries highlights the failings of some.

Another strand in the feminist critique of the state for failing to take account of women's problems is the state's failure to take action to remedy the price women pay for parenthood. Davies and Joshi's analysis of the gross cash earnings foregone by women bearing up to three children shows that the costs in Britain and Germany are extremely high. In France and Sweden, where governments are more woman-responsive, the costs are much lower (Lewis, 1993, p. 20). Joshi has also shown how many women return, after maternity leave, to lower level jobs at lower rates of pay (Joshi, 1991, p. 180). Feminists interpret this as a failure of social policy to provide adequate support services to women.

Thirdly, there is the critique of the welfare state for failing to take account of the responsibilities women assume as carers because caring is what women naturally do. It is only a peripheral issue in a male-constructed social policy. Feminists argue that the social security system too often fails to provide carers with an adequate income at the time of caring and later.

The thrust of the feminist critique of government's failure to take account of carers' needs is that caring is seen as a personal, private matter which is properly a woman's responsibility. Feminists see it as a political matter, as an issue where women should have a genuine choice and where carers should have adequate support from public policy.

Feminists are critical of many welfare states for their failure to respond to the special needs and circumstances of single mothers.

British policy neither presses nor enables such mothers to work. Britain is the only EC country where single mothers have a lower employment rate than mothers in two-parent families. In Sweden, 87 per cent of single mothers are in the labour force, nearly all working fulltime, enabled to be economically active, independent and to escape poverty by publicly provided child care (Lewis, 1992, p. 170).

Women's needs have changed in recent years as a result of a variety of economic and social changes such as women's increased involvement in the labour market, the increase in family breakdown, or the increase in the number of very elderly people needing care. Feminists see the welfare state in many countries as fundamentally unresponsive to women's particular needs.

A force for social (that is, gender) control

Another theme in the feminist critique of the welfare state is the way in which social policies function to reinforce traditional family forms and gender roles. Social policy makes assumptions about family forms and gender roles based on current norms. Such assumptions, when embedded in policy, then reinforce the assumed status quo. The problem is that the assumed status quo may represent the past rather than the present, myth rather than reality. Once embedded in policy, assumptions become almost self-fulfilling prophecies.

British feminists see the major developments in the welfare state after 1945 as reflecting an outdated model of women's role, that is, women as primarily mothers, and then functioning to reinforce women's dependent status and supposed primary role (Williams, 1989, p. 162).

Feminists see the absence of public child care, the low level of women's earnings and the difficulty of independent access to housing and income from the social security system as trapping women in dependent relations on men. Discussing the policies which make it very difficult for women to obtain housing after marriage breakdown or domestic violence, Pascall argues that 'it is difficult not to see them [such policies] also as family measures having to do with the preservation of the dependence of women in families and the discouragement of their independence from men' (Pascall, 1986, p. 163).

Feminists also interpret the policy of community care as having the function, if not the aim, of forcing women into particular roles. Order and traditional patterns are preserved and state expenditure is reduced. Elizabeth Wilson writes of 'community' as 'an ideological portmanteau word for a reactionary, conservative ideology that oppresses women by silently confining them to the private sphere without so much as even mentioning them' (Wilson, 1982, p. 55).

Feminists make the same case against welfare state policies in other countries though, obviously, the detail of the argument varies. Borchost and Siim see the expansion of the welfare state in the Scandinavian countries as simply marking a development from oppression in the family to oppression in the male-dominated patriarchal state (Borchorst and Siim, 1987). Pateman argues in exactly the same terms that 'The power and capriciousness of husbands is being replaced by the arbitrariness, bureaucracy, and power of the state, the very state that has upheld patriarchal power' (Pateman, 1988, p. 255). She sees the welfare state as reinforcing women's identity as men's dependents so confirming rather than ameliorating 'our social exile' (ibid., p. 248). Leira's judgement is that:

> The expanding Norwegian welfare state upheld the gendered division of labour in the public domain and in the private sphere, and may even have strengthened it. More or less tacitly it was assumed that women would go on coping with care. (Leira, 1990, p. 155)

Segregated labour markets help trap women in particular roles and function to maintain particular patterns of gender relations.

Langan and Ostner's judgement about what they style the Bismarckian model of welfare state policy is that it is 'a gendered status maintenance policy supporting the male "normal worker" and the female "normal wife" ' (Langan and Ostner, 1991, p. 138). Norway's social policies also supported the breadwinner-homemaker family model, as did Britain, by keeping public child care provision to a minimum.

Dominelli's assessment of family policy in a wide range of countries is also relevant here. Her judgement is that, in reality, such policies operate for 'the reinforcement of patriarchal conjugality'. They support a particular family form which traps women in dependent roles (Dominelli, 1991, ch. 3).

There is much criticism, too, in feminist literature of the way doctors and other professionals treat women. 'Doctors', say Dale

and Foster, 'not only attempt to define and control women's reproductive and sexual lives, they also often attempt to reinforce
women's caring role by the advice and treatment which they give
to both caring and uncaring patients' (Dale and Foster, 1986, p.
92). They function as part of the male state apparatus which aims –
or at least functions – to control women.

Only a limited concern about inequality

The welfare state has certainly shown a concern for gender inequalities and discrimination. The feminist accusation is that such
concern has been naive and tentative. Even if the end has been
willed – and for feminists it is a significant 'if' – then the means
have not been put in place. Four examples illustrate the lines of the
feminist critique.

First, feminists criticise the approach which has been adopted as
the answer to discrimination and inequality, that is, legislating for
equality. That has been central to the British approach to reducing
inequality. Pascall's verdict is that such legislation for equal pay
and to outlaw discrimination 'makes a small ripple on a deep pool'
(Pascall, 1986, pp. 32–3). In other countries the successes have
been similarly limited (e.g., Pateman, 1988, p. 245).

Such approaches can be helpful, as at the very least they are
public declarations of government intent, but such policies depend
on vigorous enforcement which has tended to be lacking and more
importantly, they depend on parallel policies which enable women
to take advantage of more equal opportunities. For women, private opportunities determine public ones. Services are needed to
change the division of labour to enable women to take advantage
of public opportunities and they have not followed.

Such policies can also be too restrictive to provide effective help.
For example, British legislation to protect the jobs of pregnant
women simply failed to do so. In the late 1980s, 40 per cent of all the
employed pregnant women in Britain did not meet the conditions
which gave women a statutory right to return to work after the birth
of their children. In the mid-1980s, 37 per cent of women returning
to work after the birth of their first child went into a lower level job
than their previous one (Graham, 1993, pp. 116–17).

A second feminist criticism of the lack of the welfare state's concern about equality relates to women's incomes. Women's pay remains unequal in many countries. In France, for example, women make up two-thirds of workers earning the minimum wage. Women's incomes are still on average around 25 per cent less than men's despite equal pay legislation (Hantrais, 1993, p. 132). The situation is similar in Britain.

A third criticism is of the way welfare states have contributed to segregated employment which leads inevitably to inequalities in pay. Such segregation in the public sphere reflects and supports a traditional gender division of labour in the home, which in turn perpetuates unequal public opportunities and unequal pay. Leira sees the Norwegian welfare state as illustrating this vicious circle (Leira, 1993, p. 69).

Fourthly, welfare states are criticised for continuing to accord paid work more importance than unpaid caring work. Some countries have gone some way to recognise the importance of unpaid caring work, for example, through making provision for generous parental leave as in Sweden. Others continue to define caring as essentially a private matter, for example, Britain. That limits opportunities and perpetuates inequalities.

Too little attention to the private and the personal

A central line of criticism developed by feminists is that the welfare state has given too little attention to the private and personal sphere of life – an area which is crucial to women's independence and opportunities. The feminist argument is that too often the welfare state defines as personal what are, to feminists, political issues because of their wider importance for women. Pateman, for example, has argued that women's oppression can be understood in terms of the nature of the division between the public and the private (L. Bryson, 1992, p. 191). A narrow definition of what is political serves to enforce women's subordination because of their dependence on social services for anything approaching equality of opportunity.

If women are to be liberated for employment, something which is crucial to any extension of opportunities and to their protection from poverty, then caring has to be accepted as not simply a private and personal matter. In those countries where women have achieved a significant measure of equality, for example, Denmark, Sweden and Finland, it has been to a large extent because of the provision of extensive public child care facilities. Siim writes of growing state responsibility for the care of children and the elderly as 'one of the preconditions for the integration of women into the public sphere of work' (Siim, 1990, p. 81). Anttonen describes children's day care as 'the most important social service in Finnish society today' (Anttonen, n.d., p. 33). It is so important because it makes possible women's participation in the public sphere. In the British welfare state, in contrast, as in Norway, child care is seen as a private matter. As Mrs Thatcher put it 'Women make their own arrangements now and they can carry on doing so' (Land, 1992, p. 60). In a society where more and more women with young children are in paid employment, and where such work is increasingly important to the economy and to their families, child care, feminists argue, can no longer be seen as a private matter.

The care of the elderly and handicapped people is less clear cut as an issue but is becoming of increasing importance to the lives and opportunities of many women. What is being expected of many women in 'care by the community' policies is that they take personal and private responsibility for a type and level of caring which is new in human history. Government seeks to define this responsibility as the caring which families have always undertaken. Feminists argue its novelty in scale and implications and seek to see it defined as a public issue rather than a private trouble. They are fiercely critical of the welfare state's attempt to privatise the responsibility.

The feminist argument is that caring is a political issue because of the implications it has for women's lives. It may be a private matter in the sense that it is located in the home, but the breadth of its implications for the whole shape of women's lives renders it properly a public, political issue.

The values of social service organisations

As well as being critical of welfare state policies, feminists are also critical of the ideology and values of social services organisations. They see professionalisation as a force devaluing women's knowledge and experience and pushing women into positions of dependency. While the professionalisation of teaching and social work has extended opportunities for women, at the same time, most feminists would agree with Hearn that 'the whole process of professionalisation is one of the bastions of patriarchy' (Hearn, 1985, p. 205).

Feminists are equally critical of the tide of managerialism which has swept through the British welfare state. They see what has happened as being, in Lupton's words 'an increased masculinization of the managerial process' (Lupton, 1992, p. 99). What is involved in this process is an emphasis on management and accounting skills and techniques rather than on a traditional service ideal, emphasis on the need for varied experience, 'department hopping', which may be impossible for women constrained by a partner's employment and its assumed priority.

Feminists argue the negative implications of these trends for women using personal social services. Things are done for them or to them rather than with them. Little is expected from them beyond a response to the expert or the passive consumption of the service allocated to them. Their individuality is denied, their strengths unrecognised.

Feminists also make specific criticisms of the dominant values and ideologies of particular services. 'Women give and receive health care', says Webb, 'in a male dominated setting . . . Paternalism is the hall mark of much present-day health care' (Webb, 1986, p. 9). Dale and Foster write of 'a strong sexist ideology lying just beneath the surface of medical advice and treatment' (Dale and Foster, 1986, p. 83).

Discussing education, Pascall points out the nature of the knowledge that is purveyed.

> From a history that is a history of men's wars, to a literature that is dominated by men's books, to a social science that is constructed around men's position in the division of labour, the 'knowledge' purveyed is that women have no place in the world. (Pascall, 1986, p. 131)

Women as workers in the welfare state

Rein was one of the first to point out the significance of the welfare state for the integration of women, especially married women, into paid employment (Rein, 1985, p. 37). By the beginning of the mid-1980s, 45 per cent of all employed Swedish women worked in what Rein calls the Social Welfare Industry (SWI), 18 per cent of women in West Germany, 28 per cent of working women in the United States and 26 per cent of women in Britain (ibid., pp. 40–1). Two-thirds to three-quarters of women with higher education in these four countries were employed in the SWI (ibid., p. 43). Siim, on the basis of her analysis of the Danish situation, has argued that women need a strong public service sector as a precondition for entry into the labour market (Siim, 1990, p. 102).

The welfare state is clearly a major source of employment for women and, as such, has offered many women the prospect of independence and satisfying work. Feminists, however, have raised a number of questions about the nature of women's work in the welfare state and the role of women as workers within it.

The welfare state has offered women new opportunities of employment. That has increased their independence and enhanced their citizenship. However, on the other hand, welfare states have helped to institutionalise segregated labour markets. They reinforce ideas about what is properly men's work and women's work. The divisions are very real. In Denmark, for example, two-thirds of men work in the private sector, two-thirds of women in the public sector (Siim, 1993, p. 38). Such segregation also institutionalises unequal pay by making equal pay for equal work a broken reed because it cannot be applied when work is different.

Feminists argue, too, that the fact women dominate as workers in the welfare state institutionalises the low pay which is a common characteristic of such work. The work is low paid because it is defined as unskilled. Some feminists argue that it is defined as unskilled, not because of what it is, but because it is work done by women *and* it is often no more than an extension and development of the caring, tending work women do in the home. Hallett points out that skill is in fact an ideological construct rather than an objective fact and that there are good arguments that women's caring work is, in fact, very skilled (Hallett, 1989, pp. 29–30).

The welfare state has also done much to institutionalise part-time work for women, particularly on the lower levels. This may seem to suit women and at one level it may. But part-timers are frequently gravely disadvantaged in terms of job security, sick pay, paid holidays, and the earning of social security benefits. Part-time workers remain a gravely disadvantaged group, partly, at least, because they are women.

There is massive evidence that while women predominate as workers in the lower reaches of the welfare system, it is men who predominate in management positions. This is true of infant and primary schools where most teachers are women but most head-teachers are men. It is true of nursing – a female occupation where men are massively over-represented in key top posts. Women make up the majority of those who work in personal social services but they are notably under-represented in management. There is also evidence that women who gain senior management posts are very untypical of women generally. A high proportion, for example, are single (Hudson, 1989, p. 87). Marriage and motherhood are best avoided by the ambitious.

In the area of employment we see all the ambivalence of the welfare state – it does open up opportunities but many of those opportunities have structured limitations. There is no question that job opportunities have been of benefit to women whether unskilled or highly educated. At the same time, the same oppor-tunities have helped to institutionalise segregation and inequality.

Policy-takers not policy-makers

The final criticism which feminists lay against the welfare state in a sense underlies and explains all the others. It is that although women are the major users of welfare and outnumber men as employees of the welfare state, nevertheless men dominate the policy-making process. State policies are sexist, Dale and Foster conclude, because men dominate the policy-making process – as politicians, civil servants or representatives of major interest groups (Dale and Foster, 1986, p. 61). Throughout the welfare state women are, as Hernes says of even the highly developed Scandinavian welfare states, 'the object of welfare policy and not its creators' (Lister, 1990, p. 459) policy-takers not policy-makers.

The situation varies, obviously, from nation to nation. Pateman concludes that 'The legislation, policy making and higher level administration of the welfare state have been and remain pre-dominantly in men's hands' (Pateman, 1988, p. 234). She then goes on to note how in Australia the Office of the Status of Women in the Prime Minister's Department and the Women's Budget Program require all departments to make a detailed assessment of the impact of their policies on women.

All Nordic parliaments, apart from Iceland, have now 30–40 per cent of women members which is why, in Lewis's view, women in the Scandinavian countries are optimistic about the role of the state. Such a degree of female representation means that key issues such as the status of unpaid work reach the political agenda (Lewis, 1992, p. 171). Whether it brings more power depends on where decisions are actually made. Siim argues, for example, that growing corporatism in Denmark has reduced the sphere of political decision-making. In some countries women's position in welfare state policy-making has changed; in some it may be changing. The reality is, however, that until very recently in all countries, and even now in many, women play little part in shaping and administering the policies which are much more important to their lives than to men's.

Even in countries, for example, Britain, the United States and Canada, where there is an active feminist movement, it is relatively powerless compared to other groups seeking to influence social policy (Dominelli, 1991, p. 265). Langan and Ostner stress the fragility of the Scandinavian woman-friendly state. The advances which have accrued to women are, they argue, properly seen as gifts which depend not on women's power but on the 'fragile and contingent consent of those who have always so far held state power: men' (Langan and Ostner, 1991, p. 142). Given this balance of power, it is scarcely surprising that so often welfare state policies fail to meet women's needs and seem, at times, to benefit men more than women.

Welfare and their ideal society

Chamberlayne suggests that in the 1970s and 1980s both feminism and social policy thinking can be categorised in terms of a typology of approaches to gender relations. There was the *gender neutrality* approach which took no account of the differences in women's position. Secondly, there was *gender recognition*, an approach which focused on the obstacles impeding women's equality and sought public solutions. Thirdly, *gender reconstruction* which stressed the need to change men's roles by increasing their role in reproductive activities. Finally, there was *gender reinforcement* aiming to reaffirm traditional roles and relationships (Chamberlayne, 1993, p. 172).

Different groups of feminists obviously have differing views about the kind of social policies they would like to see in their ideal society but they are in basic agreement that the aims of policy should be *gender recognition* and *gender reconstruction*. What we attempt here, hopefully without misrepresenting any particular feminist perspective, is an overview of what feminists would ideally want. We organise the discussion under three headings – principles, starting points and policies.

Principles

There are certain basic principles which underpin the policies which feminists would like to see. Seven stand out as the most important.

1. They want policies which offer women – and men – a genuine *choice* as to whether they give priority to paid work or to domestic responsibilities.
2. They want policies which accept, and seek to institutionalise, basic principles of *equality of opportunity* and to outlaw discrimination on the basis of gender.
3. They want policies which are *universalist*, that is, policies which operate to the benefit of all women not simply to the benefit of highly educated, white, middle-class, fulltime workers.
4. They want policies which are *differentiated*, which start from a recognition and acceptance of women's differences from men.
5. They want policies which are based on the idea of women's equal citizenship, which see women as *full citizens, not simply as resources* – for the care of children and the dependent, for support for men, for the labour market (Langan and Ostner, 1991, p. 141).
6. *Unpaid, caring work in the home* must be accepted as of equal standing and importance to paid work in the public sphere. Unpaid work must be seen as women's work as citizens.

7. *Social policy must not be subordinated to economic policy.* They must be integrated on an equal footing. Until that happens those who generate wealth in the formal economy will always be given priority over those whose primary concern is welfare and this has clearly disadvantageous implications for women.

Starting points

There are four starting points which need analysis. First there is the stress that feminist proposals are pragmatic not simply ideological. They are a pragmatic response to economic and social change, to a world vastly different from the one in which Beveridge enunciated his oft-quoted and much maligned statements about the role of married women in the post-war world (e.g., Beveridge, 1942, p. 49). They start from a new world. As Harman puts it 'Women have left the twentieth century behind. To the majority of young women of all backgrounds today the role of lifelong, full-time, dependent housewife is neither an option, nor an ideal' (Harman, 1993, p. 1).

Second, there is stress, with varying degrees of enthusiasm and qualification, on state action, as even those groupings who castigate the state as male, racist and capitalist make demands which depend on state action. All see the necessity and centrality of state action if women are to achieve the goals which feminists set for them (e.g. Lister, 1990, p. 459). Those optimistic about the state stress what has been achieved for, and by, women through state action in other countries. British feminists look enviously at many aspects of welfare state provision in France and the Scandinavian countries where public provision of day care, for example, seems to be the key factor liberating women for employment and full integration into the public sphere.

Frances Fox Piven contrasts feminist literature which criticises state action as 'public patriarchy' with women activists' campaigns for more state action. In her view 'the main opportunities for women to exercise power today inhere precisely in their "dependent" relationships with the state' (Piven, 1990, pp. 250–1).

Eisenstein's view is that feminists must push the state as far as it can go towards securing equality of opportunity for women to help to uncover the patriarchal structure of the state (Eisenstein, 1981,

p. 222). The use of the state is a starting point and a method but feminists are concerned that such an approach on its own, even where successful, will at best produce reform rather than social transformation.

The third starting point is the centrality of the traditionally personal and the private to the position of women in society. Feminists argue that the opportunities open to women do not simply depend on a public equality of opportunity, because the ability to take advantage of such opportunities is conditioned by domestic responsibilities. If responsibilities for care are left unshared between men and women, or between women and the state, there can be no genuine equality of opportunity, no equality of access to the public sphere on which so much depends, for example, independent access to social security benefits. 'The century gap will be bridged', says Harman, 'when men and women participate in both the worlds of work and the world of home on equal terms' (Harman, 1993, pp. 6–7) and that means the private and personal must become political.

The final starting point is an acceptance of the difficulty of the task of securing the social policies which feminists advocate. As Lewis points out 'The feminist vision of a more equal society requires a process of redefinition and change in all areas of human activity' (Lewis, 1986, p. 98). Men benefit from the situation as it exists. Women's claims are a threat to men's rights and privileges. Women have moved in ever-increasing numbers into paid employment; women's consciousness has changed. There is little evidence that men have moved in equivalent numbers, or with comparable enthusiasm, into the field of domestic labour. That must happen if genuine equality of opportunity is to be realised.

Policies

There are feminist proposals for change in all areas of social policy but there is no space here to cover them all. We shall deal with feminist proposals under five headings – income maintenance, work, care, equal opportunities/rights and service organisation.

Income maintenance

Central to feminist proposals on income is the demand for a set of policies which 'instead of institutionalising and perpetuating women's poverty, begins the process of dismantling and reversing the feminisation of poverty' (Pearce, 1990, p. 277). Dominelli sets out a number of feminist principles which she thinks should be central to a social security system and two are particularly important. The first is that provision must be universal, that is, available to all regardless of marital status, or work record. The second is that benefits must be allocated to individuals rather than aggregated (Dominelli, 1991, p. 31). This would deal with the two abiding feminist concerns, that is, that women's access to social security benefits depends on their male partner's contribution record or that it depends on their own employment history, thus taking no account of women's caring responsibilities.

Work

Paid work is central to the lives of most women in modern, industrial economies. National economies and family budgets both depend upon it. Work is also the main route to the establishment of full social integration and key rights of citizenship such as full, independent membership of the public income maintenance system.

Feminists would argue that the British welfare state has signally failed to take account of this change in the role of women. In other countries, for example, France, Denmark, Sweden and Finland, there has been a recognition of the need for social policy to come to terms with the change.

Joshi sums up the lines of feminist strategy. 'Measures to support the equal treatment of men and women in the labour market', she writes, 'cannot be effectively separated from measures to support the employment of mothers and promote egalitarian parenthood' (Joshi, 1991, p. 190). Feminists argue for policies to further these two purposes. They argue the need for a massive expansion of public day care to remedy the situation in which women's employment opportunities are limited by the availability of appropriate day care. They want a full acceptance of women's right to work and the child care policies required to make that right a reality.

Secondly, feminists seek to promote the 'egalitarian parenthood' to which Joshi refers. The argument is a simple one. The domestic division of labour which gives women the major responsibility for domestic duties is an obstacle to women's equality of opportunity in employment. Therefore, measures must be designed and adopted to create a more egalitarian pattern. Feminists propose reductions in the length of the working week which would at the same time give men more leisure and make women's work more necessary to the family income. They press the need for more effective equal pay policies to make women's work more profitable and to make the costs of women not working more obvious. They urge the case for separate taxation as a way of making it advantageous for the family income if a woman goes out to work rather than a man advancing his own career or working additional hours.

Social policy in Britain has never given significant attention to the needs of women as workers. Feminists are arguing that there are responsibilities here which the state must assume. In a world in which women want – and need to work – and in which the economy needs their labour and in which work is the best protection against dependency and poverty, enabling women to work becomes a central task for social policy – for hard economic reasons as well as for ideological reasons.

Care

Feminist proposals about caring start from three arguments. Firstly, caring is a vital task. Secondly, caring responsibilities limit women's opportunities for paid employment which in turn limits their access to important social rights. Thirdly, there is no ground for assuming that women have a primary or exclusive responsibility to care for the dependent in modern society whether they are children, the elderly or handicapped people.

Feminists make various proposals: first, there is the controversial proposal that informal carers should be paid (e.g., Ungerson, 1990, p. 23). The aim is to assert the social importance of caring and society's responsibility to compensate carers for the labour involved and to give carers access to the normal benefits of employment. All feminists are, however, wary of the potential implications of payment for carers, that is, it traps women in low paid traditional female roles and it could strengthen the traditional division of labour. Finch, for example, is in favour of more support for women who do unpaid caring but emphasises that this represents a very limited form of feminist social policy when the real goal is a change in the division of labour between men and women (Finch, 1990, pp. 52–3).

Secondly, feminists propose that care should be conceptualised very clearly as care *in* the community rather than care *by* the community, that is, community care on a non-sexist basis. Baldwin and Twigg develop proposals along these lines arguing that the real issue for feminists is the changing of the balance between public and private provision. They suggest a three-pronged policy: firstly, policies to minimise the dependency of those needing care on individual carers so that carers are not prevented from leading relatively ordinary lives; secondly, policies to ensure people with disabilities and the need for care have a choice and are not forced to rely on relatives; and finally, realistic support for women who do opt to care (Baldwin and Twigg, 1991, pp. 131–3). Such proposals, Baldwin and Twigg argue, are fully in line with the long-term aim of creating a society in which caring for vulnerable and dependent people is seen as men's as well as women's work.

Thirdly, there is the argument which is perhaps most vigorously advocated by Janet Finch (Finch, 1984) that community care is a fundamentally gendered concept and only institutional care can liberate women from the massive burden of caring and make a reality of collective responsibility. Certainly, if choice is to be a reality, residential care needs to remain an element in the care package.

As long as caring for the vulnerable and dependent is seen as primarily and centrally a woman's responsibility, many women will be deprived of access to the institutions of work and the social security system which provide independence and rights of citizenship. The central feminist argument is that long-term caring is a collective not a personal responsibility and social policies must reflect that fact.

Underlying the feminist approach to care is a conviction of the need to raise the status of caring in society, to argue its central importance in social life and social reproduction. There are those who argue the importance of caring on the basis that it is a precondition for paid work in the labour market, not an aspect of a social role but as part of the occupational system. All feminists are agreed on the social and economic importance of caring. Where they differ is on how caring is best carried out, how to make possible a genuine choice for potential carers and how to ensure proper societal recognition of its salience.

Equal opportunities/rights

Most feminists have always been critical of the equal rights/equal opportunities approach expressed by measures like the equal pay and anti-discrimination legislation. Their criticism is that such measures always promise more than they deliver. While they may help individuals, they leave the basic gendered structure of society untouched because the focus is on the individual rather than on the collective needs of women. And such legislation only relates to the public sphere.

While remaining sceptical of the possibilities of this approach, feminists see it as containing possibilities if strengthened and given teeth. Cockburn, for example, suggests a number of ways in which such legislation might be developed. She suggests mandatory positive action in fields where women are clearly under-represented or disadvantaged and an obligation on institutions found at fault to show an improved performance. Government funding, subsidies and contracts should be withheld from firms failing to take steps to end any proven disadvantage experienced by women. Finally, the Equal Opportunities Commission should be made more accountable to feminist organisations (Cockburn, 1991, pp. 228–9).

Equality legislation cannot secure fundamental changes in women's position. Equality and justice demand and depend on a recognition that women's needs are different. What is required are policies sensitive to those needs but equality policies can make a contribution and can help shape the general climate of opinion.

Service organisation

Feminists are deeply sceptical, as we saw earlier, about many aspects of social service organisation. They are sceptical about professionalisation and managerialism and see social service organisations as embodying those 'male' values to which they are profoundly antipathetic.

Feminists are very clear about the kind of organisations they would like to see in social services or health care. They would be accessible to all women, psychologically as well as physically. Staff would be organised in non-hierarchical teams. Service users would be affirmed as people with skills, experience and knowledge. Their right to know why the staff proposed what they did for them would be clearly recognised and knowledge would be shared. Users would have an active role in their treatment and not be regarded as passive clients and efforts would be made to avoid user dependency.

Morley speaks of women's refuges as constituting 'a feminist political practice – women working collectively to take control of their lives' (Morley, 1993, p. 178). Leeson and Gray describe the desired relationship between themselves as doctors and the women who consult them as that of 'skilled but sisterly helpers' (Eisner and Wright, 1986, p. 130).

This is how feminists wish to see welfare services organised. How this goal is to be generally attained in mainstream services is less clear. One way forward, however, is via separatist strategies – the establishment of specifically feminist services run by women for women. Such services, as Dale and Foster acknowledge, will never pose any serious challenge to what they describe as 'male dominated, professionally oriented mainstream welfare systems' (Dale and Foster, 1986, p. 171). What they can do, however, is to provide non-sexist (that is, feminist!) alternatives which offer a challenge to mainstream services and provide a prefigurative liberating picture of the possibilities of more egalitarian relationships between service providers and service users.

The social policies which feminists would like to put in place depend on extending women's power and influence. Women must secure an increased representation on key decision-making bodies at all levels of policy-making and administration. Change will only be achieved when women gain an increase in representation and thus in power in key places.

The picture which emerges from this sketch of the social policies which feminists would like to see is almost inevitably reformist. Radical and Marxist feminists see little point in making policy proposals which depend on a male-dominated, capitalist state and which are essentially ameliorative. On the other hand, the majority of feminists do nourish hopes of state action. In some countries, the state has certainly pursued with vigour those policies which feminists in others can only dream about.

Assessment

The feminist perspective has enormously enriched the study of social policy and our understanding of those institutions which we call, with declining confidence, 'the welfare state'. The central contribution of feminism is to give a range of new dimensions of analysis to the study of social policy. That is a contribution of enduring value. It can be summarised and assessed as follows:

1. Feminist analysis has, in Bryson's words 'revolutionised our understanding of the state' (Bryson, L., 1992, p. 191). It has added another dimension to the analysis of the state as an interested rather than a neutral body. After feminist analysis, the state and its policies have to be seen as *gendered* and probed for the biases and inequalities which follow from that.
2. Another important contribution of feminism is to alert us to the gender specific consequences of social policies. In contemporary analysis, gender is generally accepted as a basic variable. Prior to the mid-1980s it was not. This insight allows a much fuller and richer appreciation of the consequences and implications of policies such as community care.
3. Feminism has also effectively defined a range of accepted conditions as 'social problems' demanding societal action, for example, domestic violence and rape in marriage. It has also given new insights into old problems. Feminists have enriched our understanding of child abuse – physical and sexual – by a gender analysis. As regards poverty, 'The contemporary discussion of the underclass in the United States', says Gordon, 'is dulled by a lack of a gender analysis' (Gordon, 1990, p. 175) and by implication is enriched by its addition.
4. Perhaps feminism's most important contribution has been its assertion of the importance of the private and the personal in the shaping of women's opportunities in the public sphere. Feminists have gone a substantial way to persuading the academic community that, in Graham's words, caring 'should be the place we begin, and not end our analysis of modern society' (Pascall, 1986, p. 70). Caring is so crucial to social analysis because it is the key determinant of women's opportunities. Feminist analysis has given us this insight – that the personal is indeed political – and in so doing it has explained the limited impact of those liberal measures concerned with formal equality in the public sphere. Such equality is necessary but insufficient so long as the domestic division of labour remains unequal.

5. Feminists performed an important service to the study of welfare by their exploration of what might be described as the social relations of welfare, that is, the relations between providers and users and the values and ideologies which permeate and shape organisations. It was feminists who opened up the whole issue of the attitudes and approach of doctors and other medical staff in antenatal care. The issue soon widened. Feminist analysis has enriched our understanding of organisations and organisational values and gave a powerful but specific boost to the consumerism-empowerment movement in welfare services.

6. Marxists have always analysed the welfare state in terms of its role in social control. Feminists have added a new dimension to that class analysis seeing the welfare state as functioning to maintain a particular pattern of gender relations functional to capitalism and to men. They see a range of services – education, social security, health and personal social services – as all contributing to the preservation of existing inequalities which they see as exploitative.

7. Feminists have emphasised gender as a key dimension of inequality adding it to the issue of class inequality which has always been an issue in social policy analysis. They highlight three key dimensions of such inequality which cumulatively make a powerful indictment of an institution supposedly concerned with rights and inequalities. Firstly, feminists argue that in spite of their dominant position as users and providers of services they remain policy-takers rather than policy-makers with a minimal role in the policy-making process. Secondly, feminists have laid great stress on the position of women as workers in the welfare state and the inequalities they suffer through the fact that they are trapped in the lowest positions with scant access to positions higher up the hierarchy. Finally, feminists have highlighted the inequalities which afflict women as service users, that is, their unequal access to housing, education, social care and social security benefits.

There is no disputing feminism's contribution to our understanding of the welfare state. It has been stimulating and enriching, critical and constructive. That is not, of course, to say that it is above criticism. The socialist and radical strands, in particular, adopt positions which have attracted much criticism. Critics ask, for example, whether capitalism can reasonably be blamed for gender inequalities and whether separate women-only services are possible and are likely to promote equality.

What feminism is against is clear, what feminism is for is not quite so clear. There is a central, crucial tension which runs like a fault line through feminism – between emphasising equality or difference as the guiding policy principle. Lewis and Davies spell out the issue. 'Policies built on a premise of difference and of protection', they write, 'offer some amelioration for people at the bottom of the heap, but in the end seem to confirm a position of labour market inferiority.' On the other hand, policies built on a premise of equality offer some improvement for women at the top of the heap but in the end also confirm women's inferior position in the labour market (Lewis and Davies, 1991, pp. 22–3).

The choice for feminists is often posed in these terms as one between equality and difference. It is an impossible one. The terms of the debate have to be changed. Lewis and Davies advocate what they call a 'diversity model' and that expresses the reality of women's lives. There must be policies to enable women to work. Equally, there must be policies which recognise unpaid caring as of equal value to paid employment. The sheer complexity of women's lives means that simple, clear-cut proposals are inadequate. Feminism has to come to terms with this complexity and the rest of the world has to recognise that an ideology which attempts to come to terms with reality is bound to be complex.

There is, of course, no one feminist analysis; there are a range of perspectives with different arguments and insights. Many of those arguments are substantiated by research. Others could be classed as 'non-proven but critically stimulating'. The overall verdict must be that feminism has made a major contribution to our understanding of the welfare state in the 1980s and 1990s.

CHAPTER 7

GREENISM

Concern about the environment has a long, worldwide and varied history. It has featured in the writings of religious leaders, philosophers and others all through the ages but it became particularly acute during the period of the Industrial Revolution with its 'dark satanic mills'. It spawned a plethora of political and philosophical tracts and pamphlets which warned against the destruction of the environment, the blind exploitation of human and physical resources, the high rates of population growth and the wretchedness of the populace. The solutions ranged from Malthusian population controls to Marxist revolutionary struggles and, more to the point, to new libertarian or anarchical forms of societal and political organisation from such writers as Fourier, Proudhon and Kropotkin. Numerous single-issue pressure groups sprang up to support such causes as the preservation of the countryside, forests and lakes as well as the protection of animals, birds and historic buildings in several countries from the second half of the nineteenth century onwards (Gould, 1988; Goodin, 1992; Marshall, 1992).

Despite all this, the origins of contemporary Greenism as a distinct ideology are much more recent. Greenism is the product of the 1970s and if any one year has to be singled out it has to be 1972 which saw the publication of three books by internationally acknowledged experts: the Club of Rome report (Meadows *et al.*, 1972); the report for the United Nations Conference on the Human Environment (Ward and Dubois, 1972); and the special issue of *The Ecologist* magazine (Goldsmith, 1972). All three books quantified the seriousness of the environmental problems, presented them as global in nature both as regards causes and solutions and supported by a mass of data insisted that, unless action was taken, these problems would worsen at an exponential rate. Greenism was one of several post-industrial concerns of primarily the affluent world which could afford to worry about the future of planet Earth or the position of women in society. The Third World had the more immediate and pressing problem of how to feed its people and stave off starvation for millions of its citizens.

Strands of Greenism

From its very early days Greenism came in different shades usually divided into two contrasting types: shallow versus deep ecology (Naess, 1973; Young, 1992); technocratic versus ecocentric mode (O'Riordan, 1976); environmentalism versus ecologism (Porritt, 1984); green versus Green (Dobson, 1991); and generally light or weak versus dark or strong Green.

These two contrasting types of Greenism have very little in common apart from the awareness that the environment needs care and protection from wanton exploitation. The weak side of Greenism accepts the current world order with its emphasis on constantly rising rates of economic growth and consumption; all it asks for is that economic growth and consumption should be environmentally friendly. It puts its faith in complex forms of technology to achieve the economic miracle and to deal with any environmental problems that may arise in the process. Some light Greens even maintain that 'a new breed of green capitalists' and 'environmental enterpreneurs' have now emerged who do not place company profit above environmental considerations (Elkington and Burke, 1989, p. 23). Other light Greens put their faith in government taxation policies which reward the environmentally friendly products and punish the environmentally unfriendly (Pearce *et al.*, 1989). Light Greenism is above all unashamedly anthropocentric for it views humans as superior to all other forms of life on the planet with the right to exploit it as it thinks best. It is now espoused by parties of the Left and the Right as well as by industrialists and trade unionists for it is part of the established political order which it serves.

As we shall see in later sections, Greenism of the strong type stands for exactly the opposite: technological fixes cannot solve the current environmental problems; only reductions in economic growth and consumption stand any chance of achieving this; species egalitarianism means that humans are not superior to other life – they are simply one of many species on the planet; and a new world order is needed to save mankind from ecological disaster that is neither capitalist nor socialist but Green. Though Greens see some value in Green consumerism from the short-term perspective, they also fear that support for it can be dangerous in the long term for it can 'lead attention away from, even legitimate, the retention of environmentally damaging practices' (Yearley, 1991, p. 101).

Many dark Greens see no fundamental difference between capitalism and socialism for they see both as dedicated to the ideology of 'industrialism' which is committed to the pursuit of economic growth, a commitment which will inevitably lead to environmental catastrophe. The chasm between these two old ideologies on one hand and Greenism on the other is, according to one of its most eloquent exponents, unbridgeable and a new political direction is needed to save the environment.

> The politics of the Industrial Age, left, right and centre, is like a three-lane motorway, with different vehicles in different lanes, but all heading in the same direction. Greens feel it is the very direction that is wrong, rather than the choice of any one lane in preference to the others. It is our perception that the motorway of industrialism inevitably leads to the abyss – hence our decision to get off it, and seek an entirely new direction. (Porritt, 1984, p. 43)

It is the dark, strong side of Greenism that primarily forms the substance of this chapter. Naess's formulation of the principles of deep ecology in 1973 was generally accepted until the 1980s when it was challenged from two opposing directions. Bookchin's social ecology was critical of the lack of social theory, the separation of human and non-human exploitation and the non-political nature of the proposed solutions (Bookchin, 1982). Social ecologists see the roots of the exploitation of the non-human world in the stratified socio-economic system that is responsible for the overall social exploitation in human society along class, gender, race and other lines as well as the exploitation of the Third by the First

World. As a result, the solution to the problem lies in the abolition of the existing stratified, authoritarian and exploitative socio-economic system.

On the other hand, the radical group of activists established in the United States in 1980 and known as Earth First! were dissatisfied with the insufficient emphasis on the non-human world and its preservation at all costs. They engaged in direct forms of action, or monkeywrenching as they call it, to protect the environment (Foreman and Haywood, 1989) and made proposals for drastic reductions in world population, some of which were grossly insensitive such as allowing famine-stricken people in Africa or AIDS victims to die. Over the ensuing years, however, there has been a closing of ranks, for some of the disagreements between these groups proved to be mere differences of emphasis, as the debate between Bookchin and Foreman in 1989 showed (Chase, 1991). The discussion in the subsequent sections of the chapter will, however, highlight the differences of substance within the ecology movement.

Recently there have been several attempts to combine Greenism with both socialism and feminism. Green socialists have argued that Greenism and socialism share the basic commitment to egalitarianism and the preservation of the environment. Their paths converge and united they will achieve more than fighting their battles separately (Ryle, 1988). This is true as far as it goes but it ignores the basic fact that socialism is committed to increased economic growth and consumption which is anathema to Greenism. Only utopian strands of socialism, such as that of William Morris, can be combined with Greenism and this has always been very much of a minority type in both socialist ideology and everyday politics, as Chapter 4 showed.

Attempts to combine Greenism with feminism are based either on that brand of feminism which claims that women's values are closer to nature than men's values (Henderson, 1983) or on socialist/libertarian feminism which sees the oppression of women and the non-human world as part of the same process and value system (Merchant, 1990), both of which are minority positions within feminism. Mainstream socialism as well as feminism does share some objectives with Greenism but they also diverge in many more fundamental ways. It is quite feasible to envisage societies which are socialist or in which inequalities between men and women are insignificant but which are not Green. Vice versa, some versions of dark Greenism are neither socialist nor non-sexist.

The development of the welfare state

Bearing in mind the many strands of Greenism and its preoccupation with the present and the future of society, it comes as no surprise to say that it has little to say about the forces that influenced the development of the welfare state. There is no explicit, let alone coherent, discussion of this issue and what is presented here stems indirectly from the writings of Greens on other issues. With this in mind, it can be argued that Green explanations of the development of the welfare state are of three main types: industrialism, capitalism and pressure group reformism.

Running through the writings of many Greens is the idea that the powerful combination of industrialisation, technology and public craving for constantly rising rates of economic growth – what Porritt calls the logic of industrialism – has been the main driving force behind the major political and economic changes of industrial societies. As we saw in the previous section, he sees no difference between the political forces of the Left and the Right for they are both under the spell of industrialism. This kind of explanation is very similar to those we examined in previous chapters which attribute the growth of welfare to the process of industrialisation itself rather than to the political forces generated by it.

Greens with a Marxist or Democratic Socialist perspective, however, will reject the above explanation. For them, it is not industrialism as such but capitalism that accounts on the one hand for the growth of the welfare state, and on the other, for the destruction of the environment and other social problems. Weston, for instance, insists that 'it is time that greens accepted that it is capitalism rather than industrialism *per se* which is at the heart of the problems they address' (Weston, 1986, p. 5; emphasis in original). Similarly, Ryle warns his fellow Greens that even in ecological campaigns they cannot stay above traditional politics: 'relations between people and classes are at stake the moment one begins to talk about structural economic and social changes' (Ryle, 1988,

p. 20). Though neither Weston nor Ryle go into debates on the development of the welfare state, it follows from their overall stance on these issues that class conflict and the needs of capital have been the forces that shaped the welfare state over the years.

Many Greens see individuals and pressure groups as the determinants of government policies. Indeed, Green activists must believe in this for, otherwise, there would be no point in their campaigns. Porritt makes a clear reference to this kind of explanation when he writes that there is no need 'to deny the humanitarian intentions of those whose visions of material plenty and the elimination of poverty and oppression' in order to make the point that decades of economic development have created the current environmental crisis (Porritt, 1984, p. 19). Similarly, Green writers who support the idea of communes as a way forward feel that individuals acting alone or in groups *can* influence the course of events in history. Roszak's belief that the way forward for Greenism is through ecomonasticism, that is, living in communes based on the model of monasteries, is one of many examples of the faith in the power of the individual to change the course of history. He acknowledges the immense difficulties in this but he also points out that 'cultural diversity is always the province of minorities' (Roszak, 1979, p. 312).

This brief account of Green views on the development of the welfare state indicates that Greens have little original to say on this issue. Nor would one expect otherwise for Green concerns are about the future, not the past.

Attitudes towards the welfare state

Like all other ideologies, Greenism consists of a core of ideas about which there is general agreement and a periphery about which there are differences of opinion. The core ideology of Greenism makes several basic criticisms of the nature, policies and direction of advanced industrial societies with their superstructure of welfare provision. It is with these criticisms that we are concerned here rather than with all the criticisms made by Greens.

First, such societies are based on the fundamental belief that ever-expanding economic growth and consumption are both possible and desirable. The central platform of the manifestos of all political parties, other than Green, in all these countries is how to satisfy the rising economic aspirations of their electorates. Lately, they have attempted to combine this with various policies under the general umbrella of green consumerism which Greens reject as nothing but tokenism for it does not face up to the ecological dangers of exponential growth and consumption.

From the publication of the Club of Rome report in 1972, the fundamental tenet of Greenism has been that there are 'limits to growth'. As the authors of the report warned: 'If the present growth trends in world population, industrialisation, pollution, food production and resource depletion continue unchanged, limits to growth on this planet will be reached sometime within the next hundred years' (Meadows, *et al.*, 1972, p. 4).

Twenty years later, their new calculations led them to the same conclusion but this time with much more emphasis on the earth's inability to absorb the harmful waste created by constant industrial expansion. The evidence of the depletion of the ozone layer and global warming accumulated in the intervening years together with the various nuclear power disasters gave new urgency to their warning which they saw not as a prediction of doom but as a scenario of choice.

> Human use of many essential resources and generation of many kinds of pollutants have already surpassed rates that are physically sustainable. Without significant reductions in material and energy flows, there will be in the coming decades an uncontrolled decline in per capita food output, energy use, and industrial production. (Meadows, *et al.*, 1992, p. xvi)

They repeated their belief that humanity could still save itself if it changed course but to do that 'the acceptance of physical limits is the first step toward getting there' (ibid., p. xvii).

The limits to growth debate is an area where the differences of opinion between the deep Greens and the social ecologists become apparent. For the social ecologists, it is the capitalist system or at least the rich individuals or nations that are responsible for the current environmental crisis. Blaming it on humans in general or on human greed is not only theoretically unsatisfactory but grossly unfair to the poor. It is like blaming the victim. As Bookchin put it, 'when you say a black kid in Harlem is as much to blame for the ecological crisis as the President of Exxon, you are letting one off the hook and slandering the other' (Bookchin, 1991, p. 31).

Closely related to their first criticism is their objection to the use of highly complex forms of large-scale technology, be it in industry, in agriculture or in medicine. Such forms of technological organisation are wasteful in the sense that they encourage over-consumption of resources and they are often destructive of the environment because of the high probability of generating pollution in a variety of ways. They are also inappropriate as places of employment for they are usually run on bureaucratic, authoritarian lines which are alienating and dehumanising for the workforce. Contemporary reliance on such technological forms of production reflects the dominance of that type of optimistic, even aggressive, scientific thinking which sees humans as conquerors of their environment and masters over all the other species because technology is seen as having unlimited potential in wealth-creation and in problem-solving.

This is a view of science that is universally rejected by Greens, particularly the belief that it can solve all environmental problems. As the Club of Rome put it more than twenty years ago: 'We cannot expect technological solutions alone to get us out of this vicious circle' (Meadows *et al.*, 1972, p. 192). Even the use of high technology for recycling purposes is viewed with a mixture of hostility and suspicion for not only does it use up energy but it also lends support to the technocratic view that there are technological fixes to the environmental issue. As Porritt put it 'Recycling is both useful and necessary – but it is an illusion to imagine that it provides any basic answers' (Porritt, 1984, p. 183). It is, therefore, no surprise that Greens have joined forces with many others who have argued that the industrialised world commits a fundamental error in exporting its technological forms of organisation and production to Third World countries. The future of humankind lies in the contraction rather than the expansion of this form of technology.

The third related criticism of industrial society concerns its acquisitive, highly individualistic ethos. Such a dominant ideology inevitably results in competitive consumption with its obvious effects on the limits to physical resources discussed earlier. It also results in gross forms of 'exploitation within societies, between societies, and between humans and other species' (Irvine and Ponton, 1988, p. 7). Greens are not too worried about the criticism that without this competitive spirit economic growth would suffer for they do not aspire to it and also because they believe in co-operation as a spur to human action. In addition, they make the very valid point that exploitation of the Third World is not only ethically unacceptable but it also leads to environmental destruction. In their justifiable pursuit of decent standards of living, many Third World countries, for example, are forced to destroy their forests. A more equal distribution of wealth between the rich and the poor countries would do much more to save the environment, argue the Greens, than all the summit conferences of world leaders. Third World poverty is largely the result of First World affluence, argues Trainer, and world redistribution of resources coupled with significant changes in outlook towards consumption are necessary if we are 'to improve our own chances of surviving the twenty-first century' (Trainer, 1985, p. 178). Thus, if not for altruistic but for self-interest reasons, Third World poverty has to be tackled urgently through redistribution.

The fourth fundamental Green objection to industrial welfare states is that despite the presence of pressure groups and legislation to protect various aspects of the environment and non-human life, the overall outlook of these societies is grossly anthropocentric. The non-human world – animal and plant alike – is there to be used for the benefit of humans. Any protective policies or actions for the environment that may be pursued by governments, industry or individuals is based on the self-interested grounds that it is to the benefit of humankind.

Green concern for the environment is ecocentric and disinterested. 'For Greens', writes Jacobs, 'the environment is to be understood as humankind's spiritual home, not simply as its source of wealth' (Jacobs, 1991, p. xiv). The concept of anthropocentrism, however, has its weak and strong nuances with differing policy implications, as Dobson points out. If it means that humans are at the centre of the universe in the sense that they plan what is to be done with the rest of the earth's resources, then this is inevitable. If, however, it means that the non-human world is there to be exploited at will by the humans or that it should be protected for purely instrumental reasons, that is, that to do so is to human benefit and advantage, then it would be rejected by most Greens speaking as individuals but not always as politicians anxious to attract political support to their cause (Dobson, 1990, pp. 63–70).

Anthropocentrism's counterpart, that is, ecocentrism, is an even more contested concept with considerable policy implications, as we shall see in the next section.

The Green critique of industrial society inevitably contains a series of criticisms of current welfare provision. We shall simply summarise them here for they will become more apparent in the more detailed discussion of the Green vision of an ideal welfare state later in this chapter.

The first and primary criticism of the welfare state is that its services deal with the symptoms rather than the causes of social problems. Greens claim that social problems such as crime, illness, loneliness, unemployment, and polluted water stem from the very nature of industrial society. Real solutions lie in the radical re-structuring of society rather than in services dealing with the symptoms of this structural malaise. It is similar to the Marxist criticism though, naturally, both the causes and the solutions to the problems are differently defined.

The second criticism relates to the cost of public welfare provision. Since one of the central demands of Greenism is a reduction in rates of economic growth and consumption, it means that public expenditure on welfare must also be reduced. After all, expenditure on these services consumes about a third of the gross national product. What is more, it is money spent on dealing with symptoms rather than causes. Without such a reduction in costs, the pursuit of economic growth will continue with all its adverse implications for the environment.

The third criticism of current forms of welfare provision relates to the role of professionals. The Green emphasis on self-reliance implies a rejection of fulltime state-paid professionals who 'disable' their clients through their authoritarian forms of provision (Irvine and Ponton, 1988, p. 83). The fourth criticism refers to the reliance of some services, particularly medicine, on high levels of technology. As was pointed out earlier in this section, Greens associate complex technology with wasteful use of resources and the destruction of the environment.

The fifth criticism comes from the Green rejection of large units of organisation irrespective of whether these are cities, factories, hospitals, or schools. Their preference has always been for small residential and work units. Large institutions tend to become bureaucratic with the result that they inhibit individual participation and mystify decision-making in social service provision. Thus, the emphasis on self-reliance, on participation and on small units implies a system of local services run by local residents for one another, as we shall see later.

It can be argued that Green critiques of current state welfare provision amount to an argument for a return to Victorian ama-teurism and voluntarism. Greens would respond that this is a very superficial assessment of their position because their commitment to equality and participation is in marked contrast to the ineg-alitarianism and hierarchical social deference of Victorian society.

Welfare and their ideal society

Greens have been quite prepared to sketch out the contours of their ideal society despite the fact that this often leads to deep divisions of opinion among them. The foremost feature of a Green society is its ecocentricism or, as it is otherwise known, biocentricism. It is a society based on the premise that humans are only one of many species on the planet, that there is an in-built inter-dependence between these species to the advantage of all, and that there should be equality of treatment between the species in principle and, wher-ever possible, in practice, too. It is certainly a complex and problem-atic premise with immense practical day-to-day implications.

Though the 'species inter-dependence' claim can be substantiated by empirical evidence in its totality, if not in all its details, it does not necessarily lead to the 'species equality' claim. It is quite feasible to argue that there is an inter-dependence between human beings and, say, worms but this does not necessarily lead to equality of either status or treatment between them. The position becomes even more untenable when biocentrism is used to apply not only to living or-ganisms but to land, water and plants, that is, the principle of bio-spherism or the 'land ethic' as it is sometimes known in the literature (Leopold, 1968). It is one thing to claim that humans should respect the land – trees, forests, lakes, rivers, mountains – and treat it with care but it is quite another to insist that there is equality between them of either status or treatment. Indeed, most Greens take this position for, if for no other reason, it is not possible to compare the intrinsic value of plant life and human life.

Greens have been aware of these difficulties and various attempts have been made to iron out the inherent anomalies. The founder of deep ecology, Naess, attempted to do this by distinguishing between equality in principle and equality in praxis because 'any realistic praxis necessitates some killing, exploitation and suppression' of the non-human world (Naess, 1973, p. 95). However necessary and sensible this concession may be, it inevitably raises the immediate question of how much killing, exploitation and suppression is acceptable for different forms of non-human life. The various attempts made to answer this very thorny question are based on the notion that there is a hierarchy of non-human organisms which 'are entitled to moral consideration commensurate with their degree of central organisation (or capacity of richness of experience) for the duration of their existence' (Fox, 1984, p. 199). As Dobson rather harshly observes, however, this attempt at elucidation 'makes rather a mess of the principle of biospherical egalitarianism: it is in fact a principle of biospherical inegalitarianism' (Dobson, 1990, p. 56). Yet it is difficult to see what other forms of elucidation will prove more useful unless one adopts the untenable absolutist position of some of the Greens within the Earth First! group.

In brief, apart from the diehards in their midst, Greens will accept that biocentrism and biospherism are ethical principles to be always borne in mind rather than specific guidelines for individual or government action. A certain degree of divergence of behaviour between both individuals and communities in a Green society is, therefore, inevitable. What these principles amount to is, first, human respect and concern for the environment and all forms of life on it; and second, interference with the non-human world should never be taken for granted but it should have to be justified. It is only in this mild form that the principle of biocentrism can be used in political terms and it is not surprising that Green parties have watered it down even further to make it more acceptable to the public. Thus, the Green Party election manifesto for Britain for 1992 restricts its policy concerning 'other species' to animals only and makes the following points: phasing out of animal experiments and of intensive livestock farming; a halt to trading in furs, ivory, reptile skins and whale oil; banning of blood sports and animal circuses; a moratorium on the genetic manipulation of animals; and the establishment of a government commission to oversee the implementation of all this (The Green Party, 1992, p. 19).

A Green society infused by the ethic of biocentrism would be organised bioregionally. Not all Greens will agree with the details of bioregionalism as propounded by Sale though most will subscribe to the spirit behind his ideas. The fundamental underlying principle of bioregionalism is that we must live close to nature: 'be in touch with its particular soils, its waters, its winds; we must learn its ways, its capacities, its limits; we must make its rhythms our patterns, its laws our guide, its fruits our bounty' (Sale, 1985, pp. 224–5). Thus, the physical formation of the land will determine the boundaries of communities rather than the current nation states with their administrative subdivisions. There will be ecoregions of several hundred thousand square miles, subdivided into georegions of a few tens of thousands of square miles, in turn subdivided into morphoregions of only several thousand square miles. In terms of residential communities, they will be small to enable face-to-face contacts; normally of 500 to 1000 people and exceptionally larger of 5,000 to 10,000 people. Similar ideas have been expressed by Bahro who has been one of the strongest advocates of small communities to spearhead the way for the Green society of the future.

It is argued that bioregionalism will encourage conservation, reduce waste and pollution, and bring human beings closer to nature. The small community of Sale, Bahro and other Green advocates will be largely autonomous, self-sufficient and determinedly participatory. In Bahro's view, the size of small communities is 'anthropologically favourable' and it avoids the problems of both the 'neurotic-making family and the alienating big organisations' (Bahro, 1986, pp. 87–8). Communities within the same ecoregion will be able to trade and exchange goods but it is acknowledged that even then there will have to be changes and restrictions of consumption in comparison to life in today's affluent societies. This will not always be such a bad thing. In Sale's words, some bioregions will have 'to steel themselves for significant changes from their omnivorous and gluttonous habits of the present' (Sale, 1985, p. 75).

Not unnaturally, Green political parties have put the concept of bioregionalism on the backburner, as a vision of the distant future rather than as a practical proposition for the present. 'Ultimately', says the British Green Party, 'it is hoped the European Community will be replaced by a confederation of European regions, based on ecological and cultural boundaries' (The Green Party, 1992, p. 17). For the present, we have to live with nation states and larger politico-economic units and the Green task is how to disperse power, and how to make such nation states fully participatory. To achieve this, Greens have always argued for decentralising power from the centre to small local units. As early as 1972, *The Ecologist's A Blueprint for Survival* stressed the importance of decentralisation to Green objectives and recommended 'neighbourhoods of 500, represented in communities of 5,000' that will in turn be represented regionally, nationally and internationally. Such a decentralised system had very positive advantages over the current system: it could act far better as a means of social control reducing crime; it could provide a more integrated system linking agriculture and industry both catering for people's needs; it would be more self-fulfilling for individuals; and it would reduce environmental destruction (Goldsmith *et al.*, 1972, pp. 50–3). Such a system, argued the authors of the report, would not be parochial and xenophobic. Far from it: it would create '*community feeling* and *global awareness*', even though they did not explain just how or why this latter would happen.

This emphasis on local decision-making within a unitary state inevitably raises the question of the dividing line between central and local power and responsibility. The Greens have come up with two rather similar slogans which convey quite well the spirit of their intentions even though they confuse as much as they enlighten policy-making. The first from Dubois's much quoted phrase 'Think globally, act locally', similar to the above quotation from *The Ecologist* report, is a testimony to Green concerns for the world environment and to their commitment to local styles of participatory decision-making (Tokar and Miles, 1987, p. 138). Similarly, Porritt's thesis 'nothing should be done at a higher level that cannot be done at a lower' stresses the Green preference for local decisions but does not provide hard and fast rules for the division of responsibilities between central and local governments (Porritt, 1984, p. 166). Neither of these two catchy slogans provides a guarantee that local government powers and responsibilities will not inevitably be overwhelmed by the central government. Indeed, the proposals of Green parties on this issue suggest that, contrary to intentions, the outcome will be a fairly powerful central government. The Green Party of Britain proposes that district authorities would be responsible for 'taxation, benefits, social services, housing, education, health care, land reform, policing, and many aspects of justice, transport and pollution control' (The Green Party, 1992, p. 16). That means that defence, foreign affairs, security, customs and excise, communication networks, environmental conservation policies, and policies to co-ordinate the work of district councils will be the province of the central government. The hard fact is that once one rejects the bioregional solutions of Sale and Bahro and accepts the nation state, one inevitably is forced to accept that the central government will play a major, if not a deciding role, in the administration of the country.

Having discussed Green views on the appropriate relationship between humans and non-humans and on the organisational structure of their ideal society, we now move on to examine their ideas on how such a society will earn its living. There are five points that could be made which would command support from most Greens. The first is that their definition of work is much broader than the one used in industrialised societies. Work is more than just paid employment. It covers also unpaid work at home by women, unpaid caring of the sick or the disabled and generally all types of work in the informal sector. Secondly, this kind of work is good for the human spirit: it provides not only economic benefits but social and emotional satisfaction as well. Porritt, for example, declares that he is in full agreement with Saint Thomas Aquinas's belief that 'There can be no joy of life without the joy of work' and goes on to humbly confess that: 'I'm one of those who consider work to be a necessity of the human condition, a defining characteristic of the sort of people we are' (Porritt, 1984, p. 127).

Third, their preference is for labour-intensive rather than automated work for it is more satisfying; it makes fewer demands on the environment and it does not create unemployment. They are critical of the sociological theories of the post-industrial society that automation would increase economic growth as well as leisure time for us all. In fact, automation seems to be producing unemployment rather than leisure, it is creating a balkanised employment structure with some jobs being secure and well-paid while others are insecure, badly-paid and unattractive. Even if automation achieved the goal of its dreamers, it would still be unacceptable to the Greens because of the limits to growth argument, particularly when so many of the leisure activities make heavy demands on the environment.

Fourth, workers' participation is a must for Greens for the usual reasons that it increases productivity and workers' self-esteem. A system of workers' participation will be more practically possible in a Green society where industries, businesses and institutions in general are kept to a small size since they will be based on, what Schumacher called, intermediate technology. He called it intermediate because it is 'vastly superior to the primitive technology of bygone ages but . . . much simpler, cheaper and freer than the super-technology of the rich' (Schumacher, 1974, p. 154). Greens feel that their support for intermediate technology is a sufficient reply to the criticism made against them that their production methods are a throwback to the hard labour of pre-industrialised societies.

Fifth, wage inequalities will be kept to the minimum, a policy that is in line with the general tenor of a participatory, egalitarian, frugal and sustainable Green society. Those not at work will be entitled to a state universal basic income benefit that we shall be discussing in the next section.

We discussed earlier the Greens' claim that the world ecological disaster cannot be averted unless people consume less and pollute less. A society based on the principles, though not necessarily on the strict practices, of biocentrism, bioregionalism and intermediate technology will certainly reduce both consumption and pollution and thus contribute to the creation of a sustainable society. All this, however, will not have any chance of success 'if we do not tackle the most ominous factor in the equation of environmental and social ruin, namely the population explosion' (The Green Party, 1992, p. 18). It is generally agreed that the current size of world population, let alone the current rate of population growth, is not sustainable if the environment is to be saved and the dire poverty of the Third World is to be abolished. Between 1900 and 1970 the world population increased at an annual rate of 2.1 per cent from 1.6 billion to 3.6 billion, while from 1971 to 1991 it rose at the slightly slower annual rate of 1.7 per cent reaching 5.4 billion (Meadows *et al.*, 1992, pp. 23–4). Despite the reduction in growth rates, the absolute rise in population will remain high because the population base of people of reproductive age has grown. What divides the Greens is how and by how much the population of the world and of individual countries is to be reduced. Apart from Earth First!, other Greens reject compulsion in favour of education, birth control facilities, abortion and a range of government fiscal policies, applying both the carrot and the stick approach. Irvine and Ponton summarise these measures as follows:

> There could be payments for periods of non-pregnancy and non-birth; tax benefits for families with fewer than two children; sterilisation bonuses; withdrawal of maternity and similar benefits after a second child; larger pensions for people with fewer than two children; free, easily available family planning; more funds for research into means of contraception, especially for men; an end to fertility research and treatment; a more realistic approach to abortion; the banning of surrogate motherhood and similar practices; and the promotion of equal opportunities for women in all areas of life.
> (Irvine and Ponton, 1988, p. 23)

Greens recognise the grossly unequal consumption patterns between rich and poor countries and the implication of this to the limits to growth debate. Hence their recommendations for population reductions in all countries must be seen in conjunction with their proposals for redistribution of resources between rich and poor countries, as well as between rich and poor in the same country. Despite this recognition of the world maldistribution of resources, Greens come out in favour of immigration controls. This, as Dobson points out, makes 'a nonsense' of Green support for cultural diversity, equality between ethnic groups, non-discriminatory practices and the satisfaction of basic needs for all people in the world (Dobson, 1990, p. 97).

The final major ingredient of a sustainable society – the Greens' vision of their ideal society – is sustainable development. Since the publication of the report by the World Commission on Environment and Development, otherwise known as the Brundtland Report, the term sustainable development has passed into popular usage and it has been accepted by governments of the Left as well as the Right. Basically, the Brundtland Report argued for environmentally friendly methods of production and consumption, for redistribution of resources from the rich to the poor countries so as to abolish poverty and for rates of economic growth that do not over-use physical resources. Its definition that development is sustainable if it ensures that 'it meets the needs of the present without compromising the ability of future generations to meet their needs' (Brundtland, 1987, p. 43) goes some way towards the Green view but differs from it in many significant respects. This applies even more so to the largely light green approach adopted by the Report of the Thatcher Government which claimed that sustainability was the foundation stone of all government policies! (Department of Environment, 1990). Even Greens find themselves in disagreement on how to define sustainable development and all we can do here is to outline those features which we consider will command most support among them.

To begin with, sustainable development involves extreme care in the use and disposal of the earth's physical resources. In more precise terms, Daly suggests that renewable resources should not be used at a rate which is faster than that necessary for their regeneration; similarly, non-renewable resources should be used up only as fast as renewable substitutes can be developed. As for pollution creation, it should not exceed the ability of the environment to absorb it in harmless ways (Meadows *et al.*, 1992, p. 209). Sustainable development, in the second place, implies a rejection of current rates and types of production in favour of production for the satisfaction of everyone's basic needs. This raises the thorny question of who is to decide and in what ways decisions will be reached as to what these needs are. Greens have tried to grapple with this problem and, like others before them, they have failed. Porritt, for example, distinguishes between needs and wants with 'needs being those things that are essential to our survival and to civilized, humane existence, wants being the extras that serve to gratify our desires' (Porritt, 1984, p. 196). Elkins distinguishes between needs and the methods through which they are satisfied. Needs are few, uniform and universal, he claims, while methods of satisfaction are cultural and variable both between countries and between generations (Elkins, 1986, pp. 49–50). Thus food is a universal need but this can be satisfied in numerous ways. The difficulty is that the method of satisfaction can be just as important as the act of satisfaction itself. One can get the same calories from cheap as well as expensive food. The conclusion reached by students of need over the years is that the definition and method of satisfaction of needs are political rather than social scientific tasks. All this does not detract from the Greens' emphasis on bread for all before cake for some; it simply stresses the problems involved in all this. Thirdly, the process of sustainable development is important for reasons explained earlier and hence the Greens' emphasis on active participation in all aspects of society. Finally, sustainable development has to be seen in an international and not simply in a national context. This involves a substantial redirection of resources from the rich to the poor countries. Without this, poor countries have every reason not to heed calls for ecological prudence for their immediate task is to feed their people.

To sum up: the ideal Green society is ecocentric or biocentric in the sense that, to put it mildly, it does not accord humans the right to do as they please with the non-human world. It is bioregional in the sense that it at least places a great deal of emphasis on decentralisation, local communities, public participation and smaller residential centres. It is committed to intermediate technology, a broader concept of work and greater wage equality. It is anti-natalist emphasising population control at both the national and the international level with strong relevant government policies to implement this. It is committed to sustainable development that is based on the limits to growth thesis, frugality of consumption, egalitarianism and concern for future generations. In each one of these component parts of the Green utopia, there is the strong and the weak position with the political wing of Greenism associated with the latter approach for obvious electoral reasons.

Industrial societies measure their successes and failures largely through the fortunes of their gross national product which they see as a fairly valid shorthand of welfare. There have always been critics of this approach to welfare even among those who saw economic growth as paramount to welfare. The social indicators movement, for example, was an explicit attempt to broaden government approaches to the concept of welfare by adding health, education, unemployment, poverty, crime, and other such social criteria to the well-established economic criteria in order to arrive at a more composite and realistic estimation of a nation's state of welfare. The notion of welfare was too important to be measured by economic criteria alone.

Greens have added another dimension to this debate on welfare. First, they have added a series of environmental criteria to the notion of welfare – deforestation, ozone layer depletion, global warming, exhaustion of resources, and pollution. Second, they have argued that these environmental criteria are at least of equal weight as the more commonly quoted social and economic criteria of welfare. Third, they have insisted that it is far better to have disaggregated indicators of welfare so that we can all see which aspects of welfare are improving and which are getting worse (Jacobs, 1991, pp. 239–41). Individuals, using the same data, may well arrive at different conclusions. Faced with a decline in the GNP and an improvement in the pollution rates, for example, Greens will conclude that the overall rate of welfare is rising while some others might arrive at the opposite conclusion.

To the extent that environmental and social criteria are seen as similar and distinct from economic criteria, Greens will view social policy in broader terms than all the other groups we have discussed in this book. But because of their commitment to environmental factors, the traditional concerns of social policy with poverty and inequality 'will be reinterpreted and made more relevant to a society which is beginning to realise the implications of the limits to growth' (Cahill, 1991, p. 20). Moreover, as we pointed out earlier in this chapter, and as Ferris reminds us, the Green hostility to constant economic growth and to centralised administration means that social policy will be administered locally, and public expenditure on it will decline and will be replaced by a greater reliance on ordinary citizens than professionals (Ferris, 1991, p. 25). This will become clear as we discuss the Green approach to the traditional social services of social security, education, health, housing and the personal social services.

In social security, Greens aim to replace the current complex system with a streamlined Basic Income Guarantee scheme which provides benefits for all as of right.

> The Green Party would introduce a basic income scheme payable as of right to all, regardless of status. It would ensure that everyone, whether in paid employment or not, would have a guaranteed income high enough to support a full and independent life, regardless of circumstances. (Kemp and Wall, 1990, p. 92)

Such a scheme has been put forward by others before such as socialists and pragmatists, and it has received extensive coverage in the social security literature (Walter, 1989; George and Howards, 1991). The only novel aspect of the proposals of the Greens is that the benefit would not be paid to third and subsequent children in the family in response to their overall population control policy. In line with the principles of bioregionalism, the scheme would be financed and administered locally, whether this means the local units envisaged by Sale or the more traditional units put forward by Green parties. If it is the Sale prototype of communities, it is difficult to see how it would operate, or indeed whether it would be necessary, since people would work for themselves and each other with no unemployment and minimum degrees of wage inequalities. The scheme, however, fits in better in the decentralised form of government of the Green parties but it is difficult to see how it would be financed, particularly in those communities which are not so prosperous, bearing in mind its high costs. It would certainly require high rates of taxation and it would involve a substantial administrative framework. One cannot but agree with Dobson's assessment that the Greens' Basic Income Guarantee Scheme 'looks like a social democratic measure grafted unsustainably onto the ailing post-industrial body politic, rather than a radically Green measure in the spirit of solutions to the problems of sustainability raised by the spectre of limits to growth' (Dobson, 1990, p. 115). It could, of course, be argued that the scheme would be financed and administered centrally but this goes contrary to another Green principle, that is, maximum local responsibility for the finance and administration of services.

Greens' ideas on education are in line with their general principles. To begin with, education will be fully in local hands: 'Elected representatives of local government will be responsible for funding and control of educational establishments' (The Green Party, 1992, p. 16). Maximum feasible participation runs through their educational proposals with parents and pupils playing an important part in school affairs and headteachers sharing power with their staff. Some of them consider the Danish system of education as the one which most approximates to their own ideas on this issue. Close links between school and home are envisaged and 'home visits could be a legitimate part of teachers' duties, with time allowed for them' (Irvine and Ponton, 1988, p. 111). Education for life is another theme running through their proposals with perhaps a voucher system for further education to be used by individuals as they think best. There is a strong streak of egalitarianism as well as parental responsibility in many of their proposals. Thus private education would be abolished but 'Support will be provided for parents wishing to educate their children at home'

(The Green Party, 1992, p. 16). Finally, they are naturally critical of the dominance of the value of 'industrialism' in schools and they would attempt to replace it with ecological values that stress human care for the environment. Indeed, Kemp and Wall revive memories of Mao's red brigades when they suggest that social science students should spearhead this by leading 'campaigns for land reform, exposing local landowners who threaten to vandalise hedgerows, meadows and marshes' (Kemp and Wall, 1990, p. 165).

To understand Green proposals on health policies, one needs to understand first their ideas on the causes of illness in society. Their basic premise is that illness and disability in advanced industrial societies are the result largely of the ethos and practice of industrialism. In detail this means that the dominance of the industrial processes in manufacturing and agriculture, the type of food and diet, the nature of the transport system, the pollution of the environment, the emphasis on technological medicine and the general social pressures for endless production and consumption combine to produce the complex web of factors behind illness and disease. The poor are most susceptible to these factors and hence their greater incidence of illness: 'The poor suffer the worst pollution; they inhabit the dampest and most overcrowded housing; eat the worst food; and generally have lifestyles which produce unacceptable inequalities in patterns of illness and mortality' (Irvine and Ponton, 1988, p. 97).

As a result, Green health policy proposals place paramount emphasis on prevention in general with specific prevention measures for the poor. Prevention is not only better than cure but 'Health for individuals is only possible in a healthy environment' (The Green Party, 1992, p. 14). This means improvements in housing and diet for all, including the poor; clean air and unpolluted water; and changes in the pressurised industrial way of life so that there is satisfying employment for all, accidents at work are reduced and the emotional pressures of the work ethos are taken care of. There is much in common here with the ideas of some of the exponents of community medicine (McKeown, 1979; Draper, 1991) as well as with the ideas of Illich with his strong stance against technological and drug-based medicine (Illich, 1975). Greens stress that preventive health measures are not a cheap alternative to technological medicine and they will be resisted by entrenched interests who make enormous profits out of drugs and medicines.

In terms of medical services, there is strong support for free, universal government provision along the lines of the National Health Service but with several important modifications. First, the NHS should be broadened to include such traditional forms of medicine as acupuncture, chiropractice, and herbal medicine, under 'proper regulation and proper funding' (Kemp and Wall, 1990, p. 156) for they have much to offer despite the misplaced opposition from the medical establishment. Second, general practitioners should be enabled and encouraged not only to give more time to their patients but 'to deal with the whole person not just an isolated symptom' (Porritt, 1990, p. 110). Third, the trend towards larger and more technological hospitals should be reversed so that small local hospitals can play a greater role in medical care. This is clearly a reflection of the Greens' general disapproval of excessive technologism, large size and remoteness in society that we referred to earlier in the chapter. Finally, greater participation in the running of the services as well as legal recognition that both 'healers and healed should have rights' (Irvine and Ponton, 1988, p. 101) so that an egalitarian atmosphere of mutual trust between them can develop to replace the current professionally dominated relationship.

Housing policies must be seen within the wider context of urban and rural planning. As mentioned earlier, there is general agreement that large cities are undesirable for social, economic and ecological reasons. They are unfriendly places, they become breeding grounds for crime, they are wasteful of resources because of the long distances involved for travelling to work and they destroy the natural environment replacing it with huge expanses of cemented areas and millions of cars. A mixture of villages and small towns – not exceeding 50,000 in population – would be the ideal form of residential planning for most Greens. The current separation of residential and work areas is detrimental in all sorts of ways and in a Green town people should live where they work. 'City areas that suddenly become semi-deserted at half past five, because they're all shops and offices, are dangerous and unfriendly places; by contrast, nothing enhances a city's reputation more than lively, lived-in streets where there's plenty going on' (Porritt, 1990, p. 104).

Every attempt should be made to introduce agriculture and nature into city life through the provision of 'inner-city greenhouses, allotments and city farms' (Kemp and Wall, 1990, p. 149), the planting of trees and the preservation of woodland and rivers.

Human beings feel better when they live close to nature. Priority must be given to pedestrians, cyclists and public transport; the use of private cars should be restricted as far as possible. All this is not an argument for sprawling cities. The exact opposite is in fact the case: density of living is preferred but not in the unnatural form of high rise buildings. 'From an ecological and social perspective, high concentrations of people in cities are actually very desirable' because such a form of living 'allows for the most efficient use of energy; it makes it far easier and more economical to plan for proper public transport' (Porritt, 1990, p. 103).

It goes without saying that Greens would insist that all buildings should be conservationist. Natural local building materials should be used wherever possible; energy-saving devices should be given top priority; and renewable forms of energy, such as solar power, should be used along with electricity generated as far as possible by renewable sources of wind and water. It is acknowledged that such a building programme 'incurs a greater initial cost, though this would be offset by low running costs and long life' (Irvine and Ponton, 1988, p. 90).

Bearing all this in mind, Greens accept that there is a need for all forms of housing tenure even though they would prefer the co-operative type because it is in line with their ideas of public co-operation and participation. An adequate standard of housing for all is seen as top priority for social, educational and health reasons. People have a social right to good housing and 'the presence of large-scale homelessness in a "civilised" society is shameful' (The Green Party, 1992, p. 8). Government subsidies are necessary and they should be based on individual need rather than aiming to encourage one form of housing tenure in preference to others as at present.

Proposals by the Greens on the personal social services amount to very little. They begin by insisting that the causes of our current social problems such as crime, mental illness, child abuse, and neglect of the elderly are to be found in the industrial system or in the capitalist system. Porritt sees the causes of it all in the industrial system:

> Given that we have failed to reduce residual levels of violence, unhappiness and alienation, despite all our wealth-creating powers and industrial might, shouldn't we consider the possibility that there is something inherently flawed in the vision of progress which has

goaded one generation after another since the start of the Industrial Revolution? (Porritt, 1990, p. 89)

Others point the accusing finger at capitalism. Kemp, for example, argues that since 'Capitalism needs poverty in order to survive' (Kemp, 1990, p. 3), it is illusory to expect that poverty can be abolished within a capitalist society. Whether industrialism or capitalism generates the various social problems, the conclusion remains the same: these problems will continue until the system itself is changed and a Green society is created.

In the Green society of Bahro there will be no need for organised personal social services for the small communes will look after their own social casualties or deviants, if they exist. In the decentralised Green society of the Green parties, there will be an emphasis on community care with full government support for the carers, unlike the situation in many welfare states today, as the Greens claim, where community care is used as a cost-cutting exercise. What little residential care may be necessary will be in institutions which are 'small and very much part of the community. The units should be run cooperatively and with the involvement of residents, staff and the local community' (Kemp and Wall, 1990, p. 101). As for penal policy, the Green Party of Britain 'believes in "restorative justice" which, while punishing the criminal, deals constructively with both victim and offender' (The Green Party, 1992, p. 18). In brief, whether in the small communes or in the decentralised state, Green proposals on the personal social services remain an enigma.

In general, Greens envisage a major role for social policy in their ideal society to be financed and administered according to their general principles of egalitarianism, the satisfaction of basic needs for all, community and individual self-reliance, public participation, sustainability and respect for the environment. In this, as in other areas, the differences between the deep ecologists, the social ecologists and the Green parties are quite marked.

Assessment

The central theme of Green ideology, whether of the deep or social ecology kind, is that there are limits to growth as regards renewable and non-renewable resources as well as the earth's capacity to absorb pollution and waste. This is particularly the case if population growth continues at its present rate and if the standard of living in the Third World is brought anywhere near that of the affluent world. Those who oppose the Green thesis base their case on the ability of science and technology to come up with solutions to the future scarcity of resources and to the ability of the planet to absorb polluting waste. Thus, international bodies such as the World Bank and the International Monetary Fund together with the governments of industrial societies still base their policies on the traditional economic view that high rates of economic growth are not inherently environmentally unfriendly, that such rates by themselves improve the standards of all groups in all countries and that increased consumption for all, including the already over-consuming affluent world, is a desirable goal (Korten, 1991/92).

There is no objective way of impartially judging between these two claims because historical evidence can be found in support of both. Industrial and agricultural productivity has clearly benefited from technological advances and often substitutes have been found to replace exhausted natural resources. But the same process of technological innovation has caused a great deal of pollution on a world scale and it has led to the exhaustion of some resources and the extinction of many forms of animal and plant life. Moreover, technology has not been able to deal with population growth because this is the result of human as well as technical factors. The technology is there to reduce birth rates but in many countries the human and social factors outweigh technology. It is, therefore, likely that world population growth rates will remain high for some time to come. Thus, if the rich countries were to maintain their high rates of consumption as well as assist the Third World to improve its living standards whilst its population is still growing, the limits to growth thesis has to be taken very seriously. What is happening, however, is that there is no credible attempt by the rich countries to raise the standard of living of the Third World. This is the weak link in the limits to growth thesis in terms of exhaustion of resources, however unethical and deplorable the conduct of the affluent world may be. To put this more bluntly, there are enough resources to maintain the high standards of living enjoyed by the rich world so long as the Third World continues its present low levels of existence. In terms of pollution, however, the risk remains for no technological solutions to such problems as global warming or ozone layer depletion have yet been found. Moreover, without *true* aid from the rich world, Third World industrialisation will be heavily polluting and this is bound to affect the lives of people in the First World as well.

Assuming, however, that the limits to growth thesis is correct, what can one make of the proposed major Green solution of reducing production and consumption? Is it desirable and will it solve our current ecological problems? The desirability or otherwise issue is very much a personal decision. It is difficult to see why the affluent, over-consuming sections of the world will consider it desirable to accept frugality and simplicity of life in accord with nature unless they are convinced of the Green thesis *and* they are broad-minded enough to consider the plight of others today and of the generations to follow. Low rates of economic growth will also perpetuate Third World poverty. Whether a policy of low growth rates will solve the ecological problems depends very much on whether it is pursued in an environmentally friendly way.

The Green utopia, just like all other utopias, faces immense problems of public acceptability and political viability. This is particularly the case with such Green principles as biocentrism and bioregionalism as understood by either the deep or the social ecologists. Even the more moderate programme of Green parties does not at present fall 'within the "art of the possible" ' (Jones, 1990, p. 54). It is not surprising that some Greens, such as Bahro, have sought a way out of this political impasse through the establishment of communes which provide 'a new social formation and a different civilisation' (Bahro, 1986, p. 29). Communes, whether of the anarchist, the sexual liberation or the Green type, may well 'provide welcome interludes from the pressures of society' (Kanter, 1972, pp. 189–90) but they never lead to fundamental political or social change.

The most pressing need for the Green movement is to provide viable examples of a working Green society. Simply writing about the Green utopia will not get the Green movement very far. As Eckersley puts it 'the Green movement will ultimately stand or fall on its ability to generate *practical* alternatives to the advanced industrial way of life' (Eckersley, 1992, p. 186; emphasis in original).

The Greens deserve credit for raising and highlighting very serious ecological issues even if on the strict test of an impartial
assessment their case remains unproven today. This does not jus-
tify a rejection of their limits to growth thesis for the stakes are
high. It calls for a more careful and a more egalitarian use of
resources on a world basis. Green consumerism by itself is not
sufficient. It may reduce the ecological problems if it is practised
on a worldwide basis but it will not abolish Third World poverty.

The Green thesis of the limits to growth, though strictly speaking unproven, must remain a reminder to governments and people
that the current forms of production, consumption and distribution
are ethically unacceptable, environmentally destructive and may
well prove ecologically unsustainable.

CHAPTER 8

CONCLUSION

In this concluding chapter we compare and contrast the views of our six groups of thinkers on the four issues which we see as central to any position on the role of the state in welfare – attitude to the role of the state in welfare; assessment of the possibilities of politics; beliefs about the economy; and view of what constitutes the good society.

Comparing our chosen perspectives is not always easy. Four of them sit easily on the classic, easily-managed Left-Right political continuum. Greenism and feminism are different and are more accurately seen as political movements rather than as parties with easily defined attitudes to traditional political questions. Obviously, too, all our groupings, but some more obviously than others, are coalitions within which sub-groups differ sharply on particular points.

Attitudes to the role of the state in welfare

Clearly our six perspectives have very different attitudes to the role of the state in welfare and to the contemporary welfare state. The New Right's hostility to the welfare state is based on the judgement that it damages the economy by burdening corporations and individuals with levels of taxation which discourage enterprise because of the way rewards are limited. By damaging the prospects for growth, it reduces the possibility of enhancing

189

human wellbeing and reducing poverty. The New Right also see the welfare state as socially damaging as it creates a dependency culture and weakens the historic stabilising power of reward for success and punishment for failure. It undermines the authority of government because the aspirations of welfare states lead governments to extend their reach beyond their grasp and because governments come to depend on powerful groups if they are to make good their promises. Fiscal crisis inevitably follows the expansion of the welfare state expenditure which the New Right see as the result of the powerful expansionary forces built into the fabric of welfare states, for example, the self-interested pressure by professionals and bureaucrats for extended services.

The Middle Way, in contrast, see the welfare state as a powerful force for social progress and stability – removing the rough edges of the free market system, giving people a sense that the government is positively concerned about their wellbeing and so giving legitimacy to its authority. They see government management of the economy not only as crucial to the softening of potentially destructive fluctuations in economic activity but also as essential to the achievement of full employment and economic growth. They stress, too, the contribution of public expenditure to a healthy economy, for example, through investment in people as human capital. Whereas the New Right always give priority to the supposed needs of the economy, the Middle Way shy away from such an absolutist position and stress the need for a balance between economic and social policy to be determined by circumstances.

The Democratic Socialists also see the welfare state as crucial to social harmony, as providing the vital mediating force between the political rights provided by democracy and the aspirations which grow out of such rights, and the free market's neglect of considerations other than market power in the distribution of the social product. They also stress the potential of welfare state policies to reduce inequalities and promote a more equal society.

The Democratic Socialists are, however, rather ambivalent in their stance. They see the welfare state both as a way of softening the harsher aspects of the free market system and so securing social stability, and at the same time as a way of stimulating the expectations and prefiguring the relationships from which a socialist society will eventually emerge.

The dominant Marxist view is that the welfare state is a mechanism which helps to preserve capitalism. It is a *capitalist* welfare state and therefore primarily concerned with maintaining that economic system though at times that may involve making not insignificant concessions at the outworks of the system. Because of how Marxists see the state, they do not see the welfare state as a way to significantly change society. Their optimism rests not on the potential of the planned consequences of the welfare state but on the fiscal crisis to which they see it inevitably leading. To square the circle and achieve social harmony and state legitimacy, welfare states, so the Marxists think, will always have to spend more than they can afford. Crisis will follow – eventually.

Feminists see the potential of the welfare state in its ability to help women. It can offer the services which women need if they are to attain an equal position in the labour market on which any equality of citizenship realistically depends. On the other hand, feminists stress that the welfare state is a male-dominated state in which men are the policy-makers and women merely the policy-takers. They see the welfare state as dominated by male values and as functioning, even if unintentionally, to preserve particular patterns of unequal and oppressive gender relations even though at times it helps to break down such patterns.

Feminist analysis generating the idea of the male-dominated state leads to pessimism. On the other hand, the experience of several European countries shows the possibilities of public policy in extending women's opportunities. There is also a belief among feminists that it is only state action which can advance the position of women. For the liberation of most women, a recognition of the political nature of the personal is essential. So the feminist approach is a mix of critical pessimism and a struggle for a determined optimism.

For the Greens, the welfare state is fundamentally flawed because it has come to depend on economic growth and so on a particular industrial and economic system. The Greens see this system as producing short-term gains at the cost of long-term disaster. All the other perspectives we have analysed see economic growth as the way to enhance welfare either through extending private affluence or through increasing the resources for public services. The Greens see growth as the great diswelfare. It increases pollution; it leads to the consumption of capital as income;

it places values which deny the fundamentals of human nature at the heart of government concerns.

The Greens see the free market system as based on values and processes which are inherently destructive of individuals and of society. They believe that government has a major role to play in promoting the welfare of people and of society but they start their analysis from premises which are totally different from those of our other groups.

Our six perspectives show a full range of opinion on the welfare state. There is support ranging from the enthusiastic (Democratic Socialists) to the more qualified (Middle Way and feminists). There is strong opposition – from the New Right because of what the welfare state might do to the free market and social stability, from the Marxists because of the little the welfare state can be expected to achieve in a capitalist society and because it may, temporarily at least, prop up an inequitable system, and from the Greens because of its dependence on the pursuit of economic growth.

The possibilities of politics

Secondly, our groups of thinkers take very different positions on the possibility of achieving desirable social change through political action. They are both optimistic and pessimistic about politics as a means and a method.

There are sharply differing views on the possibility of achieving a sense of common purpose in society. The Middle Way have few doubts about this. The New Right deny the possibility except in times of war, as do the Marxists though for rather different reasons. The Democratic Socialists do not rule out the possibility. The feminists would differ among themselves, some seeing women's and men's interests as fundamentally in conflict, others seeing common action on some issues as possible. There are also differences about the legitimacy of majorities enforcing policies in the face of minority objections.

These differing views on the role of politics stem, firstly, from the sharp differences between our groups about the nature of the state as reviewed in the previous section.

Secondly, our groups have different views about human capacity to plan, co-ordinate and implement policies of any kind. The New Right and the Middle Way share doubts about human beings' capacity to plan comprehensively because of human intellectual limitations. The New Right doubts are the stronger; they are clear that such planning is impossible. The knowledge is simply not available, and, if it were, human beings would lack the capacity to use it. The Middle Way would agree that planning a new world is impossible but believe that planning to deal with manifest social ills can achieve beneficial results.

In contrast, the Democratic Socialists and the Marxists have enormous faith in human capacity to design and plan a new social order. Greens believe a new order to be possible but many see it, not as something to be planned and directed from above but, as something which can only be rebuilt from below. Many Greens would share many of the New Right doubts about attempts at sophisticated planning. Like Hayek, they prefer wisdom and experience to the assumed knowledge of experts.

Thirdly, our groups' attitude to politics is shaped by their views on the nature of professionals and bureaucrats. This judgement is at the heart of any views on the possibilities of political action to remedy social ills. Professionals and bureaucrats are the key instruments for translating policies into practice. For the New Right, they are inherently self-interested and self-serving. They are also inefficient because they lack the competitive spur of market systems. They are ineffective because they provide what someone thinks people need rather than what potential and actual consumers actually want.

In contrast, Democratic Socialists have enormous confidence in the judgement, expertise and service ethic of these key institutions, particularly when they are made properly accountable to the public. They are also confident that government can control them and hold them accountable. The Middle Way share this optimistic view though they are less enthusiastic than the Socialists and lay more emphasis on the problems of securing control.

The feminists and the Greens are sceptics. The former stress how bureaucratic systems and professional hierarchies are dominated by men and infected by priorities and value systems which are inherently male. They see the organisations which constitute the welfare state as gendered systems expressing a particular and pervasive male sexuality. The Greens dislike and distrust large, hierarchical organisations. They see them as remote and alienating, embodying the false values of industrial society. Professionals are indicted for largely ignoring the wisdom, experience and knowledge of ordinary people on issues on which they are the real experts.

Fourthly, our groups differ on the fundamental question of whether or not it is possible to eliminate or even significantly alleviate those ills which historically have always been endemic in the human situation such as want, disease, unemployment, bad housing, homelessness, and inequalities of educational opportunity. For the New Right these are facts of life. It may be possible to ease them marginally through government action but they are basically inherent in the human situation – the price to be paid for all the benefits of the free market system and a price which cannot be avoided. The Democratic Socialists, the Middle Way and the Marxists all believe in the possibility of remedying such ills through political action and do not see them as inevitable. Feminists would see them as the price to be paid for a society dominated by men and male values and/or capitalism. Greens see such ills as the product of industrialism – the drive for growth, the stress on large-scale organisations, the low value placed on people and human-scale organisations, the emphasis on gratifying wants rather than meeting needs which is a key element in capitalism.

Attitudes to the possibilities of politics depend also on judgements about human moral capacities and potential. Our perspectives reflect very different views. The Democratic Socialists, the Marxists and the Greens are basically optimistic. The first two believe that people will respond to pleas for self-sacrifice and to put the common good first and that welfare state policies can promote altruistic types of behaviour. The Greens, for example, believe that people can be persuaded to put the future first, to put it before the present, to sacrifice their present interests for the assumed long-term interests of their own and other people's children.

The New Right stress human beings' moral imperfection. They see people as basically self-centred and unresponsive to the needs of others and to vague concepts such as the general good. They think policy-makers must accept these as givens not ignore them or try to change them – these are *facts*. The only way forward is for politics to try to harness and use self-interest for the common good and this is what the market does. The Middle Way accept the possibility of a modicum of human altruism but regard it as safer to assume individuals are primarily self- and family-centred and that it is extremely difficult, if not totally impossible, to change that orientation.

These basically different positions lead to different views about how people will respond to welfare state policies, and thus to different views about the possibilities of politics. Those who stress people's moral imperfection emphasise the potentially corrupting influence of the offer of something for nothing and how people will 'abuse' the system. If people can get something for nothing, the argument runs, then they will. Political action cannot, therefore, make for a better society. Some ills may be remedied at the cost of generating others. On the other hand, those who dismiss notions of the corrupting nature of welfare provision such as the Democratic Socialists, for example, have a much more positive and optimistic view of what might be achieved through political action.

Beliefs about the economy

The third area we need to explore is different beliefs about the economy. In some ways, the key issue which divides perspectives on the proper role of the state in welfare is the judgement about whether or not government can successfully manage the economy to achieve certain economic and social purposes. The post-Second World War welfare state in Britain was based very explicitly on this assumption – that the economy could be managed to secure full employment and such an economy could afford a developing welfare state. The Middle Way are quite confident on this. They see government management of the economy as necessary because markets are not self-regulating. They are also confident that it is possible for governments to do better than market forces. Democratic Socialists agree though they want to move beyond a managed capitalism to socialism. Marxists are clear that a state-managed economy is more efficient but they do not believe that such management can be successful or effective in a free market system. The state has to be transformed before the economy can be managed. The New Right stance is that the state's attempt to manage the economy will be disruptive rather than helpful. Markets do not need states and governments can do little constructive beyond providing a secure legal and monetary framework within which market forces can operate.

Our groups hold very different views, too, on the potential of economic growth to solve social problems, firstly because of how they assess the impact of growth on society and also because of how they see the distributional impact of growth. For the New Right, economic growth is the main engine of welfare – a rising tide which raises all boats. For the Middle Way, growth is crucial, but will need to be accompanied by measures to protect its inevitable casualties and by measures to ensure a fair distribution of its fruits. For Democratic Socialists, growth is desirable and necessary but its use for social purposes is crucial to welfare. For the Greens, growth is the problem not the solution, and talk of redistribution of the fruits of growth as the way to solve the problems to which growth leads is potentially dangerous because it distracts attention from the real problem, which is the relentless pursuit of the growth which threatens to destroy us all. Greens are strongly in favour of redistribution at both the national and the international level. They see it as the only way to pre-empt further environmental pressures but they firmly reject the approach which says that redistribution must depend on growth.

There are also very different views among our groups on what it is that actually generates economic vitality. For the New Right and the Middle Way, it is inequality and financial incentives. These are seen as altogether essential to a healthy economy, the necessary spurs to effort, recognitions of the realities of human motivation and behaviour. People will only experiment, take risks and work hard when there are strong rewards in prospect and the threat of poverty for those who fail to join the race or fail in it.

The Democratic Socialists lay much more stress on the motivating power of collective purposes. They see the prospect of individual reward as no more important than the incentive of promoting the public good. They see reductions in inequality as posing no threat to economic vitality in a society which is committed to the pursuit of shared goals. The Marxists would lay even greater stress on the pursuit of collective purposes as the spur to economic development particularly when the communist society has been achieved. That can, of course, only happen when the individualistic, competitive values of capitalism have been superseded. The Green view would be that concern for a dynamic economy is wrong because of its destructive potential. The real concern must be for sustainability so that if inequality and incentives are indeed engines of growth then they are at the same time forces which threaten human survival. Sustainability and the long-term common good rather than the pursuit of economic growth are the Green principles for the good life.

Competitive markets are central to economic wellbeing for the New Right and the Middle Way as they generate innovation and efficiency. Because they must sell, producers must be responsive to consumer wishes and they must sell at competitive prices or else their rivals will destroy them. Markets are democratic because of the way they give power to consumers. They are also an essential element in a free society because a market society means only a limited role for government. What distinguishes both the New Right and the Middle Way from our other groups is their deepseated faith in the competitive mechanism. To them it is the crucial guiding and driving force.

Traditionally, Democratic Socialists have adopted an ambivalent attitude towards markets. Though they accept them, they also see market systems as failing to deliver most of the benefits claimed for them. They see capitalism as both useful and wasteful, as no inevitable guarantee of efficiency, as persuading consumers of what they need rather than responding democratically to consumer wants. They see other ways of securing efficiency in the provision of basic goods and services which they see as superior to markets. Marxists, of course, have always been hostile to markets, emphasising their destructive nature. Greens see the free market system as fostering the competitive relationships between individuals, groups and institutions which both are wasteful of natural resources and deny the co-operative relationships which for the Greens are vital to the good life and to survival.

In the 1980s and 1990s, of course, markets have been rehabilitated. Governments in Britain and elsewhere have introduced market mechanisms into the heartlands of social service provision as the way to stimulate efficiency and reduce producer power. The Left have expressed a wary acceptance of the potential benefits of market mechanisms and a reluctant belief that they can, perhaps, be harnessed to social objectives.

Another central economic issue which sharply divides our groups is their assessment of the supposed impact of a large public sector on economic performance. The New Right see public spending as inherently destructive, and as always threatening the health of the economy. It absorbs resources which could be used more productively in other parts of the economy and it punishes success by the taxes which are necessary to fund its programmes. Those programmes, by cushioning the effects of failure, are a further disincentive to effort and initiative. The Middle Way, on the other hand, see such spending as socially necessary and economically beneficial as long as commonsensical limits are maintained. The Democratic Socialists and the Marxists take an equally positive view of public spending and would set their commonsensical limits rather above those of the Middle Way.

For the New Right, the free market system has a peculiar sanctity. They see it as reflecting fundamental realities of human nature and human relations. The Middle Way regard it with enthusiasm but without such veneration. They think it is the best way of running an economy but that it needs judicious control, direction and modification. Socialists, Marxists and feminists regard it as a system which has developed and survived because it serves the needs of the powerful. Its supposed inherent logic is used to legitimate exploitation and oppression. Their view would be that people behave as they do in market systems not because such systems reflect unalterable realities of human nature, but because the system encourages them to behave in certain ways and rewards them for doing so. The Greens take a similar view but their opposition to market systems is more fundamental than that of Democratic Socialists. For them, market systems are a crucial element in the unsustainable society. Ultimately, the issue is whether the market system reflects some ultimate realities or whether it is no more than a human construct which is modifiable just as are all such human creations.

Different approaches to the good society

Implicit in what we have said so far is the fact that all our groups have very different ideas about what constitutes the good society. These ideas shape their differing perspectives on the role which they believe the state should play in welfare. They differ fundamentally, for example, on the desirable relationship between the individual and society. For the New Right, individual fulfilment is a private matter most likely to be achieved when the individual is left to his/her own devices. For the Democratic Socialist, individual fulfilment depends on action by society to make real a range of freedoms and opportunities which remain a fiction until, and unless, brought about by collective action. This Democratic Socialist perspective derives from a strong sense of the person as a social being and from a sense of how market systems can narrow and constrain opportunities for most individuals. The Middle Way, too, lay a very strong emphasis on people as social beings. For them, the good life for the individual depends very much on the way society is ordered. People are not islands capable of an isolated self-fulfilment. They are members of a collectivity which can constrain or enhance opportunities.

The feminist perspective is fiercely critical of the way in which many societies prioritise and individualise responsibilities which traditionally fall on women. By accident or design, this traps women in a position of dependency on men and thus keeps them in a position of inequality. Until there is a collective responsibility for the tasks traditionally assumed by individual women, women cannot take their place in the public sphere. This depends on a recognition and acceptance of the feminist demand that the personal be seen as political.

There are very clear and sharp divisions between our chosen perspectives on the issue of equality and inequality. The New Right and the Middle Way regard the pursuit of economic and social equality as economically and socially damaging and as doomed to failure. The only equality in which they believe is equality of opportunity by which they mean simply equality of access.

In contrast, the Democratic Socialists and the Marxists see inequality as economically and socially damaging, as wasteful of potential and as socially divisive. They want to see reductions in substantive inequalities and the promotion of a genuine equality of opportunity which they see as requiring a wide range of economic and social policies, not simply equality of access. Their concern has been with the removal of manifest and socially destructive inequalities rather than the advancement of a theoretical equality.

The feminists advance a wide range of arguments for policies to further women's equality. At the heart of their case is the insistence that extending equality in the public sphere alone will not remedy women's current unequal position because women's public inequality depends substantially on inequalities in the private sphere of the home. A concern for equality, therefore, means that the personal must become the subject of social, that is, public, policy.

The Greens take a much broader view. For them, human survival depends on reductions in a range of inequalities. They see the rich, whether individuals or nations, as over-consumers – consuming more than they need and more than they have any right to consume. They want to see reductions in inequalities within industrial societies and between the First and the Third World. A viable future depends on the First World reducing its levels of consumption and raising levels of living in the Third World so that those nations are not driven to pursue globally destructive policies in the pursuit of growth.

The Green's specific contribution to the idea of the good society is twofold. First, there is the concept of sustainability. The good society must be *sustainable*, that is, it must not consume capital as income by depleting non-renewable resources. It must not leave to the next generation a poorer inheritance than the one into which it entered – poorer in the sense of depleted resources or increased or yet to be solved – problems of pollution. This gives the Greens a different and longer timescale than other groups and they are highly critical of the short-termism which characterises the thinking of other ideologies.

Secondly, the Greens try to reconcile their belief that co-operative relationships are the basis of the sustainable society with their commitment to individual freedom. Because of their heavy emphasis on how *society* must conduct its affairs the Greens have been accused of totalitarianism. But at the same time as making this emphasis, Greens also stress human individuality and the need for self-realisation. Reconciling these beliefs is vital to the Green's good society and to any good society.

Conclusion

Approaches to the proper role of the state in welfare are a mix of ideological judgements and judgements of relevant evidence. We do not have the space properly to evaluate how research supports or contradicts the various positions we have been exploring. On some issues, however, research findings clearly contradict, or do not support, firmly held opinions, for example, the New Right belief that welfare state policies are inevitably economically damaging.

The perspectives we have explored are about means and ends. Ends are matters of judgements about what constitutes the good society. Means are susceptible to research and evaluation and they can often be shown to be right or wrong.

Our own judgement is that the kind of society we want to see, that is, democratic, with genuine equality of opportunity, with greater equality of wealth and income, with enhanced choice and freedom, and with a proper regard for sustainability, can only be achieved through a major role for the state in welfare. We judge that to be an inescapable necessity in our kind of society.

We do not, however, simply want more of the same welfare state policies of the last fifty years. That is no way to meet the social needs of a very different and rapidly changing society and is to ignore all that has been learned by research and experience. What we do want, quite simply, is a commitment to use the powers and resource of the state, that is, of society – for the common good. We want a recognition of the truth which Beveridge asserted in 1944 – that social ills such as want, disease, ignorance and squalor must be regarded 'as common enemies of all of us, not as enemies with whom each individual may seek a separate place, escaping himself to personal prosperity, while leaving his fellow in their clutches' (Beveridge, 1944, pp. 254–5). They are common enemies because they diminish all our lives whether or not they seem to affect us directly.

We believe that there is such a thing as the common good and that the good life for individuals depends on asserting its reality and on pursuing it. Certainly, it is an abstraction, but its neglect diminishes the lives of individuals. It is our view that an enlightened welfare state can both express and enhance the common good and individual wellbeing.

Industrial, urban, free market societies simultaneously generate the affluence which makes it possible to abolish many historic human ills and a self-regarding, individualistic, fragmented way of life with a lack of respect for people which threatens the improvements in the quality of life which affluence makes possible. To realise the gains which markets make possible, markets need states.

The state's role is to assert common purposes, to organise a collective assault on historic social ills, to use and redistribute the economic product for the social good. Social order and sustainability and a high quality of life depend on the state assuming a major role in welfare. Neither markets nor societies are self-regulating and self-sustaining. The health and wellbeing of both depends on state action. Such action is not just desirable but is essential to sustain complex economic and social orders. We also believe that it is possible. Humankind has the skills and the knowledge. They have to be harnessed to a vision which only the state can articulate and take forward. Of course, there will be mistakes and failures and the task is immensely complex. But history shows what can be done by public action to reconstruct societies and the need for such social engineering has never been greater. We are firmly committed to its possibility.

BIBLIOGRAPHY

Abel-Smith, B. (1984) 'Social welfare' in *Fabian Essays in Socialist Thought*, Pimlott, B. (ed.), Heinemann: London.

Adams, I. (1993) *Political Ideology Today*, Manchester University Press: Manchester.

Addison, P. (1975) *The Road to 1945*, Cape: London.

Antonnen, A. (n.d.) *The Nordic Welfare State: Is it really woman-friendly?*. Unpublished paper.

Arnot, M. (1986) 'State education policy and girls' educational experience' in *Women in Britain Today*, Beechy, V. and Whitelegg, E. (eds), Open University Press: Milton Keynes.

Arnot, M. (1987) 'Political lip service or practical reform?' in *Gender and the Politics of Schooling*, Arnot, M. and Weiner, G. (eds), Hutchinson: London.

Bacon, R. and Eltis, W. (1976) *Britain's Economic Problem: Too few producers*, Macmillan: London.

Bahro, R. (1986) *Building the Green Movement*, trans. Mary Tyler, Heretic Books: London.

Baldwin, S. and Twigg, J. (1991) 'Women and community care' in *Women's Issues in Social Policy*, Maclean, M. and Groves, D. (eds), Routledge: London.

Ball, T. and Dagger, R. (1991) *Ideals and Ideologies: A reader*, Harper Collins: New York.

Banks, O. (1981) *Faces of Feminism*, Martin Robertson: Oxford.

Barnett, C. (1986) *The Audit of War*, Macmillan: London.

Barry, N. (1987) *The New Right*, Croom Helm: London.

Barry, N. (1990) *Welfare*, Open University Press: Milton Keynes.

Barry, N. (1991) 'Understanding the market' in *The State or the Market*, Loney, M. (ed.), 2nd edn, Sage: London.

Beer, S.H. (1982a) *Modern British Politics*, 2nd edn, Faber: London.

Beer, S.H. (1982b) *Britain Against Itself: The political contradictions of collectivism*, Faber: London.

Bell, D. (1960) *The End of Ideology*, Free Press: New York.

Bell, D. (1973) *The Coming of Post-Industrial Society*, Free Press: New York.

Beveridge, W.H. (1942) *Social Insurance and Allied Services*, Cmd 6404, HMSO: London.

Beveridge, W.H. (1944) *Full Employment in a Free Society*, Allen & Unwin: London.

Beveridge, W.H. (1948) *Voluntary Action*, Allen & Unwin: London.

Bookchin, M. (1982) *The Ecology of Freedom*, Cheshire Books: Palo Alto, California.

Bookchin, M. (1991) 'Looking for common ground' in *Defending the Earth*, Chase, S. (ed.), South End Press: Boston.

Boothby, R. (1962) *My Yesterday, Your Tomorrow*, Hutchinson: London.

Borchorst, A. (1990) 'Political motherhood and child care policies' in *Gender and Caring*, Ungerson, C. (ed.), Harvester Wheatsheaf: Hemel Hempstead.

Borchorst, A. and Siim, B. (1987) 'Women and the advanced welfare state – a new kind of patriarchal power', in *Women and the State: The shifting boundaries between public and private*, Sassoon, A.S. (ed.), Hutchinson: London.

Bowles, S. and Gintis, H. (1986) *Democracy and Capitalism*, Basic Books: New York.

Boyle, E. (1973) 'Introduction' in *Iain Macleod*, Fisher, N. (ed.), Deutsch: London.

Boyne, R. and Rattansi, A. (eds) (1990) *Postmodernism and Society*, Macmillan: London.

Brundtland, G. (1987) *Our Common Future*, Oxford University Press: Oxford.

Bryson, L. (1992) *Welfare and the State*, Macmillan: London.

Bryson, V. (1992) *Feminist Political Theory*, Macmillan: London.

Buchanan, J.M. (1986) *Liberty, Market and the State*, Harvester Wheatsheaf: Hemel Hempstead.

Burns, E.M. (1963) *Ideas in Conflict*, Methuen: London.

Cahill, M. (1991) 'The Greening of social policy' in *Social Policy Review, 1990–91*, Manning, N. (ed.), Longman: London.

Carling, A. (1986) 'Rational choice Marxism', *New Left Review*, no. 160, November–December, pp. 24–62.

Carrillo, S. (1978) *Eurocommunism and the State*, Lawrence Hill: Westport, USA.

Castles, F.G. (1978) *The Social Democratic Image of Society*, Routledge and Kegan Paul: London.

Chamberlayne, P. (1993) 'Women and the state' in *Women and Social Policy in Europe*, Lewis, J. (ed.), Elgar: Aldershot.

Chase, S. (1991) *Defending the Earth*, South End Press: Boston.

Chilcote, E. and Chilcote, C. (1992) 'The crisis of Marxism', *Rethinking MARXISM*, vol. 5, no. 2, pp. 84–107.

Cockburn, C. (1991) *In the Way of Women*, Macmillan: London.

Cole, G.D.H. (1954) 'Socialism and the welfare state', *Dissent*, Autumn.

Conley, T. (1989) 'State social work: a socialist-feminist contribution' in *Women And Social Services Departments*, Hallett, C. (ed.), Harvester Wheatsheaf: Hemel Hempstead.

Coote, A. (1987) 'Social and economic change: two sides of the policy coin' in *Feminist Theory and Practical Policies*, Ashton, F. and Whiting, G. (eds), School of Advanced Urban Studies: University of Bristol.

Corrigan, P. (1979) 'Popular consciousness and social democracy', *Marxism Today*, vol. 23, no. 12, pp. 14–18.

Crick, B. (1984) *Socialist Values and Time*, Fabian Tract No 495, Fabian Society: London.

Critchley, J. (1988) *Heseltine: The Unauthorised Biography*, Hodder & Stoughton: London.

Crosland, C.A.R. (1956) *The Future of Socialism*, Cape: London.

Crosland, C.A.R. (1974) *Socialism Now*, Cape: London.

Crowley, B.L. (1987) *The Self, the Individual and the Community*, Clarendon: Oxford.

Dale, J. and Foster, P. (1986) *Feminists and State Welfare*, Routledge and Kegan Paul: London.

Daly, H. (1977) 'The steady-state economy' in *The Sustainable Society*, Pirages, D. (ed.), Praeger: New York.

David, M. and Land, H. (1983) 'Sex and social policy' in *The Future of the Welfare State*, Glennerster, H. (ed.), Heinemann: London.

Davies, S. (1991) 'Towards the remoralization of society' in *The State or the Market*, Loney, M. (ed.), 2nd edn, Sage: London.

Deacon, A. (1977) 'Concession and coercion: the politics of unemployment insurance in the Twenties' in *Essays in Labour History 1918–1939*, Briggs, A. and Saville, J. (eds), Croom Helm: London.

Deakin, N. (1987) *The Politics of Welfare*, Methuen: London.

Dean, H. and Taylor-Gooby, P. (1992) *Dependency Culture*, Harvester Wheatsheaf: Hemel Hempstead.

Deem, R. (1985) 'State policy and ideology in the education of women 1944–1980' in *Women and Social Policy*, Ungerson, C. (ed.), Macmillan: London.

De Jasay, A. (1980) *Market Socialism: A scrutiny*, Institute of Economic Affairs: London.

Delphy, C. (1984) *Close to Home: A materialist analysis of women's oppression*, Hutchinson: London.

Department of Environment (1990) *This Common Inheritance*, Cm 1200, HMSO: London.

Department of Social Security (1992) *Social Security Statistics*, HMSO: London.

Dobson, A. (1990) *Green Political Thought*, Unwin Hyman: London.

Dobson, A. (ed.) (1991) *The Green Reader*, Deutsch: London.

Dominelli, L. (1991) *Women Across Continents*, Harvester Wheatsheaf: Hemel Hempstead.

Doyal, L. and Gough, I. (1984) 'A theory of human needs', *Critical Social Policy*, vol. 4, no. 1, pp. 6–38.

Draper, P. (1991) *The Greening of Public Health*, Green Print: London.

Dunleavy, P. and O'Leary, B. (1987) *Theories of the State*, Macmillan: London.

Eccleshall, R. (1990) *English Conservatism Since the Restoration*, Unwin Hyman: London.

Eccleshall, R., Georghegan, V., Jay, R. and Wilford, R. (1984) *Political Ideologies*, Hutchinson: London.

Eckersley, R. (1992) *Environmentalism and Political Theory*, University College London Press: London.

Eisenstein, Z. (1981) *The Radical Future of Liberal Feminism*, Longman: New York.

Eisner, M. and Wright, M. (1986) 'A feminist approach to general practice' in *Feminist Practice in Women's Health Care*, Webb, C. (ed.), Wiley: Chichester.

Elkington, J. and Burke, T. (1989) *The Green Capitalists*, Gollancz: London.

Elkins, P. (ed.) (1986) *The Living Economy*, Routledge & Kegan Paul: London.

Elster, J. (1985) *Making Sense of Marx*, Cambridge University Press: New York.

Engels, F. (1936) *The Housing Question*, Lawrence and Wishart: London.

Esping-Andersen, G. (1990) *The Three Worlds of Welfare Capitalism*, Polity Press: Cambridge.

Faludi, S. (1992) *Backlash*, Chatto and Windus: London.

Ferris, J. (1991) 'Green politics and the future of welfare' in *Social Policy Review* 1990–91, Manning, N. (ed.), Longman: London.

Finch, J. (1984) 'Community care: developing non-sexist alternatives' *Critical Social Policy*, vol. 9, no. 1, pp. 6–18.

Finch, J. (1990) 'The politics of community care in Britain' in *Gender and Caring*, Ungerson, C. (ed.), Harvester Wheatsheaf: Hemel Hempstead.

Finch, J. and Groves, D. (1980) 'Community care and the family: a case of equal opportunities' *Journal of Social Policy*, vol. 9, no. 4, pp. 487–511.

Finnie, R. (1988) 'Changes in well-being and inequality, 1960–1988' in *Starting Even*, Haverman, R. (ed.), Simon and Schuster: New York.

Fisher, N. (1973) *Iain Macleod*, Deutsch: London.

Fitzgibbons, A. (1990) *Keynes's Vision*, Clarendon: Oxford.

Forbes, I. (1986) *Market Socialism: Whose choice?*, Fabian Tract no. 516, Fabian Society: London.

Foreman, D. and Haywood, B. (1989) *Ecodefence: A field guide to monkeywrenching*, Ned Ludd Books: Tuckson.

Foster, P. (1991) 'Well Women's clinics' in *Women's Issues in Social Policy*, Maclean, M. and Groves D. (eds), Routledge: London.

Fox, W. (1984) 'Deep Ecology: a new philosophy of our time', *The Ecologist* vol. 14, no. 5/6, pp. 194–200.

Friedman, M. (1962) *Capitalism and Freedom*, University of Chicago Press: Chicago.

Friedman, M. and Friedman, R. (1984) *Tyranny of the Status Quo*, Harcourt Brace: New York.

Fukuyama, F. (1992) *The End of History and the Last Man*, Hamish Hamilton: London.

Furniss, N. and Tilton, T. (1979) *The Case for the Welfare State*, Indiana University Press: Bloomington.

Galbraith, J.K. and Menshikov, S. (1989) *Capitalism, Communism and Coexistence*, Hamish Hamilton: London.

Gallie, W. (1955/56) *Essentially Contested Concepts, Proceedings of the Aristotelian Society*, Supplement to vol. 48.

Gamble, A. and Walton, P. (1976) *Capitalism in Crisis*, Macmillan: London.

George, V. and Howards, I. (1991) *Poverty Amidst Affluence: Britain and the United States*, Elgar: Aldershot.

George, V. and Miller, S. (eds) (1993) *Social Policy Towards 2000: Squaring the welfare circle*, Routledge: London.

George, V. and Wilding, P. (1976) *Ideology and Social Welfare*, Routledge and Kegan Paul: London.

Gilbert, B. (1970) *British Social Policy 1914–1939*, Batsford: London.

Gilder, G. (1981) *Wealth and Poverty*, Basic Books: New York.

Gilmour, I. (1978) *Inside Right*, Quartet: London.

Gilmour, I. (1983) *Britain Can Work*, Martin Robertson: Oxford.

Gilmour, I. (1992) *Dancing with Dogma*, Simon and Schuster: London.

Ginsburg, N. (1979) *Class, Capital and Social Policy*, Macmillan: London.

Glazer, N. (1988) *The Limits of Social Policy*, Harvard University Press: Cambridge, Mass.

Glendinning, C. (1992) 'Community care: the financial consequences for women' in *Women and Poverty in Britain in the 1990s*, Glendinning, C. and Millar, J. (eds), Harvester Wheatsheaf: Hemel Hempstead.

Goldsmith, E., Meadows, D.A., Meadows, M.D.L., Randers, J. and Behrens, W. (1972) *A Blueprint for Survival*, special issue of *The Ecologist*, Stacey: London.

Goodin, R. (1992) *Green Political Thought*, Cambridge University Press: Cambridge.

Goodin, R. and Le Grand, J. (1987) *Not Only the Poor*, Allen and Unwin: London.

Gordon, L. (1990) 'The welfare state: towards a Socialist–Feminist perspective' in *Socialist Register 1990*, Miliband, R. (ed.), Merlin Press: London.

Gorz, A. (1982) *Farewell to the Working Class*, Pluto Press: London.

Gough, I. (1979) *The Political Economy of the Welfare State*, Macmillan: London.

Gould, P. (1988) *Early Green Politics*, Harvester Wheatsheaf: Hemel Hempstead.

Graham, H. (1993) *Hardship and Health in Women's Lives*, Harvester Wheatsheaf: Hemel Hempstead.

Gray, J. (1986) *Hayek on Liberty*, Blackwell: Oxford.

Gray, J. (1990) 'Hayek on the market economy and the limits of state action' in *The Economic Burden of the State*, Helm, D. (ed.), Oxford University Press: Oxford.

Gray, J. (1992) *The Moral Foundations of Market Institutions*, Institute of Economic Affairs: London.

Green D.G. (1988) *Everyone a Private Patient*, Institute of Economic Affairs: London.

Greenleaf, W.H. (1973) 'The character of modern British Conservatism' in *Knowledge and Belief in Politics*, Benewick, R., Berki, R.N. and Parekh, B., Allen and Unwin: London.

Green Party (1992) *New Directions: Policies for a Green Britain now*, Green Party: London.

Griffiths, B. (1982) *Morality and the Market Place: Christian alternatives to capitalism and socialism*, Hodder & Stoughton: London.

Griffiths, B. (1984) *The Creation of Wealth*, Hodder & Stoughton: London.

Griffiths, B. (1990) 'The Conservative quadrilateral' in *Christianity and Conservatism*, Alison, M. and Edwards, D.L. (eds), Hodder & Stoughton: London.

Groves, D. (1992) 'Occupational pension provision and women's poverty in old age' in *Women and Poverty in Britain, the 1990s*, Glendinning, C. and Millar, J., Harvester Wheatsheaf: Hemel Hempstead.

Hailsham, Viscount (1959) *The Conservative Case*, Penguin: London.

Hallett, C. (1989) 'The gendered world of the social services departments' in *Women and Social Services Departments*, Hallett, C. (ed.), Harvester Wheatsheaf: Hemel Hempstead.

Hamilton, M.B. (1987) 'The elements of the concept of ideology', *Political Studies*, vol. 35, no. 1, pp. 18–38.

Hanmer, J. and Statham, D. (1988) *Women and Social Work*, Macmillan: London.

Hantrais, L. (1993) 'Women, work and welfare in France' in *Women and Social Policies in Europe*, Lewis, J. (ed.), Edward Elgar: Aldershot.

Harman, H. (1993) *The Century Gap*, Vermillion: London.

Harrington, M. (1972) *Socialism*, Bantam Books: New York.

Harris, J. (1991) 'Enterprise and the welfare state: a comparative perspective' in *Britain Since 1945*, Gourvish, T. and O'Day, A. (eds), Macmillan: London.

Harris, R. (1990) 'Poverty and wealth creation' in *Christianity and Conservatism*, Alison, M. and Edwards, D.L. (eds), Hodder & Stoughton: London.

Hattersley, R. (1987) *Choose Freedom: The future of Democratic Socialism*, Penguin: London.

Hayek, F.A. (1960) *The Constitution of Liberty*, Routledge and Kegan Paul: London.

Hayek, F.A. (1967) *Studies in Philosophy, Politics and Economics*, Routledge and Kegan Paul: London.

Hayek, F.A. (1976) *Law, Legislation and Liberty, Vol. 2, The Mirage of Social Justice*, Routledge and Kegan Paul: London.

Hayek, F.A. (1988) *The Fatal Conceit*, Routledge: London.

Hearn, J. (1985) 'Patriarchy, professionalism and the semi professions' in *Women and Social Policy*, Ungerson, C. (ed.), Macmillan: London.

Henderson, H. (1983) 'The warp and the weft' in *Reclaim the Earth*, Caldecot, L. and Leland, S. (eds), Women's Press: London.

Heseltine, M. (1987) *Where There's a Will*, Hutchinson: London.

Hewitt, M. (1992) *Welfare, Ideology and Need*, Harvester Wheatsheaf: Hemel Hempstead.

Hindess, B. (1987) *Freedom, Equality and the Market*, Tavistock: London.

Hobsbawm, E. (1992) 'The crisis of today's ideologies', *New Left Review*, no. 122, March/April, pp. 55–64.

Hogg, Q. (1947) *The Conservative Case*, Penguin: London.

Honderich, T. (1991) *Conservatism*, Penguin: London.

Hoover, K. and Plant, R. (1989) *Conservative Capitalism in Britain and the United States*, Routledge: London.

Hudson, A. (1989) 'Changing perspectives: feminism, gender and social work' in *Radical Social Work Today*, Langan, M. and Lee, P. (eds), Unwin Hyman: London.

Hunt, A. (1992) 'Can Marxism survive?', *Rethinking MARXISM*, vol. 5, no. 2, pp. 45–63.

Illich, I. (1975) *Medical Nemesis*, Calder and Boyars: London.

Irvine, S. and Ponton, A. (1988) *A Green Manifesto*, Optima: London.

Isaac, J. (1987) *Power and Marxist Theory: A realist view*, Cornell University Press: Ithaca.

Jacobs, M. (1991) *The Green Economy*, Pluto Press: London.

James, R.R. (1987) *Anthony Eden*, Macmillan: London.

James, R.R. (1991) *Bob Boothby*, Hodder & Stoughton: London.

Jones, B. (1990) 'Green thinking', *Talking Politics*, vol. 2, no. 2, pp. 50–4.

Jones, B. (1991) 'Understanding ideology', *Talking Politics*, vol. 3, no. 3, pp. 98–103.

Joseph, K. (1976) *Stranded on the Middle Ground*, Centre for Policy Studies: London.

Joshi, H. (1991) 'Sex and motherhood as handicaps in the labour market' in *Women's Issues and Social Policy*, Maclean, M. and Groves, D. (eds), Routledge: London.

Joshi, H. (1992) 'The costs of caring' in *Women and Poverty in Britain, the 1990s*, Glendinning, C. and Millar, J., Harvester Wheatsheaf: Hemel Hempstead.

Kanter, R. (1972) *Commitment and Community*, Harvard University Press: Harvard.

Kavanagh, D. and Morris, P. (1989) *Consensus Politics from Attlee to Thatcher*, Blackwell: Oxford.

Kemp, P. (1990b) 'Forward' in *Getting There: Steps to a Green economy*, Wall, D. (ed.), Green Print: London.

Kemp, P. and Wall, D. (1990a) *A Green Manifesto for the 1990s*, Penguin: London.

Kenny, M. (1993) 'Ladies of the Right', *The Spectator*, 3 July 1993.

Keynes, J.M. (1927) *The End of Laissez Faire*, Hogarth: London.

Kingas, O. (1991) 'The bigger the better?', *Acta Sociologica*, vol. 34, no. 1, pp. 33–44.

Kolberg, J.E. (1991–2) 'The gender dimensions of the welfare state', *International Journal of Sociology*, vol. 21, no. 2, pp. 119–48.

Korpi, W. (1989) 'Power, politics and state autonomy in the development of citizenship', *American Sociological Review*, vol. 53, no. 3, pp. 309–28.

Korten, D. (1991/92) 'Sustainable development: a review essay', *World Policy Journal*, vol. IX, no. 1, pp. 157–90.

Kukathas, C. (1989) *Hayek and Modern Liberalism*, Clarendon: Oxford.

Kumar, K. (1983) 'Factors in the development of capitalism' in *Dilemmas of Liberal Democracy*, Ellis, A. and Kumar, K. (eds), Tavistock: London.

Laclau, E. and Mouffe, C. (1985) *Hegemony and Socialist Strategy*, Verso Books: London.

Land, H. (1978) 'Who cares for the family?' *Journal of Social Policy*, vol. 7, no. 3, pp. 257–84.

Land, H. (1987) 'Social policies and women in the labour market' in *Feminist Theory and Radical Policies*, Ashton, F. and Whiting, G. (eds), School of Advanced Urban Studies, University of Bristol: Bristol.

Land, H. (1992) 'Whatever happened to the social wage?' in *Women and Poverty in Britain, the 1990s*, Glendinning, C. and Millar, J. (eds), Harvester Wheatsheaf: Hemel Hempstead.

Langan, M. and Ostner, I. (1991) 'Gender and welfare' in *Towards a European Welfare State*, Room, G. (ed.), School of Advanced Urban Studies, University of Bristol: Bristol.

Laski, H. (1934) *The State in Theory and Practice*, Allen and Unwin: London.

Leach, R. (1991) *British Political Ideologies*, Philip Allan: Hemel Hempstead.

Lee, P. and Raban, C. (1983) 'Welfare and ideology' in *Social Policy and Social Welfare*, Loney, M., Boswell, D. and Clarke, J. (eds), Open University Press: Milton Keynes.

Lee, P. and Raban, C. (1988) *Welfare Theory and Social Policy*, Sage: London.

Le Grand, J. (1982) *The Strategy of Equality*, Allen and Unwin: London.

Le Grand, J. (1989) 'Markets, welfare and equality' in *Market Socialism*, Le Grand, J. and Estrin, S. (eds), Clarendon Press: Oxford.

Leira, A. (1990) 'Coping with care: mothers in a welfare state', in *Gender and Caring*, C. Ungerson (ed.), Harvester Wheatsheaf: Hemel Hempstead.

Leira, A. (1993) 'The woman-friendly welfare state? The case of Norway and Sweden' in *Women and Social Policies in Europe*, Lewis, J. (ed.), Edward Elgar: Aldershot.

Leopold, A. (1968) *A Land County Almanac*, Oxford University Press: Oxford.

Lewis, J. (1984) *Women in England*, Harvester Wheatsheaf: Hemel Hempstead.

Lewis, J. (1986) 'Feminism and welfare' in *What is Feminism?*, Mitchell, J. and Oakley, A. (eds), Blackwell: Oxford.

Lewis, J. (1991) *Women, Family, Work and the State since 1945*, Blackwell: Oxford.

Lewis, J. (1992) 'Gender and the development of welfare regimes', *Journal of European Social Policy*, vol. 2, no. 3, pp. 159–73.

Lewis, J. (1993) 'Introduction' in *Women and Social Policy in Europe*, Lewis, J. (ed.), Elgar: Aldershot.

Lewis, J. and Davies, C. (1991) 'Protective legislation in Britain, 1870–1990', *Policy and Politics*, vol. 19, no. 1, pp. 13–25.

Lipset, S. (1963) *Political Man*, Heinemann: London.

Lister, R. (1990) 'Women, economic dependency and citizenship', *Journal of Social Policy*, vol. 19, no. 4, pp. 445–67.

Lowe, R. (1993) *The Welfare State in Britain Since 1945*, Macmillan: London.

Lupton, C. (1992) 'Feminism, managerialism and performance measurement' in *Women, Oppression and Social Work*, Langan, M. and Day, L. (eds), Routledge: London.

Lyotard, F. (1984) *The Postmodern Condition*, Manchester University Press: Manchester.

Macmillan, H. (1938) *The Middle Way*, Macmillan: London.

MacPherson, C.B. (1962) *The Political Theory of Possessive Individualism*, Oxford University Press: Oxford.

Macridis, R.C. (1992) *Contemporary Political Ideologies*, Harper Collins: New York.

Major, J. (1992) *The Next Phase of Conservatism: The privatisation of choice*, Speech to the Adam Smith Institute, 16 July, London.

Mandel, E. (1986) 'In defence of socialist planning', *New Left Review*, no. 159, September/October, pp. 5–37.

Mann, K. (1986) 'The making of a claiming class', *Critical Social Policy*, vol. 15, no. 5, pp. 62–75.

Mannheim, K. (1936) *Ideology and Utopia*, Routledge and Kegan Paul: London.

Manning, D. (ed.) (1980) *The Form of Ideology*, Allen and Unwin: London.

Marshall, P. (1992) *Nature's Web: An Exploration of Ecological Thinking*, Simon and Schuster: Hemel Hempstead.

Marsland, D. (1992) 'The roots and consequences of paternalist collectivism', *Social Policy and Administration*, vol. 26, no. 2, pp. 144–50.

Marx, K. (1947) *The German Ideology*, New York International Publishers: New York.

Marx, K. (1963) *The Eighteenth Brumaire of Louis Bonaparte*, International Publishers: New York.

Marx, K. (1964) *Selected Works, Vol II*, Progress: Moscow.

Marx, K. (1970) 'Preface to a contribution to the critique of political economy' in *Marx and Engels Selected Works*, one volume, Lawrence and Wishart: London.

Marx, K. (1973) 'The revolutions of 1848' in *Political Writings, Vol 2*, Pelican: London.

Marx, K. (1976) *Capital, Vol 1*, Penguin: London.

Mayo, M. and Weir, A. (1993) 'The future of feminist social policy' in *Social Policy Review 5*, Page, R. and Baldock, J. (eds), Social Policy Association: Canterbury.

McKenzie, S. (1990) 'Foreword' in *Women Losing Out: Access to housing in Britain today*, Sexty, C. (ed.), Shelter: London.

McKeown, T. (1979) *The Role of Medicine*, Blackwell: London.

McLaughlin, E. (1991) 'Work and welfare benefits', *Journal of Social Policy*, vol. 20, no. 4, pp. 485–509.

McLellan, D. (1986) *Ideology*, Oxford University Press: Oxford.

Meacher, M. (1992) *Diffusing Power: The key to socialist revival*, Pluto Press: London.

Mead, L. (1986) *Beyond Entitlement: The social obligations of citizenship*, Free Press: New York.

Meadows, D.A., Meadows, M.D.L., Randers, J. and Behrens, W. (1972) *The Limits to Growth*, Pan Books: London.

Meadows, D. (1992) *Beyond the Limits*, Earthscan: London.

Merchant, C. (1992) *Radical Ecology*, Routledge: London.

Miliband, R. (1969) *The State in Capitalist Society*, Weidenfeld and Nicholson: London.

Miliband, R. (1977) *Marxism and Politics*, Oxford University Press: Oxford.

Miliband, R. (1991) *Divided Societies: Class struggle in contemporary capitalism*, Oxford University Press: Oxford.

Miliband, R. (1992) 'Fukuyama and the socialist alternative', *New Left Review*, no. 193, May/June, pp. 108–13.

Millar, J. and Glendinning, C. (1992) 'It all really starts in the family' in *Women and Poverty in Britain, the 1990s*, Glendinning, C. and Millar, J. (eds), Harvester Wheatsheaf: Hemel Hempstead.

Miller, D. (1989) *Market, State and Community*, Clarendon Press: Oxford.

Mishra, R. (1977) *Society and Social Policy*, Macmillan: London.

Mishra, R. (1984) *The Welfare State in Crisis*, Harvester Wheatsheaf: Hemel Hempstead.

Mishra, R. (1993) 'Social policy in the postmodern world' in *New Perspectives on the Welfare State in Europe*, Jones, C. (ed.), Routledge: London.

Morley, R. (1993) 'Recent responses to domestic violence against women: a feminist critique' in *Social Policy Review 5*, Page, R. and Baldock, J. (eds), Social Policy Association: Canterbury.

Moggridge, D.E. (1980) *Keynes* (2nd edn), Macmillan: London.

Muller, W. and Neussus, C. (1978) 'The welfare state illusion' in *State and Capital – a Marxist Debate*, Holloway, J. and Picciotto, S. (eds), Arnold: London.

Murray, C. (1984) *Losing Ground*, Basic Books: New York.

Naess, A. (1973) 'The shallow and the deep, long-range ecology movements: a summary', *Inquiry*, no. 16, pp. 95–100.

Norton, P. and Aughey, A. (1981) *Conservatives and Conservatism*, Temple Smith: London.

Novak, M. (1990) *Morality, Capitalism and Democracy*, Institute of Economic Affairs: London.

Nove, A. (1983) *The Economics of Socialism*, Allen and Unwin: London.

O'Connor, J. (1973) *The Fiscal Crisis of the State*, St. Martin's Press: New York.

Offe, C. (1972) 'Advanced capitalism and the welfare state', *Politics and Society*, Summer, vol. 2, no. 4, pp. 479–88.

Offe, C. (1982) 'Some contradictions of the modern welfare state', *Critical Social Policy*, vol. 2, no. 2, pp. 7–17.

Offe, C. (1987) 'Democracy against the welfare state?', *Political Theory*, vol. 15, no. 4, pp. 501–38.

O'Gorman, F. (1986) *British Conservatism*, Longman: London.

O'Riordan, T. (1976) *Environmentalism*, Pion Press: London.

Ostner, I. (1993) 'Slow motion: women, work and the family in Germany' in *Women and Social Policies in Europe*, Lewis, J. (ed.), Edward Elgar: Aldershot.

O'Sullivan, N. (1976) *Conservatism*, St. Martin's Press: New York.

Page, R. (1984) *Stigma*, Routledge and Kegan Paul: London.

Parker, R. (1975) 'The study of social policy' in *Change, Choice and Conflict in Social Policy*, Hall, P., Land, H., Parker, R. and Webb, A. (eds), Heinemann: London.

Parsons, T. (1951) *The Social System*, The Free Press: New York.

Pascall, G. (1986) *Social Policy: A feminist analysis*, Tavistock: London.

Pateman, C. (1988) 'The patriarchal welfare state' in *Democracy and the Welfare State*, Gutmann, A. (ed.), Princeton University: Princeton.

Patten, C. (1983) *The Tory Case*, Longman: London.

Patten, C. with Marquand, D. (1991) 'The power to change', *Marxism Today*, February, pp. 20–3.

Pearce, D. (1990) 'Welfare is not for women' in *Women, the State and Welfare*, Gordon, L. (ed.), University of Wisconsin: Wisconsin.

Pearce, D.W., Markandya, A. and Barbier, E.B. (1989) *Blueprint for a Green Economy*, Earthscan: London.

Pierson, C. (1991) *Beyond the Welfare State*, Polity: Cambridge.

Pinker, R. (1979) *The Idea of Welfare*, Heinemann: London.

Piven, F. (1990) 'Ideology and the state: women, power and the welfare state' in *Women, the State and Welfare*, Gordon, L. (ed.), University of Wisconsin: Wisconsin.

Plant, R. (1988) *Citizenship, Rights and Socialism*, Fabian Tract no. 531, Fabian Society: London.

Plant, R. (1990) 'Citizenship and rights' in *Citizenship and Rights in Thatcher's Britain: Two Views*, Plant, R. and Barry, N., IEA: London.

Plant, R. (1992) 'Citizenship, rights and welfare' in *The Welfare of Citizens*, Coote, A. (ed.), Rivers Oram Press: London.

Plant, R. (1993) *Social Justice, Labour and the New Right*, Fabian Pamphlet 556, Fabian Society: London.

Plant, R. and Barry, N. (1990) *Citizenship Rights in Thatcher's Britain: Two views*, Institute of Economic Affairs: London.

Porritt, J. (1984) *Seeing Green*, Blackwell: Oxford.

Porritt, J. (1990) *Where on Earth Are We Going?* BBC Publications: London.

Powell, E. (1972) *Still to Decide*, Elliot Right Way Books: London.

Prior, J. (1986) *A Balance of Power*, Hamish Hamilton: London.

Pugh, M. (1992) *Women and the Women's Movement in Britain 1914–57*, Macmillan: London.

Pym, F. (1984) *The Politics of Consent*, Hamish Hamilton: London.

Rein, M. (1985) 'Women, employment and social welfare' in *The Future of Welfare*, Klein, R. and O'Higgins, M. (eds), Blackwell: Oxford.

Rejai, M. (1990) 'Ideology' in *Contemporary Political Ideologies: A reader*, Sargent, L.T. (ed.), Brooks/Cole: California.

Rengger, N.J. (1992) 'No time like the present: postmodernism and political theory', *Political Studies*, vol. XL, no. 3, pp. 561–70.

Ritchie, J. (1990) *Thirty Families: Their living standards in unemployment*, HMSO: London.

Roemer, J. (1982) *A General Theory of Exploitation and Class*, Harvard University Press: Cambridge.

Room, G. (1979) *The Sociology of Welfare*, Blackwell: Oxford.

Rowbotham, S. (1989) *The Past is Before Us*, Penguin: London.

Roszak, T. (1979) *Person/Planet: The creative disintegration of industrial society*, Paladin: London.

Rupnik, J. (1988) *The Other Europe*, Weidenfeld and Nicolson: London.

Rustin, M. (1980) 'The New Left and the crisis', *New Left Review*, no. 121, May–June, pp. 63–89.

Ruzeck, S. (1986) 'Feminist visions of health: an international perspective' in *What is Feminism?*, Mitchell, J. and Oakley, A. (eds), Blackwell: Oxford.

Ryle, M. (1988) *Ecology and Socialism*, Radius: London.

Sale, K. (1985) *Dwellers in the Land: The bioregional vision*, Sierra Club Books: San Francisco.

Sapiro, V. (1990) 'The gender basis of American social policy' in *Women, The State and Welfare*, Gordon, L. (ed.), University of Wisconsin: Wisconsin.

Saville, J. (1957/58) 'The welfare state: an historical approach', *New Reasoner*, vol. 3, no. 1, pp. 5–25.

Schumacher, E. (1974) *Small is Beautiful*, Abacus: London.

Scruton, R. (1984) *The Meaning of Conservatism*, Macmillan: London.

Segalman, R. and Marsland, D. (1989) *Cradle to Grave*, Macmillan: London.

Seldon, A. (1990) *Capitalism*, Blackwell: Oxford.

Shaw, G.B. (1896) *Report on Fabian Policy*, Fabian Tract no. 10, Fabian Society: London.

Sieber, S.D. (1981) *Fatal Remedies*, Plenum: New York.

Siim, B. (1990) 'Women and the welfare state' in *Gender and Caring*, Ungerson C. (ed.), Harvester Wheatsheaf: Hemel Hempstead.

Siim, B. (1993) 'The gendered Scandinavian welfare states' in *Women and Social Policies in Europe*, Lewis, J. (ed.), Edward Elgar: Aldershot.

Skidelsky, R. (1979) 'The decline of Keynesian politics' in *State and Economy in Contemporary Capitalism*, Crouch, C. (ed.), Croom Helm: London.

Skidelsky, R. (1992) *John Maynard Keynes 1920–37*, Macmillan: London.

Stephens, J.D. (1980) *The Transition from Capitalism to Socialism*, Humanities Press: London.

Tawney, R.H. (1921) *The Acquisitive Society*, Bell: London.

Tawney, R.H. (1931) *Equality*, Unwin: London.

Tawney, R.H. (1964) *The Radical Tradition*, Pelican: London.

Taylor-Gooby, P. and Dale, J. (1981) *Social Theory and Social Welfare*, Arnold: London.

Thane, P. (1991) 'Visions of gender in the making of the British welfare state' in *Modernity and Gender Policies*, Bock, G. and Thane, P. (eds), Routledge: London.

Thatcher, M. (1990) 'Address to the General Assembly of the Church of Scotland, 21 May 1988' in *Christianity and Conservatism*, Alison, M. and Edwards, D. (eds), Hodder & Stoughton: London.

Therborn, G. and Roebroek, J. (1986) 'The irreversible welfare state', *International Journal of the Health Services*, vol. 16, no. 3, pp. 319–39.

Therborn, G. and Roebroek, J. (1992) 'The life and times of socialism', *New Left Review*, no. 194, July/August, pp. 17–33.

Titmuss, R.M. (1958) *Essays on the Welfare State*, Allen and Unwin: London.

Titmuss, R.M. (1965) 'Goals of today's welfare state' in *Towards Socialism*, Anderson, P. and Blackburn, R. (eds), Fontana: London.

Titmuss, R.M. (1968) *Commitment to Welfare*, Allen and Unwin: London.

Titmuss, R.M. (1970) *The Gift Relationship*, Pelican: London.

Titmuss, R.M. (1974) *Social Policy: An introduction*, Allen and Unwin: London.

Tokar, B., Miles, E. and Miles, R. (1987) *The Green Alternative*, San Pedro: California.

Townsend, P. (1979) *Poverty in the United Kingdom*, Penguin: London.

Trainer, F. (1985) *Abandon Affluence*, Zed Books: London.

Ungerson, C. (1985) 'Introduction' in *Women and Social Policy*, Ungerson, C. (ed.), Macmillan: London.

Ungerson, C. (1990) 'The language of care' in *Gender and Caring*, Ungerson, C. (ed.), Harvester Wheatsheaf: Hemel Hempstead.

Vaisanen, I. (1992) 'Conflict and consensus in social policy development', *European Journal of Political Research*, vol. 22, no. 3, pp. 307–27.

Vincent, A. (1992) *Modern Political Ideologies*, Blackwell: Oxford.

Walby, S. (1990) *Theorizing Patriarchy*, Blackwell: Oxford.

Waldergrave, W. (1978) *The Binding of Leviathan*, Hamish Hamilton: London.

Walker, A. (1982) 'The meaning and social division of community care' in *Community Care*, Walker, A. (ed.), Blackwell: Oxford.

Walker, A. (1983) 'Care for elderly people' in *A Labour of Love*, Finch, J. and Groves, D. (eds), Routledge and Kegan Paul: London.

Walker, P. (1987) *Trust the People: Selected essays and speeches*, Collins: London.

Walter, T. (1989) *Basic Income*, Boyars: London.

Ward, B. and Dubois, R. (1972) *Only One Earth*, Deutsch: London.

Webb, C. (ed.) (1986) *Feminist Practice in Women's Health Care*, Wiley: Chichester.

Wedderburn, D. (1965) 'Facts and theories of the welfare state' in *The Socialist Register*, Miliband, R. and Saville, J. (eds), Merlin Press: London.

Weisskopf, T.E. (1992) 'Challenges to market socialism: a response to critics', *Dissent*, Spring, pp. 250–61.

Westergaard, J. and Resler, H. (1975) *Class in a Capitalist Society*, Heinemann: London.

Weston, J. (ed.) (1986) *Red and Green: The new politics of the environment*, Pluto Press: London.

Wetherly, P. (1988) 'Class struggle and the welfare state', *Critical Social Policy*, vol. 8, no. 1, pp. 24–40.

White, R.J. (1950) *The Conservative Tradition*, Nicholas Kaye: London.

Wicks, M. (1987) *A Future for All: Do we need a welfare state?*, Penguin: London.

Wiener, M.J. (1981) *English Culture and the Decline of the Industrial Spirit*, Cambridge University Press: Cambridge.

Wilding, P. (1976) 'Richard Titmuss and social welfare', *Social and Economic Administration*, vol. 10, no. 3, pp. 147–66.

Wilensky, H. (1975) *The Welfare State and Equality*, University of California Press: California.

Willetts, D. (1992) *Modern Conservatism*, Penguin: London.

Williams, F. (1989) *Social Policy: A critical introduction*, Polity Press: Cambridge.

Wilson, E. (1977) *Women and the Welfare State*, Tavistock: London.

Wilson, E. (1980) 'The political economy of welfare', *New Left Review*, no. 122, July–August, pp. 79–90.

Wilson, E. (1982) 'Women, community and the family' in *Community Care*, Walker, A. (ed.), Blackwell: Oxford.

Wilson, M. (ed.) (1991) *Girls and Young Women in Education*, Pergamon: London.

Wood, M. (1989) *The Retreat From Class: A new 'true' socialism*, Verso Books: London.

Wright, A. (1987) *Socialisms: Theories and practices*, Oxford University Press: Oxford.

Wright, E.D. (1985) *Classes*, New Left Books: London.

Yearley, S. (1991) *The Green Case*, Harper Collins: London.

Young, S.C. (1992) 'The different dimensions of Green politics', *Environmental Politics*, vol. 1, no. 1, pp. 9–45.

INDEX